W9-BKA-968

THE DOG BREED BIBLE

THE
DOG
BREED
BIBLE

D. Caroline Coile, Ph.D.

with Full-Color Photographs

BARRON'S

About the Author: Caroline Coile is an award-winning author of several hundred articles and 29 books, including multiple editions of *Barron's Encyclopedia of Dog Breeds*. She has participated in a variety of canine sports and studied dogs for more than 30 years.

Acknowledgments: The author is grateful for the editorial expertise of Mark Miele, and for the advice of members of the many AKC parent breed clubs concerning their breeds.

Cover Credits: Front cover: The Image Bank: GK Hart/Vikki Hart; Back cover: Tara Darling.

Photo Credits: All photos by Tara Darling except the following: GeHy/Digital Vision: page i; Norvia Behling: pages 1 and 147; Kent Dannen, page 53; Isabelle Francais, page 107; Cheryl A. Ertelt, page 129.

© Copyright 2007 by Barron's Educational Series, Inc.

All rights reserved.

No part of this book may be reproduced in any form, by photostat, microfilm, xerography, or any other means, or incorporated into any information retrieval system, electronic or mechanical, without the written permission of the copyright owner.

All inquiries should be addressed to:
Barron's Educational Series, Inc.
250 Wireless Boulevard
Hauppauge, New York 11788
http://www.barronseduc.com

ISBN-13: 978-0-7641-6000-4
ISBN-10: 0-7641-6000-1

Library of Congress Catalog Card No. 2006036904

Library of Congress Cataloging-in-Publication Data
Coile, D. Caroline.
 The dog breed bible / D. Caroline Coile.
  p. cm.
 Includes index.
 ISBN-10: 0-7641-6000-1 (alk. paper)
 ISBN-13: 978-0-7641-6000-4 (alk. paper)
 1. Dog breeds. 2. Dogs. I. Title.

SF426.C64 2007
636.7′1--dc22   2006036904

Printed in China

19 18 17 16 15 14 13 12 11

Important Note
This book describes the typical traits of the breeds recognized by the American Kennel Club. Not all members of a breed will act or look as the majority do, but a dog has a greater chance of behaving typically if it comes from a responsible breeder who has raised and socialized it optimally and has used parents who are good breed representatives. In all cases, buyers are urged to do further research into their breeds of interest before making a decision and before undertaking to raise and care for a new dog. More information is available in a variety of Barron's breed-specific books, as well as from each breed's parent club, which can be located through the AKC (*www.akc.org*).

Contents

Introduction   vi

The Sporting Group   1

The Hound Group   28

The Working Group   53

The Terrier Group   79

The Toy Group   107

The Non-Sporting Group   129

The Herding Group   147

Miscellaneous Class   167

Glossary
Definitions of Medical Conditions   175
Definitions of Color Terms   185

Appendix
Genetic Health Resources   186
Dog Anatomy   189

Index   190

Introduction

No breed of mammal is as diverse as is the one that has gained the title of man's best friend. The dog you choose as your best friend may be a tiny tornadic fluff-ball or a sleek giant with the activity level of furniture. And while either one has the capacity to capture your heart, chances are only one will really mesh with your lifestyle. With the hundreds of variations and combinations domestic dog breeds have to offer, it only makes sense to narrow your search to those having traits that fit you.

HISTORY These combinations of traits arose because people through the ages have needed dogs that could perform different jobs under different conditions. By Roman times, most of the main families of modern breeds were in existence, with dogs specifically bred as guard, sheep, hunting, and lap dogs. They differed not only in physical characteristics, but behavioral tendencies. The history of a breed contains clues about its genetic heritage and thus, its genetic propensities.

TEMPERAMENT Selection for behavior was one of the most formative pressures in the creation of most breeds. These behavioral differences are just as breed-specific as are physical ones, yet too many prospective dog owners choose their next best friend based on looks, not personality. Few people give up a dog because it didn't turn out to look as they had hoped, but many dog owners give up their dogs because it didn't turn out to behave as they had hoped. Knowing what a breed is developed to do and how it is inclined to act can greatly increase the odds of choosing the right dog and sharing a long life together. Not all dogs within a breed act the same, but most dogs within a breed have a tendency to act in certain ways, especially if those traits were important ones for performing the job they were bred to do.

PRACTICAL CONSIDERATIONS Besides temperament, every breed has practical considerations involved in caring for it and living with it. A giant breed may seem exotic, but giant dogs need spacious sleeping quarters, adequate transportation, and lots of money for increased food, veterinary, and board bills. A dog with long locks may seem glamorous, but not when they are matted and dirty. A high-energy breed may seem sporty, but only if you really do have the time to get out and exercise it as it needs. Even a smart breed can be a bad choice unless you plan to challenge that dog mentally every day rather than leave it up to the dog to figure out something to do.

HEALTH Every breed of dog comes from a limited gene pool, and as such, is subject to a different set of hereditary health disorders. Some breeds, in addition, have physical traits that predispose them to certain health problems. In some cases, health screening tests can help lower the chance of a dog exhibiting a particular problem. Knowing the health concerns of a particular breed and the tests that are suggested for that breed are essential for any prospective purebred dog owner.

RATINGS Every breed profile is accompanied by a series of ratings for a variety of categories set in a small box beside the text. Entries in this section range from low (represented by one) to high (represented by five). Most breeds vary over several rankings, and as such each ranking should be considered to be approximate for that breed. Individual dogs, like people, can show marked deviations from the average.

The information supplied in this section pertains to adult dogs. Even dogs of the calmest and least playful breeds, for example, are energetic and playful (and destructive) as puppies.

Energy level. Most people think they want an energetic dog. Think twice before you choose a high-energy breed, however, because a dog in constant motion may be unnerving or annoying to you. A very low-energy dog, however, may be frustrating for children or to an owner who wants an enthusiastic jogging companion. Note that even in breeds with low energy levels as adults, puppies will have high energy. There is no such thing as a low-energy puppy (or even adolescent), and buyers who need a low-energy dog from the outset are advised to consider a mature dog.

Exercise requirements. Exercise requirements are a combination of a dog's energy requirements and size or athleticism. The Greyhound is athletic, but quiet; its requirements can be met with short running bursts. The Miniature Pinscher is small, but energetic, and can get a lot of exercise indoors. Even a dog with very low requirements needs daily exercise.

Playfulness. Playfulness is related to energy level but focuses on whether that energy is aimed at interacting with people. Most people want a playful dog; however, the constant thud of a tennis ball dropped in your lap may be too demanding for busy people.

Affection level. Not everybody wants a dog that jumps all over them and licks them in the face. Some dogs, although devoted to their owners, are less demonstrative or fawning. People differ in which type of dog they prefer. A dog that ranks lower in this category does not mean that it does not need or thrive on attention and affection; it simply means that it may be less extroverted in its exhibition of it.

Friendliness toward other pets. All dogs can chase cats, and all dogs can learn to live peacefully with cats if they are raised with them. Some breeds, however, were bred to chase and kill small mammals, and these breeds are more likely to chase cats or other animals outside.

Friendliness toward strangers. Some breeds have never met a stranger. Some tend to be naturally aloof, or tend to be shy, or tend to be suspicious. Not everybody wants to see their darling dog seemingly adoring a complete stranger as much as it loves them! A friendly dog is a great way to meet people, however.

Ease of training. Training ease does not necessarily reflect intelligence. Some dogs combine intelligence with a high energy level and a willingness to please that, taken together, result in a dog that learns quickly. Such dogs may be hard to live with if not trained, however, because they enjoy mental stimulation and need it in order to avoid boredom.

Grooming requirements. This ranking is determined by coat type as well as size of the dog. A tiny dog with a lot of hair would generally get a lower ranking than a large dog with a lot of hair.

IMPORTANT NOTE: In all cases these ratings are based upon the assumption that a dog has been acquired from a reputable, qualified breeder. Qualified breeders will be willing to discuss temperament and health problems of their breed and will have proven their breeding stock in some sort of competitive area as well as screening it for breed typical health problems. They will have pictures of many of your potential puppy's ancestors. They will raise your puppy with plenty of human contact and proper health care. They will stand behind their dog and be available to you for advice for the rest of that puppy's life. They will screen potential buyers and make it clear that you will not be able to recoup your money by breeding your pup in the future.

Height and weight are the suggested values given in the AKC standards. Height is measured as the distance from the ground to the top of the withers. Weight is considered to be that of a dog in ideal weight for its bone structure; that is, neither thin nor fat. Note that in any case, average values within a breed may differ from suggested values. Some breeders boast of weights or sizes that differ markedly from the AKC standard weights; such breeders should generally be avoided. See the section on upkeep to interpret the significance of size when evaluating a breed.

With the dog, you can choose both your family and your friend. Choose well!

THE AMERICAN KENNEL CLUB GROUPS The breeds in this book are those recognized by the American Kennel Club (AKC), and they are divided into the seven AKC groups plus the Miscellaneous Class.

SPORTING GROUP: Sporting breeds are also known as gundogs in some countries. They specialize in hunting with a human partner, extending the hunter's capabilities by locating, flushing, or retrieving birds. Breeds that specialize in locating birds include the pointers and setters, those that specialize in flushing them include the spaniels, and those that specialize in retrieving them are the retrievers. Many of the Sporting breeds perform more than just one task. For example, spaniels tend to locate, flush, and even retrieve. Most Sporting breeds, especially those that need to locate game, are very active. They also tend to be fairly biddable, with the retrievers especially so.

Currently the Sporting Group consists of the following breeds:

Brittany	Spaniel (American Water)
Pointer	Spaniel (Clumber)
Pointer (German Shorthaired)	Spaniel (Cocker)
Pointer (German Wirehaired)	Spaniel (English Cocker)
Retriever (Chesapeake Bay)	Spaniel (English Springer)
Retriever (Curly-Coated)	Spaniel (Field)
Retriever (Flat-Coated)	Spaniel (Irish Water)
Retriever (Golden)	Spaniel (Sussex)
Retriever (Labrador)	Spaniel (Welsh Springer)
Retriever (Nova Scotia Duck Tolling)	Spinone Italiano
Setter (English)	Vizsla
Setter (Gordon)	Weimaraner
Setter (Irish)	Wirehaired Pointing Griffon

HOUND GROUP: Hound breeds specialize in pursuing mammals. The scenthounds, which include the coonhounds and foxhounds, do so by trailing them while the sighthounds, which include the greyhound-like breeds, do so by running after them. Some hounds hunt by both scent and sight. Because their hunting style means they must make independent decisions and often hunt on their own, they tend to be independent.

Currently the Hound Group consists of the following breeds:

Afghan Hound
Basenji
Basset Hound
Beagle
Black and Tan Coonhound
Bloodhound
Borzoi
Dachshund
Foxhound (American)
Foxhound (English)
Greyhound
Harrier

Ibizan Hound
Irish Wolfhound
Norwegian Elkhound
Otterhound
Petit Basset Griffon Vendéen
Pharaoh Hound
Plott
Rhodesian Ridgeback
Saluki
Scottish Deerhound
Whippet

WORKING GROUP: Working breeds have traditionally been employed for their bravery or brawn. They include guarding and protection breeds, which may guard people, places, or livestock; draft breeds, which may pull sleds or carts; and rescue breeds, which may pull people from snowdrifts or water. They are generally self-assured and intelligent.

Currently the Working Group consists of the following breeds:

Akita	Komondor
Alaskan Malamute	Kuvasz
Anatolian Shepherd Dog	Mastiff
Bernese Mountain Dog	Neapolitan Mastiff
Black Russian Terrier	Newfoundland
Boxer	Portuguese Water Dog
Bullmastiff	Rottweiler
Doberman Pinscher	Saint Bernard
German Pinscher	Samoyed
Giant Schnauzer	Siberian Husky
Great Dane	Standard Schnauzer
Great Pyrenees	Tibetan Mastiff
Greater Swiss Mountain Dog	

TERRIER GROUP: Terrier breeds can be roughly divided into the vermin hunters and the bull-and-terrier types. The vermin hunters include dogs that kill small mammals often considered to be pests. They may go into their quarry's den and pull them from it. Because they hunt on their own, they tend to be independent and feisty. The bull-and-terrier breeds were often used for bull baiting or pit fighting. They tend to be biddable but tough.

Currently the Terrier Group consists of the following breeds:

Airedale Terrier	Manchester Terrier (Standard)
American Staffordshire Terrier	Miniature Bull Terrier
Australian Terrier	Miniature Schnauzer
Bedlington Terrier	Norfolk Terrier
Border Terrier	Norwich Terrier
Bull Terrier	Parson Russell Terrier
Cairn Terrier	Scottish Terrier
Dandie Dinmont Terrier	Sealyham Terrier
Fox Terrier (Smooth)	Skye Terrier
Fox Terrier (Wire)	Soft Coated Wheaten Terrier
Glen of Imaal Terrier	Staffordshire Bull Terrier
Irish Terrier	Welsh Terrier
Kerry Blue Terrier	West Highland White Terrier
Lakeland Terrier	

TOY GROUP: Toy breeds are often miniaturized versions of larger breeds. Since their ancestors may come from any of the other groups, they include a mixed bag of physical and behavioral characteristics. They have been selected with companionship as a priority, however, so most are biddable and friendly.

Currently the Toy Group consists of the following breeds:

Affenpinscher	Miniature Pinscher
Brussels Griffon	Papillon
Cavalier King Charles Spaniel	Pekingese
Chihuahua	Pomeranian
Chinese Crested Dog	Poodle (Toy)
English Toy Spaniel	Pug
Havanese	Shih Tzu
Italian Greyhound	Silky Terrier
Japanese Chin	Toy Fox Terrier
Maltese	Yorkshire Terrier
Manchester Terrier (Toy)	

NON-SPORTING GROUP: Non-Sporting breeds are sometimes called companion breeds because they no longer perform their original functions but are kept almost exclusively as companions. The breeds in this group come from such a variety of backgrounds, however, that it's impossible to apply generalities to them.

Currently the Non-Sporting Group consists of the following breeds:

American Eskimo Dog	Keeshond
Bichon Frise	Lhasa Apso
Boston Terrier	Löwchen
Bulldog	Poodle
Chinese Shar-Pei	Schipperke
Chow Chow	Shiba Inu
Dalmatian	Tibetan Spaniel
Finnish Spitz	Tibetan Terrier
French Bulldog	

HERDING GROUP: The Herding breeds were developed to control and move herds and flocks, usually cattle or sheep. Different breeds have different styles of herding. Some crouch and intimidate, while others are more upright. Some tend to gather while others tend to drive. Herding breeds are energetic and biddable.

Currently the Herding Group consists of the following breeds:

Australian Cattle Dog	Canaan Dog
Australian Shepherd	Collie
Bearded Collie	German Shepherd Dog
Beauceron	Old English Sheepdog
Belgian Malinois	Polish Lowland Sheepdog
Belgian Sheepdog	Puli
Belgian Tervuren	Shetland Sheepdog
Border Collie	Welsh Corgi (Cardigan)
Bouviers des Flandres	Welsh Corgi (Pembroke)
Briard	

MISCELLANEOUS CLASS: Miscellaneous breeds are those breeds that will probably become regular AKC breeds in the next few years. Most breeds stay in the class for three to five years before joining one of the AKC groups as a recognized member.

Currently the Miscellaneous Class consists of the following breeds:

Dogue de Bordeaux   Pyrenean Shepherd
Irish Red and White Setter   Redbone Coonhound
Norwegian Buhund   Swedish Vallhund

Note: This book is a condensed version of
Barron's Encyclopedia of Dog Breeds, 2nd Edition.
Readers who want more information about breeds should consult the larger volume.

SPORTING

Brittany

Area of Origin: France
Original Function: Pointing, retrieving
Coat: Flat or wavy, medium length
Color: Orange and white, liver and white, or tricolored
Height: 17.5–20.5″
Weight: 30–40 lb

Energy level:	**1 2 3 4**
Exercise requirements:	**1 2 3 4 5**
Playfulness:	**1 2 3 4**
Affection level:	**1 2 3 4 5**
Friendliness toward other pets:	**1 2 3**
Friendliness toward strangers:	**1 2 3 4 5**
Ease of training:	**1 2 3 4**
Grooming requirements:	**1**

HISTORY In the mid-1800s, French sportsmen crossed small land spaniels with English Setters, producing excellent woodcock hunters with strong noses, many with stub tails. These dogs soon became popular not only with the French gentry, but with poachers, as they would both point and retrieve, and were extremely obedient—essential qualities for their clandestine activities. At first, those born with tails were considered inferior, but eventually they were accepted as long as their tails were docked. The first Brittany (or *Epagneul Breton*) was registered in France in 1907. The Brittany arrived in America around 1925. Hunters did not initially accept the breed, but the Brittany is now the most popular breed at pointing field trials.

TEMPERAMENT The Brittany is quick and curious. It has an independent nature, yet is sensitive and responsive to direction.

UPKEEP Brittanys need at least an hour of exertion every day. The Brittany coat is not particularly thick or long, but does requires brushing once or twice weekly.

HEALTH Concerns: Hip dysplasia, epilepsy
Suggested tests: Hip
Life span: 12–13 years

Nose some shade of brown or pink

Medium length, rounded skull

Short, straight back

Tailless to about 4″ long

Short, triangular ears, set high

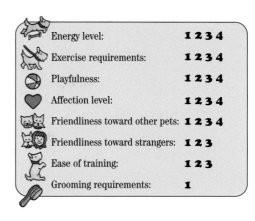

	Energy level:	**1 2 3 4**
	Exercise requirements:	**1 2 3 4**
	Playfulness:	**1 2 3 4**
	Affection level:	**1 2 3 4**
	Friendliness toward other pets:	**1 2 3 4**
	Friendliness toward strangers:	**1 2 3**
	Ease of training:	**1 2 3**
	Grooming requirements:	**1**

Pointer

Area of Origin: England
Original Function: Pointing
Coat: Short, sleek
Color: Liver, lemon, black, orange, either solid or mixed with white
Height: Male: 25–28″; Female: 23–26″
Weight: Male: 55–75 lb; Female: 45–65 lb

HISTORY The earliest Pointers were used in the 17th century to point hare. When wing-shooting became popular in the 18th century, the Pointer found its place. It would find and indicate birds, remaining still until the hunter could shoot—a fairly slow affair with flintlock guns. With the advent of self-loading guns in the 19th century, hunters began to prefer faster-working Pointers. They became popular for recreational hunting on large estates. Ideally, two Pointers were used so the hunter could locate the bird precisely by cross-referencing the dogs' points. When dog shows came in vogue in the late 19th century, Pointers were among the most prominent of the breeds shown. Pointers remain very popular as competitive field trial dogs and recreational hunters, but are less popular as pets than many other sporting breeds.

TEMPERAMENT Pointers are gentle and sweet, but may be too boisterous for small children. Pointers come in field or show types, with field types generally more active.

UPKEEP Pointers need at least an hour of exertion every day, preferably hunting or running. They require only an occasional brushing to remove dead hair.

HEALTH Concerns: Entropion, hip dysplasia
Suggested tests: Eye, hip
Life span: 12–15 years

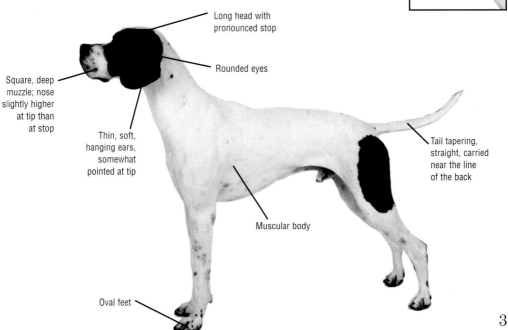

Long head with pronounced stop

Rounded eyes

Square, deep muzzle; nose slightly higher at tip than at stop

Thin, soft, hanging ears, somewhat pointed at tip

Tail tapering, straight, carried near the line of the back

Muscular body

Oval feet

Pointer (German Shorthaired)

Area of Origin: Germany
Original Function: General hunting
Coat: Short, smooth
Color: Liver or combinations of liver and white
Height: Male: 23–25″; Female: 21–23″
Weight: Male: 55–70 lb; Female: 45–60 lb

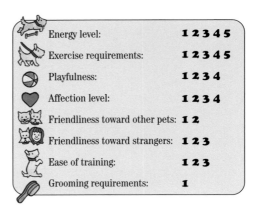

Energy level:	1 2 3 4 5
Exercise requirements:	1 2 3 4 5
Playfulness:	1 2 3 4
Affection level:	1 2 3 4
Friendliness toward other pets:	1 2
Friendliness toward strangers:	1 2 3
Ease of training:	1 2 3
Grooming requirements:	1

HISTORY This versatile hunter combines pointing, retrieving, trailing, and even game-killing abilities. It arose through blending of breeds beginning in the 17th century. Crosses of Spanish Pointers with trailing hounds produced a dog that could trail and point both birds and mammals. In 1883 two German Shorthaired Pointers, Nero and Treff, distinguished themselves against other pointing breeds at the German Derby, and through the success of their descendents, are often credited as the modern Shorthair's foundation. The breed was recognized in the late 1800s in Germany. The first Shorthairs came to America in the 1920s, and they gained AKC recognition in 1930. The breed soon gained a reputation as the ideal dog for the hunter who wanted only one dog. Its handsome looks and obedient nature helped it also become a popular companion.

TEMPERAMENT These active dogs love to run, hunt, and investigate. They are adventurous, biddable, responsive, sensitive, and devoted.

UPKEEP German Shorthaired Pointers need a long walk and a chance to run every day. Coat care consists only of weekly brushing.

HEALTH Concerns: Lymphedema, hip dysplasia, entropion, gastric torsion, vWD
Suggested tests: Eye, hip, vWD
Life span: 12–14 years

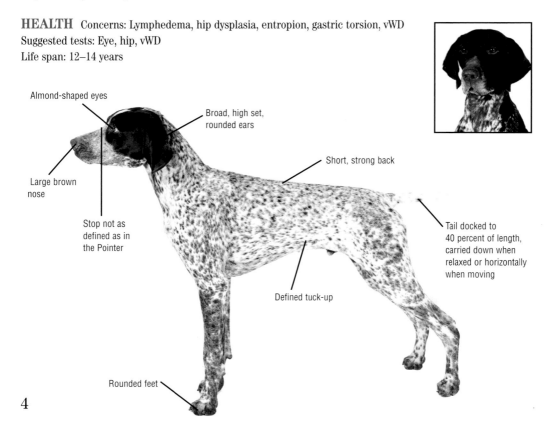

Almond-shaped eyes

Broad, high set, rounded ears

Short, strong back

Large brown nose

Stop not as defined as in the Pointer

Tail docked to 40 percent of length, carried down when relaxed or horizontally when moving

Defined tuck-up

Rounded feet

Pointer
(German Wirehaired)

Area of Origin: Germany
Original Function: General hunting, watchdog
Coat: Harsh, straight, and flat
Color: Liver and white, with ears and head solid liver, sometimes with a white blaze
Height: Male: 24–26″; Female: smaller, but not under 22″
Weight: 45–75 lb

Energy level:	**1 2 3 4 5**
Exercise requirements:	**1 2 3 4 5**
Playfulness:	**1 2 3 4**
Affection level:	**1 2 3**
Friendliness toward other pets:	**1 2 3**
Friendliness toward strangers:	**1 2**
Ease of training:	**1 2 3**
Grooming requirements:	**1 2 3**

HISTORY When game-bird shooting became accessible to persons of average means, demand for both specialist and versatile hunting breeds soared. The quest for versatile breeds reached its height in Germany, and the German Wirehaired Pointer represents one of its most successful results. Hunters wanted a dog that would hunt any kind of bird or mammal over any kind of terrain, and retrieve equally well on land and water. A rough, wiry coat was needed to hunt through dense brambles. The breed, known as the Drahthaar in Germany, has since become the most popular hunting breed in Germany. Nonetheless, it was not recognized there officially until the 1920s, the same time the first Wirehaireds came to America. German Wirehaired Pointers were recognized in America in 1959.

TEMPERAMENT German Wirehaired Pointers are energetic, amiable and responsive, but can be stubborn. They retain a guarding instinct, so tend to be aloof , even protective, toward strange people and dogs.

UPKEEP German Wirehaired Pointers need a long walk or a strenuous run every day. The wire coat requires occasional hand-stripping to maintain a sleek outline; otherwise, brushing about once a week will suffice.

HEALTH Concerns: Hip dysplasia
Suggested tests: Hip
Life span: 12–14 years

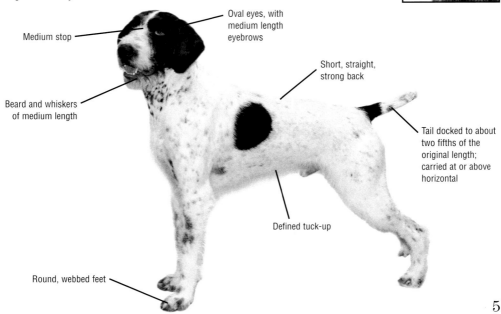

Medium stop

Oval eyes, with medium length eyebrows

Beard and whiskers of medium length

Short, straight, strong back

Tail docked to about two fifths of the original length; carried at or above horizontal

Defined tuck-up

Round, webbed feet

Retriever (Chesapeake Bay)

Area of Origin: United States
Original Function: Water retriever
Coat: Wooly undercoat; outercoat short, with a tendency to wave on back. Oily.
Color: Any color of brown, sedge, or deadgrass
Height: Male: 23–26″; Female: 21–24″
Weight: Male: 65–80 lb; Female: 55–70 lb

Energy level:	**1 2 3**
Exercise requirements:	**1 2 3**
Playfulness:	**1 2 3**
Affection level:	**1 2 3 4**
Friendliness toward other pets:	**1 2 3**
Friendliness toward strangers:	**1 2**
Ease of training:	**1 2 3**
Grooming requirements:	**1 2**

HISTORY In 1807 an American ship rescued the crew and cargo from a shipwrecked English brig off the coast of Maryland. Among the rescued were two presumably Newfoundland pups that were given to the rescuers. These pups (one black and one red) later proved to be skilled water retrievers, and as their reputations grew, many local retrievers of uncertain background came to be bred to them. It is not clear whether later purposeful crosses were made with other pure breeds, although curly-coated retrievers, Irish Water Spaniels, setters, pointers, and Indian dogs may have played a role. Whatever the means, gradually a distinct local breed emerged, a dog that would repeatedly swim through the rough icy waters of the Chesapeake Bay and unerringly retrieve ducks. By 1885 the breed was recognized by the AKC.

TEMPERAMENT Chesapeake Bay Retrievers are hardy, protective, strong-willed, and can be stubborn. They are reserved with strangers, and can be aggressive toward strange dogs.

UPKEEP Chessies need a long walk or good work out daily. Their oily coat needs weekly brushing but seldom needs washing.

HEALTH Concerns: Hip dysplasia, gastric torsion, PRA
Suggested tests: Eye, hip
Life span: 10–13 years

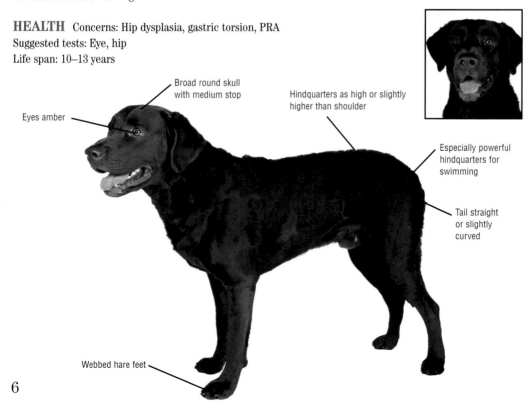

Broad round skull with medium stop

Hindquarters as high or slightly higher than shoulder

Eyes amber

Especially powerful hindquarters for swimming

Tail straight or slightly curved

Webbed hare feet

Retriever (Curly-Coated)

Area of Origin: England
Original function: Water retrieving
Coat: Tightly curled
Color: Black or liver
Height: Male: 25–27″; Female: 23–25″
Weight: 60–70 lb

Energy level:	**1 2 3**
Exercise requirements:	**1 2 3**
Playfulness:	**1 2 3**
Affection level:	**1 2 3**
Friendliness toward other pets:	**1 2 3 4**
Friendliness toward strangers:	**1 2**
Ease of training:	**1 2 3**
Grooming requirements:	**1**

HISTORY The Curly-Coated Retriever was used in England for retrieving by the 1700s. By the mid-1800s it was the most popular retriever in England, prized both for retrieving abilities and companionship. It was among the first breeds to be exhibited at English dog shows. Exports to Australia and New Zealand were well received, and the breed still enjoys great popularity there. The first exports to America were in 1907, with the breed receiving AKC recognition in 1924. During the 1900s the popularity of the Curly waned in some countries, possibly because several Curlies gave the breed the undeserved reputation as hard-mouthed retrievers, causing newer hunters to choose other retrievers. Those who give the Curly a chance have found the breed is actually quite soft-mouthed.

TEMPERAMENT Curly-Coated Retrievers are sensitive and gentle, responsive to commands. They are reserved with strangers, and one of the more courageous retrievers.

UPKEEP Curlies need daily exercise, preferably involving swimming and retrieving. Their coat requires no unusual care. Brushing loosens the tight curls, so it is best done right before getting wet.

HEALTH Concerns: Hip dysplasia
Suggested tests: Hip
Life span: 8–12 years

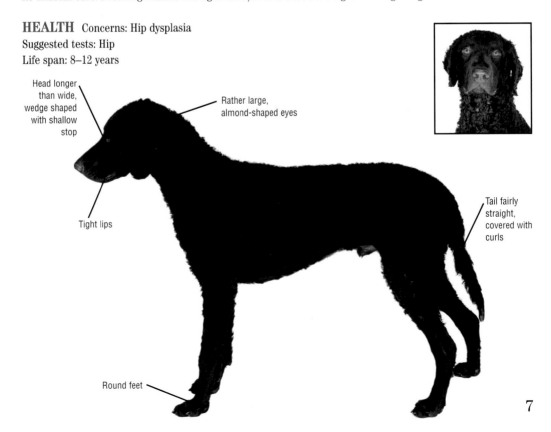

Head longer than wide, wedge shaped with shallow stop

Rather large, almond-shaped eyes

Tight lips

Tail fairly straight, covered with curls

Round feet

7

Retriever (Flat-Coated)

Area of Origin: England
Original function: Water retrieving
Coat: Straight, flat-lying, medium length
Color: Solid black or liver
Height: Male: 23–24.5″; Female: 22–23.5″
Weight: 60–70 lb

Energy level:	**1 2 3**	
Exercise requirements:	**1 2 3**	
Playfulness:	**1 2 3 4**	
Affection level:	**1 2 3 4 5**	
Friendliness toward other pets:	**1 2 3 4**	
Friendliness toward strangers:	**1 2 3 4**	
Ease of training:	**1 2 3 4 5**	
Grooming requirements:	**1 2**	

HISTORY In the 19th century retrieving dogs helped fishermen retrieve fish and objects from the water. With the development of advanced firearms, hunters were able to shoot "on the wing," but they needed dogs to mark the fallen bird and bring it back. The fishery dogs were unrivaled swimmers and natural retrievers, and crosses with setters or pointers honed their bird sense. The result was the Wavy-Coated Retriever. Near the end of the 1800s crosses with a straighter-haired breed created the Flat-Coated Retriever, which became extremely popular. By the end of the World War II, though, the number of Flat-Coats had dwindled to the point that they were threatened with extinction. Concerted efforts to bring the breed back slowly succeeded.

TEMPERAMENT Flat-Coated Retrievers are sweet, exuberant, and lively. They love to play and retrieve, but are quiet indoors. They are sensitive and responsive to training.

UPKEEP Flat-Coats need daily exercise, and especially enjoy hunting or swimming. Their coat needs weekly brushing.

HEALTH Major concerns: Hip dysplasia, cancers, gastric torsion, glaucoma
Suggested tests: Hip, eye
Life span: 10–13 years

Long head with slight stop

Almond-shaped eyes

Small, hanging, thickly feathered ears

Long deep muzzle

Fairly straight tail, carried near horizontal

Retriever (Golden)

Area of Origin: England
Original Function: Retrieving
Coat: Straight or wavy, medium length
Color: Various shades of gold
Height: Male: 23–24″; Female: 21.5–22.5″
Weight: Male: 65–75 lb; Female: 55–65 lb

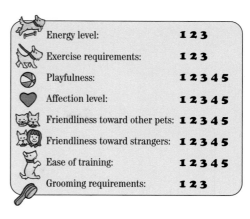

Energy level:	1 2 3
Exercise requirements:	1 2 3
Playfulness:	1 2 3 4 5
Affection level:	1 2 3 4 5
Friendliness toward other pets:	1 2 3 4 5
Friendliness toward strangers:	1 2 3 4 5
Ease of training:	1 2 3 4 5
Grooming requirements:	1 2 3

HISTORY The Golden Retriever was developed largely by Lord Tweedmouth, who, in 1868 bred Nous, a yellow Wavy-Coated Retriever to Belle, a Tweed Water Spaniel. They produced four puppies. Subsequent judicious crosses were made with other black retrievers, Tweed Spaniels, setters, and even a Bloodhound. The breed was first considered to be a yellow variety of Flat-Coated Retrievers, but was recognized as a separate breed, the Yellow or Golden Retriever, in 1912. A few of these dogs had come to America by way of Lord Tweedmouth's sons by 1900, but the AKC did not register them as a separate breed until 1927. Initially valued as hunting dogs, they later became popular as companions and obedience competitors. The Golden is one of the most popular of all breeds in America.

TEMPERAMENT Goldens are exuberant, obedient, tough, and willing to please. They are among the most accomplished obedience competitors. They especially enjoy swimming and retrieving.

UPKEEP Challenging obedience lessons, active games, or lively retrieving sessions are all good ways to exercise the Golden's mind and body every day. The coat needs twice-weekly brushing.

HEALTH Concerns: Hip dysplasia, elbow dysplasia, skin problems, heart problems, PRA, mast cell tumors
Suggested tests: Hip, heart, eye
Life span: 10–13 years

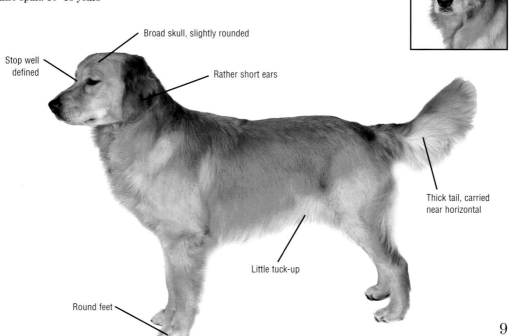

Broad skull, slightly rounded

Stop well defined

Rather short ears

Thick tail, carried near horizontal

Little tuck-up

Round feet

Retriever (Labrador)

Area of Origin: Canada
Original Function: Water retrieving
Coat: Short, straight, and fairly hard
Color: Solid black, yellow, or chocolate
Height: Male: 22.5–24.5″; Female: 21.5–23.5″
Weight: Male: 65–80 lb; Female: 55–70 lb

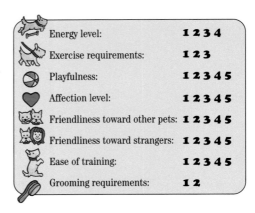

Energy level:	**1 2 3** 4
Exercise requirements:	**1 2 3**
Playfulness:	**1 2 3 4 5**
Affection level:	**1 2 3 4 5**
Friendliness toward other pets:	**1 2 3 4 5**
Friendliness toward strangers:	**1 2 3 4 5**
Ease of training:	**1 2 3 4 5**
Grooming requirements:	**1 2**

HISTORY The original Labradors were all-purpose water dogs from Newfoundland, not Labrador. The Newfoundland of the early 1800s came in different sizes, one of which was the "Lesser" or "St. John's" Newfoundland—the earliest incarnation of the Labrador. These medium-sized black dogs retrieved game and fish, pulled small fishing boats through icy water, and helped the fisherman in any task involving swimming. The breed died out in Newfoundland but it continued on in England, where several had been taken in the middle 1800s. The first yellow Lab appeared in a litter of blacks in 1899; all modern yellow Labs descend from this dog. Chocolate Labs appeared as a result of crosses with other breeds of that color. The breed was recognized by the AKC in 1917, and is the most popular breed in America.

TEMPERAMENT Devoted, obedient, and amiable, Labradors are good with everyone. They are eager to please and enjoy learning, but they can be hardheaded. They love to swim and retrieve.

UPKEEP Labradors need daily exercise, preferably retrieving and swimming, as well as mental exercise. The Lab coat needs weekly brushing to remove dead hair.

HEALTH Concerns: Hip dysplasia, elbow dysplasia, PRA, obesity
Suggested tests: Hip, eye
Life span: 10–12 years

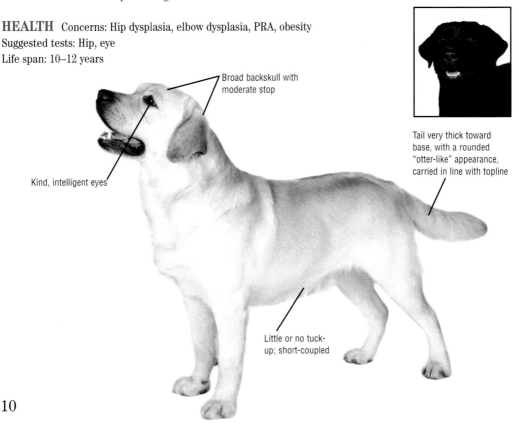

Broad backskull with moderate stop

Kind, intelligent eyes

Tail very thick toward base, with a rounded "otter-like" appearance, carried in line with topline

Little or no tuck-up; short-coupled

Retriever (Nova Scotia Duck Tolling)

Area of Origin: Nova Scotia
Original Function: Duck tolling and retrieving
Coat: Straight (sometimes with slight wave on back), medium length
Color: Any shade of red, usually with white markings on the tail tip, feet, chest, or blaze
Height: Male: 18–21″; Female: 17–20″
Weight: Male: 45–52 lb; Female: 35–42 lb

Energy level:	**1 2 3 4 5**
Exercise requirements:	**1 2 3 4 5**
Playfulness:	**1 2 3 4 5**
Affection level:	**1 2 3 4 5**
Friendliness toward other pets:	**1 2 3 4 5**
Friendliness toward strangers:	**1 2 3**
Ease of training:	**1 2 3 4**
Grooming requirements:	**1 2**

HISTORY The Nova Scotia Duck Tolling Retriever was developed in the southern tip of Nova Scotia in the early 19th century. Tolling is done by frolicking along the shore, chasing sticks, and occasionally disappearing from sight, an activity that draws curious ducks to the area. The tolling dog must continue in its animated fashion, ignoring the ducks. Originally known as the Little River Duck Dog or the Yarmouth Toller, the breed later became known as the Nova Scotia Duck Tolling Retriever. The first Tollers came to the United States in the 1960s, and joined the AKC Sporting group in 2003.

TEMPERAMENT Tollers are very energetic and playful. They are affectionate and gentle, and amiable to everyone. They learn fast and are generally willing to please.

UPKEEP Tollers need a long walk and a good play session daily. Grooming consists of weekly brushing.

HEALTH Concerns: Hip dysplasia, PRA
Suggested test: Hip, eye
Life span: 11–13 years

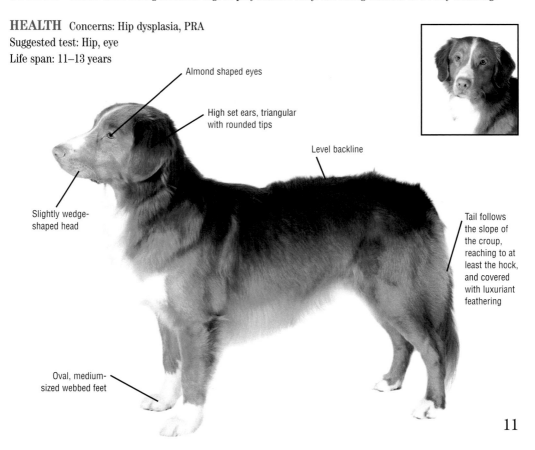

Almond shaped eyes

High set ears, triangular with rounded tips

Level backline

Slightly wedge-shaped head

Tail follows the slope of the croup, reaching to at least the hock, and covered with luxuriant feathering

Oval, medium-sized webbed feet

Setter (English)

Energy level:	**1 2 3 4**	
Exercise requirements:	**1 2 3 4**	
Playfulness:	**1 2 3**	
Affection level:	**1 2 3 4**	
Friendliness toward other pets:	**1 2 3 4**	
Friendliness toward strangers:	**1 2 3 4 5**	
Ease of training:	**1 2 3**	
Grooming requirements:	**1 2 3**	

Area of Origin: England

Original Function: Bird setting and retrieving

Coat: Flat, medium length

Color: Orange, liver, lemon, or black ("blue") flecks over a white ground color; also a combination of black and tan flecks on white ("tricolor"). Liver and lemon colors are rarely seen today. Puppies are born white, except for those with solid patches.

Height: Male: about 25″; Female: about 24″

Weight: Male: 60–65 lb; Female: 50–55 lb (field types about 10 lb less)

HISTORY The English Setter was developed to locate game on the moors, and then to freeze until the game was dispatched. Their forerunners were "sitters" or "setters," dogs that were trained to sit when they found game. The English Setter is the oldest known of this group, perhaps dating to the 14th century. The modern cultivation of the English Setter was undertaken by Edward Laverack beginning around 1825. Another influential breeder, Purcell Llewellin, obtained his foundation stock from Mr. Laverack, but based his breeding on field ability alone. To this day the breed is divided into show type, descending from the Laveracks, and field type, descending from the Llewellins. The show type is a larger dog, with a deeper muzzle, and only flecks of color. The field type tends to have patches of color, and to carry its tail higher.

TEMPERAMENT English Setters (especially field-type ones) are lively dogs that love to hunt and run. With daily exertion they can be calm and tractable housedogs. They are amiable and easygoing.

UPKEEP English Setters need at least an hour of hard exertion daily. The coat needs brushing every two to three days, and optimally, some clipping and trimming every few months.

HEALTH Concerns: Deafness, hip dysplasia, elbow dysplasia

Suggested tests: Hearing, hip, elbow

Life span: 10–12 years

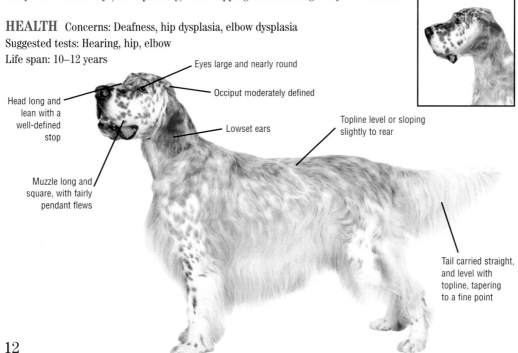

Eyes large and nearly round

Occiput moderately defined

Head long and lean with a well-defined stop

Lowset ears

Topline level or sloping slightly to rear

Muzzle long and square, with fairly pendant flews

Tail carried straight, and level with topline, tapering to a fine point

Setter (Gordon)

Area of Origin: Great Britain (Scotland)
Original Function: Bird setting and retrieving
Coat: Straight or slightly waved, medium length
Color: Black and tan
Height: Male: 24–27″; Female: 23–26″
Weight: Male: 55–80 lb; Female: 45–70 lb

Energy level:	**1 2 3 4**	
Exercise requirements:	**1 2 3 4**	
Playfulness:	**1 2 3**	
Affection level:	**1 2 3 4**	
Friendliness toward other pets:	**1 2 3 4**	
Friendliness toward strangers:	**1 2**	
Ease of training:	**1 2 3**	
Grooming requirements:	**1 2 3**	

HISTORY Black and tan setters existed in Scotland by the 1600s. In the late 1700s, the fourth Duke of Gordon bred a strain known as Gordon Castle Setters. The name was changed to Black and Tan Setter around 1900, but was restored to Gordon Setter when the English Kennel Club registered them. Gordon Setters first arrived in America in the middle 1800s, and were among the first breeds recognized by the AKC, receiving the nod in 1892. Gordon Setters are the heaviest and slowest-working of the setter breeds. Unlike many sporting breeds, little division between show and field-type Gordons exists. The breed is a favorite among hunters demanding a one-man shooting dog, though it generally lacks the flash and speed of the other setter breeds.

TEMPERAMENT Gordon Setters are lively, enthusiastic companions. Somewhat more protective than the other setters, they are reserved toward strangers and occasionally aggressive toward strange dogs.

UPKEEP The Gordon needs strenuous exercise every day. Its coat needs brushing every two to three days. Optional clipping and trimming add to good looks.

HEALTH Concerns: Hip dysplasia, gastric torsion
Suggested tests: Hip
Life span: 10–12 years

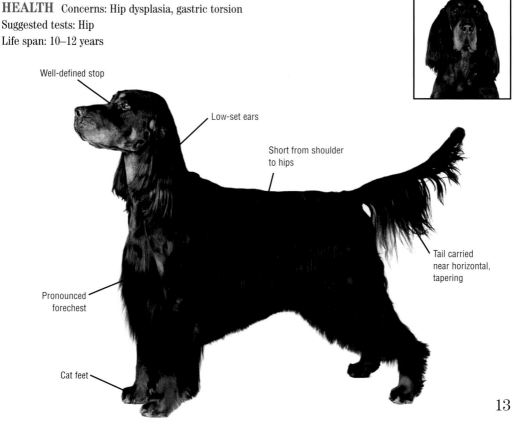

Well-defined stop

Low-set ears

Short from shoulder to hips

Tail carried near horizontal, tapering

Pronounced forechest

Cat feet

Setter (Irish)

Area of Origin: Ireland
Original Function: Bird setting and retrieving
Coat: Straight, medium length
Color: Mahogany or rich chestnut red
Height: Male: about 27″; Female: about 25″
Weight: Male: about 70 lb; Female: about 60 lb

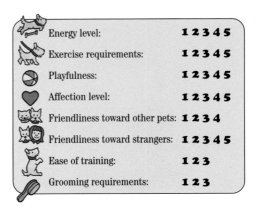

Energy level:	1 2 3 4 **5**
Exercise requirements:	1 2 3 4 **5**
Playfulness:	1 2 3 4 **5**
Affection level:	1 2 3 4 **5**
Friendliness toward other pets:	1 2 3 **4**
Friendliness toward strangers:	1 2 3 4 **5**
Ease of training:	1 2 **3**
Grooming requirements:	1 **2** 3

HISTORY Irish hunters who needed a fast-working, keen-nosed dog found it in the red and white setters produced from crosses of spaniels, pointers, and other setters. The first kennels of solid red setters appeared around 1800, and the first ones came to America by the mid-1800s. Around 1862 a dog was born in Ireland that would forever change the breed: Champion Palmerston. He was considered too slight for the field, so his owner ordered him drowned. Another fancier interceded and Palmerston became a sensation as a show dog, also siring an incredible number of offspring. Virtually every modern Irish Setter can be traced to Palmerston. As interests changed from field trials to dog shows, emphasis changed from hunting ability to glamour. The Irish Setter was among the most popular breeds in America in the 1970s.

TEMPERAMENT Irish Setters were bred to be tireless and eager hunters, and they approach life with gusto. Without ample exercise, they can be overly active inside or become frustrated. They are amiable and eager to please. Although good with children, they can be too rambunctious for small children.

UPKEEP Irish need lots of strenuous exercise. The coat needs regular brushing and combing every two to three days, plus some clipping and trimming to look its best.

HEALTH Concerns: Hip dysplasia, gastric torsion, PRA
Suggested tests: Hip, eye
Life span: 12–14 years

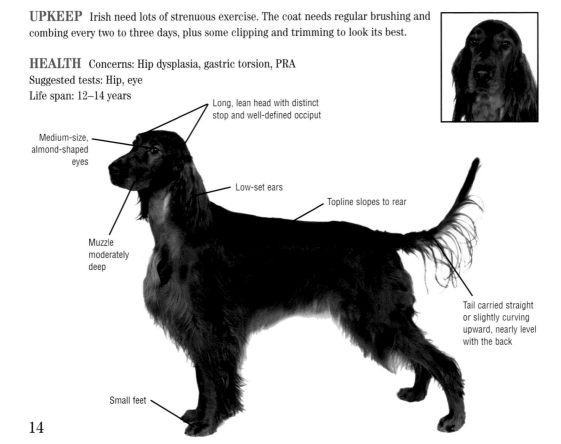

Long, lean head with distinct stop and well-defined occiput

Medium-size, almond-shaped eyes

Low-set ears

Topline slopes to rear

Muzzle moderately deep

Tail carried straight or slightly curving upward, nearly level with the back

Small feet

Spaniel (American Water)

Area of Origin: United States
Original Function: Bird flushing and retrieving
Coat: Wavy to curly, medium length
Color: Solid liver, brown, or dark chocolate
Height: 15–18″
Weight: Male: 30–45 lb; Female: 25–40 lb

Energy level:	**1 2 3 4**
Exercise requirements:	**1 2 3**
Playfulness:	**1 2 3 4**
Affection level:	**1 2 3**
Friendliness toward other pets:	**1 2 3**
Friendliness toward strangers:	**1 2**
Ease of training:	**1 2 3**
Grooming requirements:	**1 2 3**

HISTORY The American Water Spaniel first became established as a recognizable breed in the midwestern parts of the United States, where it was unsurpassed as a hunting companion. This small dog with the water-proof coat and keen nose could hunt through rough thickets, could spring game, and could retrieve all manner of game from land or water, often marking several fallen birds before retrieving them all unfailingly. Until it was recognized by the AKC in 1940, no one ever considered breeding these dogs for anything but hunting ability. Even after recognition, the breed's forte remained in the field, and it is a rarity in the show ring, or even the home. Today, the American Water Spaniel is among the rarest of AKC-recognized breeds, despite being one of only two sporting breeds developed in America.

TEMPERAMENT These skilled retrievers are also tractable fun-loving family dogs, sensitive and willing to please. Some can be aggressive toward strange dogs. Barking can be a problem.

UPKEEP American Water Spaniels need a long walk daily. The oily coat needs weekly brushing.

HEALTH Concerns: Heart problems, hip dysplasia
Suggested tests: Heart, hip
Life span: 10–12 years

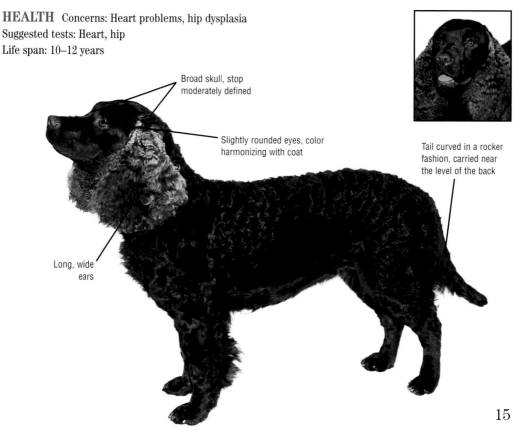

Broad skull, stop moderately defined

Slightly rounded eyes, color harmonizing with coat

Tail curved in a rocker fashion, carried near the level of the back

Long, wide ears

Spaniel (Clumber)

Area of Origin: England
Original function: Bird flushing and retrieving
Coat: Straight, flat, medium length
Color: White dog with lemon or orange markings (the fewer the markings on body, the better)
Height: Male: 19–20″; Female: 17–19″
Weight: Male: 70–85 lb; Female: 55–70 lb

Energy level:	**1 2**
Exercise requirements:	**1 2**
Playfulness:	**1 2 3**
Affection level:	**1 2 3 4**
Friendliness toward other pets:	**1 2 3 4**
Friendliness toward strangers:	**1 2 3**
Ease of training:	**1 2 3**
Grooming requirements:	**1 2 3**

HISTORY The stockiest of the spaniels, the Clumber is also one of the oldest, dating to the late 1700s. The breed did not get its name until around the time of the French Revolution, when it is believed that the *Duc de Noailles* of France moved his spaniel kennels to the Duke of Newcastle's English estate, Clumber Park. Clumber Spaniels appealed to the English nobility, who appreciated this slow-moving but especially keen-nosed hunter that was also an adept retriever. The breed was not readily available to commoners, as the nobility discouraged its popularity except among higher society. As befitting their high status, Clumbers were among the earliest breeds to be shown. They came to America in the late 1800s. They remain one of the rarest of AKC breeds.

TEMPERAMENT Clumber Spaniels are among the most low-keyed and easygoing of sporting breeds. They like to hunt, but they are generally quiet in the house. Clumbers make good companions, tending to be especially devoted to one person.

UPKEEP Clumbers enjoy daily outings, but their exercise requirements can be met with a long leisurely walk. The coat needs brushing two to three times weekly. In dirty areas the coat may need frequent bathing to stay bright white. Clumbers tend to drool and at times, snore.

HEALTH Concerns: Intervertebral disk disease, entropion
Suggested tests: Eye
Life span: 10–12 years

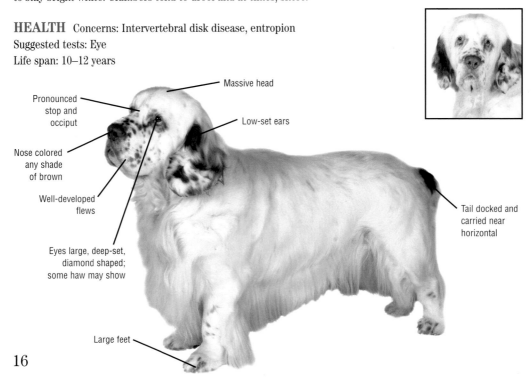

Massive head

Pronounced stop and occiput

Low-set ears

Nose colored any shade of brown

Well-developed flews

Eyes large, deep-set, diamond shaped; some haw may show

Tail docked and carried near horizontal

Large feet

Spaniel (Cocker)

Energy level:	**1 2** 3	
Exercise requirements:	**1 2** 3	
Playfulness:	**1 2 3** 4	
Affection level:	**1 2 3 4 5**	
Friendliness toward other pets:	**1 2 3 4 5**	
Friendliness toward strangers:	**1 2 3** 4	
Ease of training:	**1 2 3** 4	
Grooming requirements:	**1 2 3** 4	

Area of Origin: United States
Original Function: Bird flushing and retrieving
Coat: Flat or wavy, medium length
Color: Black variety: solid black or black and tan; ASCOB variety: any solid color other than black, including cream, red, brown, and brown with tan points; Particolor variety: any of the allowed solid colors broken up on a white background; also roans
Height: Male: 14.5–15.5″; Female: 13.5–14.5″
Weight: 24–28 lb

HISTORY The American version of the Cocker Spaniel is derived from the English Cocker Spaniel. In the late 1800s many English Cockers were brought to America, but American hunters preferred a slightly smaller dog to hunt quail and other small game birds. Just how this smaller Cocker was developed is not entirely clear; some credit the dog Obo 2nd, born around 1880, as the first true American Cocker. Initially, English and American Cocker Spaniels were considered varieties of the same breed, but were officially separated by the AKC in 1935. Although Cockers were already popular, after the separation the American Cocker surged in popularity and has remained one of the most popular breeds of all time in America. So popular was it that it was eventually divided into three color varieties: black, particolor, and ASCOB, which stands for Any Solid Color Other than Black.

TEMPERAMENT Cocker Spaniels are merry, sensitive, active, and responsive. Some bark a lot; some are overly submissive.

UPKEEP Cockers need a moderate walk daily. The coat requires brushing two to three times a week, plus clipping every two to three months. The ears require special attention.

HEALTH Concerns: Eye problems, ear problems, patellar luxation, seborrhea
Suggested tests: Eye
Life span: 12–15 years

Rounded skull with pronounced stop

Expression alert, soft, and appealing

Long, low-set, lobular ears

Topline slopes slightly to rear

Tail docked and carried in line or slightly higher than the topline

Round feet

17

Spaniel (English Cocker)

Area of Origin: England
Original Function: Bird flushing and retrieving
Coat: Flat or wavy, medium length
Color: Solid black, liver, or red, black and tan, liver and tan, and any of these colors on a white background either particolored, ticked, or roan
Height: Male: 16–17″; Female: 15–16″
Weight: Male: 28–34 lb; Female: 26–32 lb

Energy level:	**1 2 3**
Exercise requirements:	**1 2 3**
Playfulness:	**1 2 3 4**
Affection level:	**1 2 3 4 5**
Friendliness toward other pets:	**1 2 3 4 5**
Friendliness toward strangers:	**1 2 3 4**
Ease of training:	**1 2 3 4**
Grooming requirements:	**1 2 3**

HISTORY The English Cocker Spaniel is one of the land spaniels, of which larger specimens were better for springing game and smaller ones better for hunting woodcock. These sizes appeared in the same litters. Only in 1892 were the two sizes considered separate breeds, with the smaller size (under 25 lb) designated as the Cocker Spaniel. Cocker Spaniels became extremely popular in England, but American breeders changed the breed in ways that traditional English Cocker Spaniel enthusiasts objected to. One of the initial goals of the English Cocker Spaniel Club of America (formed in 1935) was to discourage the interbreeding of the American and English Cockers. Once the breeds were separated, the American Cocker eclipsed the English in popularity—but only in America. In England, the English Cocker is by far the more popular of the two breeds.

TEMPERAMENT English Cocker Spaniels are cheerful, inquisitive, demonstrative, devoted, biddable, and sensitive. They retain more of their hunting nature than do American Cockers, and also need more exercise.

UPKEEP English Cockers need daily exercise, either a long walk or vigorous run. The coat needs brushing two to three times week, plus clipping every three months. The ears should be cleaned weekly.

HEALTH Concerns: Ear problems, PRA, cataracts, patellar luxation, hip dysplasia, (deafness in particolors)
Suggested tests: Knee, hip
Lifespan: 12–14 years

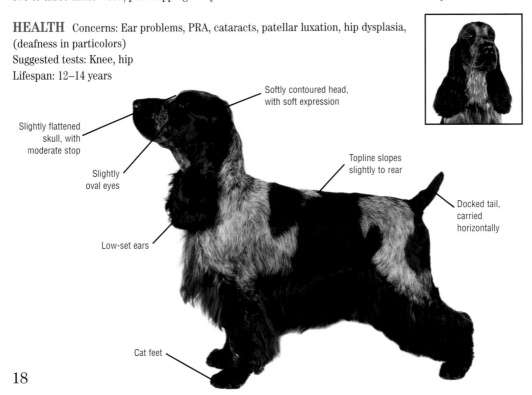

Softly contoured head, with soft expression

Slightly flattened skull, with moderate stop

Slightly oval eyes

Topline slopes slightly to rear

Docked tail, carried horizontally

Low-set ears

Cat feet

Spaniel (English Springer)

Energy level:	**1 2 3**	
Exercise requirements:	**1 2 3 4**	
Playfulness:	**1 2 3 4**	
Affection level:	**1 2 3 4 5**	
Friendliness toward other pets:	**1 2 3 4 5**	
Friendliness toward strangers:	**1 2 3 4**	
Ease of training:	**1 2 3 4 5**	
Grooming requirements:	**1 2 3 4**	

Area of Origin: England
Original Function: Bird flushing and retrieving
Coat: Flat or wavy, medium length
Color: Black or liver with white, black or liver roan, or
tricolored (black or liver and white with tan markings);
also white with black or liver markings
Height: Male: 19–21″; Female 18–20″
Weight: Male: about 50 lb; Female: about 40 lb

HISTORY The first reference to "springers" referred to land spaniels in the late 1500s. Before the advent of shotguns, the game was flushed, or sprung, into nets or to be chased by falcons or greyhounds. Around 1800 distinct strains of springers began to develop; one of the best known were Norfolk Spaniels bred by the Duke of Norfolk. The name was changed to Springer Spaniels in 1900. The matter is complicated by the fact that the larger Springer and smaller Cocker spaniels were simply size variations of the same breed. Only in 1902 did the English Kennel Club recognize the Springer as a distinct breed. In America, the American Spaniel Club was formed in 1880 and began the task of separating the Springer and Cocker sizes. After separation the Springer continued to thrive. It has remained popular with hunters demanding a versatile gun dog that ranges fast and far, and that can also flush and retrieve.

TEMPERAMENT English Springer Spaniels are cheerful, playful, and energetic, ready for a day in the field and an evening by the hearth. They do everything with gusto, and can be overly enthusiastic unless given plenty of exercise. They are amiable with strangers.

UPKEEP Springers need daily runs or long walks. The coat needs brushing or combing once or twice weekly, plus clipping and scissoring every three months.

HEALTH Concerns: Hip dysplasia, ear problems, elbow dysplasia, PRA
Suggested tests: Hip, eye
Life span: 10–14 years

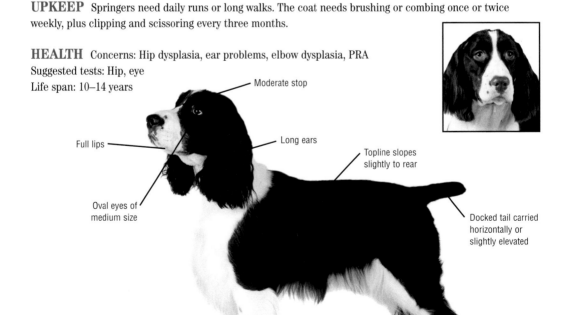

Moderate stop

Full lips

Long ears

Topline slopes slightly to rear

Oval eyes of medium size

Docked tail carried horizontally or slightly elevated

Spaniel (Field)

Area of Origin: England
Original Function: Bird flushing and retrieving
Coat: Flat or wavy, medium length
Color: Black, liver, golden liver; solid or
  bicolored; roaned or ticked in white areas. Tan points
  allowed. White allowed on throat, chest, or brisket
Height: Male: 18″; Female: 17″ (±1 inch)
Weight: 35–50 lb

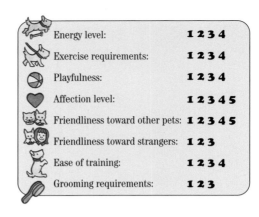

Energy level:	**1 2 3 4**
Exercise requirements:	**1 2 3 4**
Playfulness:	**1 2 3 4**
Affection level:	**1 2 3 4 5**
Friendliness toward other pets:	**1 2 3 4 5**
Friendliness toward strangers:	**1 2 3**
Ease of training:	**1 2 3 4**
Grooming requirements:	**1 2 3**

HISTORY The Field Spaniel shares its early history with the Cocker Spaniel, the only difference between the two breeds initially being one of size. The Field Spaniels were designated as those land spaniels weighing over 25 pounds. These larger Field Spaniels were originally required to be black. After becoming recognized as a separate breed in the late 1800s, the Field Spaniel succumbed to breeding for exaggeration, and the repeated infusion of Sussex Spaniel blood resulted in dogs of excessive length, overly heavy bone, and short legs. Crosses to Irish Water Spaniels, which were made in an effort to gain greater leg length, helped popularize the liver color. Other crosses with Cocker and Springer Spaniels helped recreate the breed, although it was difficult to obtain registration for them at first. The modern Field Spaniel is not only a handsome replica of its former self, but an able hunter.

TEMPERAMENT Field Spaniels are tireless and talented bird hunters. Though independent, they are devoted, docile, and willing to please. Always cheerful and affectionate, they are excellent family companions. They are typically reserved with strangers.

UPKEEP Field Spaniels need daily exercise, either vigorous runs or long walks. The coat needs brushing and combing once or twice weekly. The ears should be cleaned regularly.

HEALTH Concerns: Hip dysplasia, ear problems
Suggested tests: Hip
Life span: 12–14 years

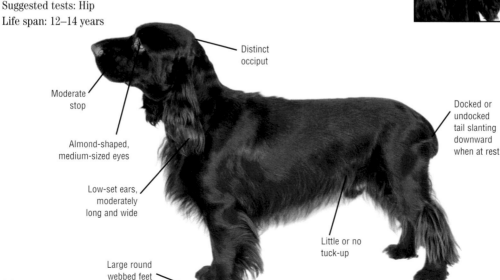

Distinct
occiput

Moderate
stop

Almond-shaped,
medium-sized eyes

Low-set ears,
moderately
long and wide

Large round
webbed feet

Little or no
tuck-up

Docked or
undocked
tail slanting
downward
when at rest

Spaniel (Irish Water)

Energy level:	1 2 3 4 5
Exercise requirements:	1 2 3 4 5
Playfulness:	1 2 3 4 5
Affection level:	1 2 3
Friendliness toward other pets:	1 2 3
Friendliness toward strangers:	1 2
Ease of training:	1 2 3 4 5
Grooming requirements:	1 2 3

Area of Origin: Ireland
Original Function: Water retrieving
Coat: Tight ringlets, medium length
Color: Solid liver
Height: Male: 22–24″; Female: 21–23″
Weight: Male: 55–65 lb; Female: 45–58 lb

HISTORY Irish Water Spaniels may be one of the oldest spaniels, perhaps dating to the 1100s, and almost certainly by the 1600s. At that time, several similar spaniels existed in Ireland; the Southern Irish Spaniel, also called McCarthy's Breed, is credited with being the eventual major forebear of today's Irish Water Spaniel. In the mid-1800s the appearance of the prolific sire Boatswain so influenced the breed that he is often credited as being the progenitor of the modern Irish Water Spaniel. The breed entered the show ring in both Britain and America by the late 1800s. In 1875 it was the third-most popular sporting dog. Despite its enchantingly clownish appearance and adept water retrieving ability, the Irish Water Spaniel lost popularity, and is not commonly seen in the show ring and rarely found in the pet home at present.

TEMPERAMENT Irish Water Spaniels approach everything with enthusiasm. They love to swim, run, hunt, and play. They are clowns, and can be stubborn and independent. They tend to be reserved with strangers.

UPKEEP Irish Water Spaniels need a daily hour of strenuous activity. Their coat needs combing two to three times a week, plus scissoring every few months. Shed hairs tend to become trapped in the coat, which can cause matting.

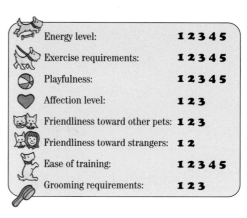

HEALTH Concerns: Hip dysplasia, ear problems
Suggested tests: Hip
Life span: 10–12 years

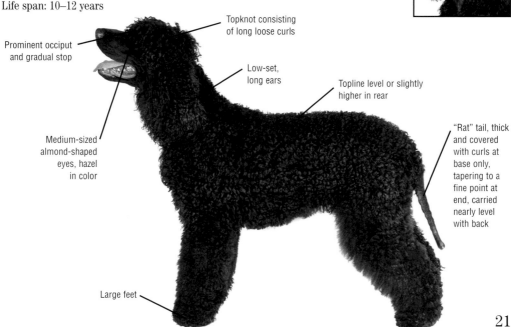

Topknot consisting of long loose curls

Prominent occiput and gradual stop

Low-set, long ears

Topline level or slightly higher in rear

Medium-sized almond-shaped eyes, hazel in color

"Rat" tail, thick and covered with curls at base only, tapering to a fine point at end, carried nearly level with back

Large feet

Spaniel (Sussex)

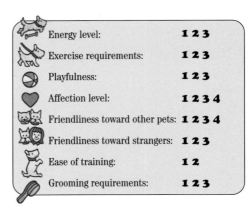

Energy level:	**1 2 3**
Exercise requirements:	**1 2 3**
Playfulness:	**1 2 3**
Affection level:	**1 2 3 4**
Friendliness toward other pets:	**1 2 3 4**
Friendliness toward strangers:	**1 2 3**
Ease of training:	**1 2**
Grooming requirements:	**1 2 3**

Area of Origin: England
Original Function: Small game tracking and flushing
Coat: Flat or wavy, medium length
Color: Rich golden liver
Height: 13–15″
Weight: 35–45 lb

HISTORY The first important breeder of the "Spaniels of Sussex" was established around 1795 in Sussex County, where the breed became quite popular. They were adept as upland shooting dogs, slow working but with a good nose and apt to give tongue when on scent. This latter trait hurt the breed at field trials in the early 1900s, when quiet hunters were preferred. In addition, American hunters usually preferred a faster hunter. Although one of the earliest breeds to compete at dog shows, the Sussex Spaniel has been perilously close to extinction throughout most of the 20th century. At times the breed had so few individuals that inbreeding had to be practiced more than was otherwise desirable. In 1954 a cross was made with the Clumber Spaniel to expand the gene pool. It remains among the rarest of AKC breeds.

TEMPERAMENT Sussex Spaniels are lower energy and less demonstrative than most spaniels. They are calm, steady, and easygoing, but some tend to bark. They may be aggressive to strange dogs.

UPKEEP The Sussex needs at least one good walk or romp daily. The coat needs brushing and combing two to three times a week, plus scissoring every few months.

HEALTH Concerns: Hip dysplasia, intervertebral disk disease, ear problems, heart problems
Suggested tests: Hip, heart
Life span: 11–13 years

Eyes soft and languishing, fairly large, hazel colored

Large, low-set ears

Tail docked from 5 to 7″

Somewhat pendulous lips

Large round feet, with long feathering

Spaniel (Welsh Springer)

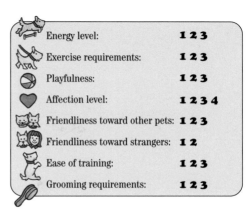

	Energy level:	**1 2 3**
	Exercise requirements:	**1 2 3**
	Playfulness:	**1 2 3**
	Affection level:	**1 2 3 4**
	Friendliness toward other pets:	**1 2 3**
	Friendliness toward strangers:	**1 2**
	Ease of training:	**1 2 3**
	Grooming requirements:	**1 2 3**

Area of Origin: Wales
Original Function: Bird flushing and retrieving
Coat: Flat, medium length
Color: Rich red and white
Height: Male: 18–19″; Female: 17–18″
Weight: 35–50 lb

HISTORY Land spaniels were used in Wales long before the Welsh Springer emerged as a recognized breed. In fact, at the first dog shows in England, English and Welsh Springers were shown together as one breed, since the only difference at that time was in their color. The breed came to America and was recognized by the AKC in 1906. But the Welsh failed to gain the support it needed, and by the end of World War II it may have totally disappeared from America. New imports arrived and fortunately, new supporters, and the Welsh has since enjoyed a steady, if modest, popularity. Not as flashy in the show ring as the English Springer, the Welsh makes up for it in the field. It is an all-purpose all-terrain hunter with a keen nose that can flush and retrieve over land and water.

TEMPERAMENT Less exuberant than English Springers, Welsh Springer Spaniels are steady and easygoing. They are extremely devoted family dogs, but reserved with strangers. Their great love is hunting, and they make good hiking companions.

UPKEEP Welsh Springer Spaniels need long walks or strenuous games every day. The coat needs brushing once or twice weekly, and also needs occasional scissoring to tidy stragglers.

HEALTH Concerns: Hip dysplasia, ear problems, glaucoma, epilepsy
Suggested tests: Hip, eye
Life span: 12–15 years

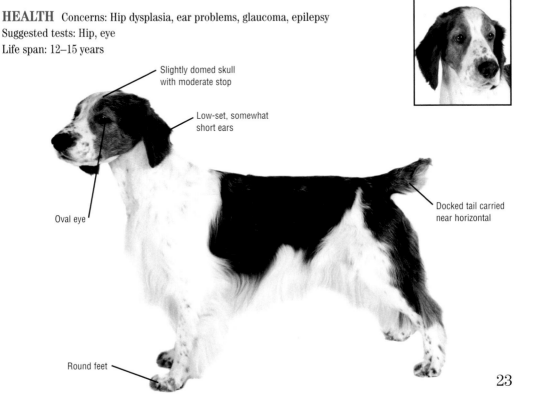

Slightly domed skull with moderate stop

Low-set, somewhat short ears

Oval eye

Docked tail carried near horizontal

Round feet

Spinone Italiano

Area of Origin: Italy

Original Function: Pointing and retrieving

Coat: Stiff and flat or slightly crimped; short to medium length

Color: All white or white with orange or chestnut markings; orange or brown roan with or without larger markings

Height: Male: 23–27″; Female: 22–25″

Weight: Male: 71–82 lb; Female: 62–71 lb

Energy level:	**1 2 3**
Exercise requirements:	**1 2 3**
Playfulness:	**1 2 3**
Affection level:	**1 2 3 4**
Friendliness toward other pets:	**1 2 3 4**
Friendliness toward strangers:	**1 2 3 4**
Ease of training:	**1 2 3**
Grooming requirements:	**1 2**

HISTORY Present-day Spinoni trace back principally to Italy's Piedmont region. They proved themselves adept at penetrating thorny cover and finding feathered or fur game. During World War II, the Spinone further distinguished itself by tracking German patrols. The end of the war found the breed in trouble, however, because its numbers had been decimated and many of the remaining dogs crossed with other breeds. The Spinone was in danger of being lost. In the 1950s, breeders began a concerted effort to reconstruct the Spinone Italiano. Its hunting abilities are well worth the effort. This is a dog that can point, set, and retrieve, aided by a good nose and good sense. It is noted for hunting at a fast trot in a diagonal pattern that keeps it fairly close to the hunter, and is classified as a versatile hunting breed.

TEMPERAMENT Spinoni are devoted and gentle, very willing to please. They are affectionate and get along well with everyone. The Spinone is calmer and more easygoing than most pointing breeds.

UPKEEP The Spinone needs a long walk or good run daily. Coat care consists of weekly brushing, plus occasional hand-stripping to tidy the face and feet.

HEALTH Concerns: Hip dysplasia, gastric torsion, ear problems
Suggested tests: Hip
Life span: 12–14 years

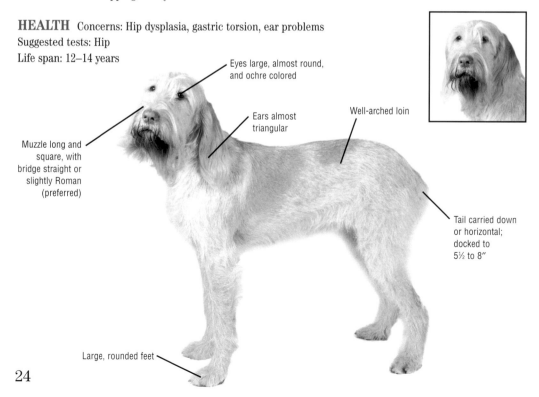

Eyes large, almost round, and ochre colored

Ears almost triangular

Well-arched loin

Muzzle long and square, with bridge straight or slightly Roman (preferred)

Tail carried down or horizontal; docked to 5½ to 8″

Large, rounded feet

Vizsla

Area of Origin: Hungary
Original Function: Pointing, falconry, trailing
Coat: Smooth, short
Color: Solid golden rust
Height: Male: 22–24″; Female: 21–23″
Weight: 45–65 lb

Energy level:	**1 2 3**
Exercise requirements:	**1 2 3**
Playfulness:	**1 2 3 4**
Affection level:	**1 2 3 4 5**
Friendliness toward other pets:	**1 2 3 4**
Friendliness toward strangers:	**1 2 3 4 5**
Ease of training:	**1 2 3**
Grooming requirements:	**1**

HISTORY The Vizsla's forebears may have included breeds that the Magyars collected as they swarmed across Europe before settling in Hungary over 1,000 years ago. The Hungarian plains were rich in game, and hunters wanted a fast but close-working dog that could not only point and retrieve birds but trail mammals over thick ground cover. The breed was unquestionably established by the 18th century, having found special favor with barons and warlords. After World War I the breed almost died out, but World War II may have ultimately saved the Vizsla as Hungarians fleeing Russian occupation took their pointing dogs to other countries. The breed came to America in the 1950s, with AKC recognition in 1960.

TEMPERAMENT Vizslas are gentle, affectionate, and sensitive. They can be protective and stubborn, and some can be overly excitable.

UPKEEP Vizslas need strenuous exercise, such as a long jog or vigorous workout, every day. The coat requires little care except an occasional brushing to remove dead hair.

HEALTH Concerns: Epilepsy, hip dysplasia, lymphosarcoma
Suggested tests: Hip
Life span: 10–14 years

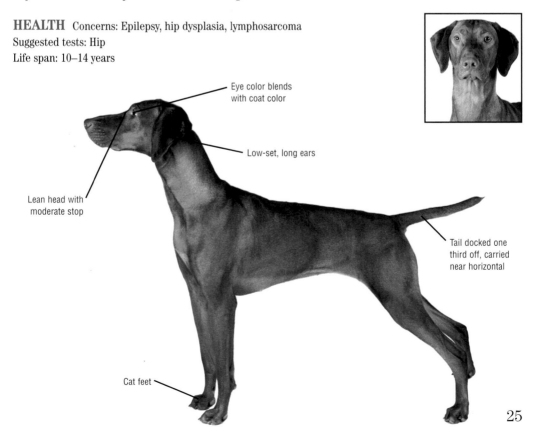

Eye color blends with coat color

Low-set, long ears

Lean head with moderate stop

Tail docked one third off, carried near horizontal

Cat feet

Weimaraner

Area of Origin: Germany
Original Function: Large game trailing
Coat: Smooth, short
Color: Mouse-gray to silver-gray
Height: Male: 25–27″; Female: 23–25″
Weight: 55–90 lb

Energy level:	**1 2 3 4 5**
Exercise requirements:	**1 2 3 4**
Playfulness:	**1 2 3 4**
Affection level:	**1 2 3**
Friendliness toward other pets:	**1 2**
Friendliness toward strangers:	**1 2**
Ease of training:	**1 2 3 4**
Grooming requirements:	**1**

HISTORY The Weimaraner was produced in the 19th century by a concerted effort to create the ideal all-round gundog that could hunt game of all sizes, including deer and bear. This effort was sponsored by the court of Weimer, and the breed was initially known as the Weimar Pointer. The origin of the Weimaraner's distinctive gray color is unknown, but it was an early feature of the breed. The breed's progress was strictly overseen by the German Weimaraner Club. Only when an American gained entry to the club, and was allowed to take two dogs back to America in 1929, did the Weimaraner leave its native land. As American hunters discovered its remarkable abilities in the field, and pet owners discovered its companionable nature, the breed gained admirers.

TEMPERAMENT Weimaraners are bold and rambunctious. They love to run, hunt, and explore. They can be headstrong.

UPKEEP Daily strenuous exertion is a must, at least an hour daily. Coat care consists of occasional brushing to remove dead hair.

HEALTH Concerns: Gastric torsion, hip dysplasia
Suggested tests: Hip
Life span: 10–13 years

Prominent occiput

Eyes shaded light amber, gray, or blue-gray

Nose gray

High-set, long ears

Topline slopes slightly to rear

Tail docked to 6″

Webbed feet

Wirehaired Pointing Griffon

Area of Origin: France
Original Function: Pointing, retrieving
Coat: Straight, wiry, medium length
Color: Preferably steel-gray with brown markings, also chestnut brown, or roan, white and brown. Less desirable is solid brown, solid white, or white and orange.
Height: Male: 22–24"; Female: 20–22"
Weight: 50–60 lb

Energy level:		1 2 3 4
Exercise requirements:		1 2 3 4
Playfulness:		1 2 3
Affection level:		1 2 3
Friendliness toward other pets:		1 2 3
Friendliness toward strangers:		1 2 3
Ease of training:		1 2 3
Grooming requirements:		1 2 3

HISTORY In 1874, Edward Korthals of Holland crossed 20 dogs representing several breeds (Griffon, Spaniel, Water Spaniel, German and French Pointer, and Setter) and then traveled extensively in France to popularize his new breed. The Korthals Griffon, as it is still known in many parts of the world, gained a reputation as a deliberate, careful hunter with a good nose. A breed standard was published in 1887. Its popularity grew steadily, only to be halted by World War II. The initiation of competitive field trials, in which faster-paced breeds dominated, caused many competitive hunters to turn away from the Griffon. Today its popularity remains low, but its followers consider it the supreme gun dog, able to point and retrieve, as well as serve as an excellent companion.

TEMPERAMENT Wirehaired Pointing Griffons are devoted, willing to please, amiable, and often, comical. They are reserved with strangers.

UPKEEP Wirehired Pointing Griffons need a long walk or good run daily. The harsh coat needs combing or brushing once or twice a week, plus hand-stripping to remove dead hair twice a year.

HEALTH Concerns: Hip dysplasia, ear problems
Suggested tests: hip
Life span: 12–14 years

Abundant mustache and eyebrows

Nose brown

Eyes large and rounded, in all shades of yellow and brown

High-set, medium-sized ears

Topline slopes slightly to rear

Tail docked to two-thirds to one-half length, carried straight or slightly raised

Round webbed feet

Afghan Hound

Area of Origin: Afghanistan
Original Function: Coursing hare and gazelle
Coat: Long, silky
Color: All colors permissible except spotted
Height: Male: 27″; Female: 25″ (±1″)
Weight: Male: 60 lb; Female: 50 lb

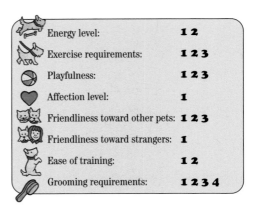

Energy level:	**1 2**
Exercise requirements:	**1 2 3**
Playfulness:	**1 2 3**
Affection level:	**1**
Friendliness toward other pets:	**1 2 3**
Friendliness toward strangers:	**1**
Ease of training:	**1 2**
Grooming requirements:	**1 2 3 4**

HISTORY The Afghan Hound is an ancient breed derived from the group of Middle Eastern sighthounds. It was used by nomadic tribes as a coursing hound capable of providing hare and gazelle meat for the pot. Generations of hunting in the harsh mountainous terrain of Afghanistan produced a fast dog that also had a good deal of stamina, but most of all, had incredible leaping ability and nimbleness. Its long coat protected it from the cold climate. These dogs remained isolated for centuries, hidden in the impenetrable Afghanistan mountains. The first Afghan Hounds came to England in the early 1900s. The breed's standard of perfection was modeled on Zardin, a particularly striking dog. Popularity grew slowly, with the dog appealing mostly to the glamour set. In the 1970s the Afghan became a fad breed with the public, but it has since dwindled in popularity.

TEMPERAMENT Afghan Hounds are independent hunters, with a tendency to chase small animals, keep on running, and not come when called. They are sensitive, yet not overly demonstrative, with a gay, clownish side.

UPKEEP Afghans need daily exertion, either a long walk or some short sprints in a fenced area. The coat requires brushing every two to three days, more often when shedding the puppy coat.

HEALTH Concerns: Cataract
Suggested tests: Eye
Life span: 12–14 years

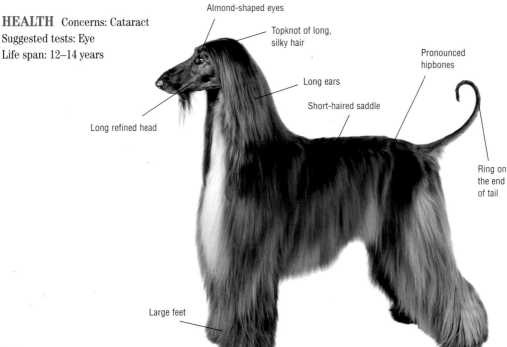

Almond-shaped eyes

Topknot of long, silky hair

Pronounced hipbones

Long ears

Short-haired saddle

Long refined head

Ring on the end of tail

Large feet

Basenji

Area of Origin: Central Africa (Zaire and the Congo)
Original Function: Hunting small game
Coat: Smooth, short
Color: Red, black, black and tan, or brindle, all with white feet, chest, and tail tips; white legs, blaze, and collar optional
Height: Male: 17″; Female: 16″
Weight: Male: 24 lb; Female: 22 lb

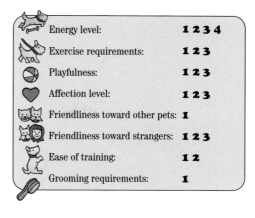

Energy level:	**1 2 3 4**
Exercise requirements:	**1 2 3**
Playfulness:	**1 2 3**
Affection level:	**1 2 3**
Friendliness toward other pets:	**1**
Friendliness toward strangers:	**1 2 3**
Ease of training:	**1 2**
Grooming requirements:	**1**

HISTORY   The Basenji is among the most primitive of breeds, discovered living in the African Congo with Pygmy hunters. The native tribes used the dogs as pack hunters, driving game into nets, often wearing a large bell. Early attempts to bring the dogs to England in the late 1800s and early 1900s were unsuccessful, as they all succumbed to distemper. In 1929 a few dogs were successfully brought back to England and became the foundation (along with subsequent imports from the Congo and Sudan) of the breed outside of Africa. The name *Basenji* was chosen, meaning "bush thing." The early imports attracted much attention, and soon after, dogs were brought to America. The Basenji retains several primitive characteristics, most notably its lack of barking ability and its yearly, rather than twice yearly, estrus cycle.

TEMPERAMENT   Basenjis don't bark, but they chortle and yodel. They are clever, inquisitive, stubborn, independent, and reserved. They are often described as catlike.

UPKEEP   Basenjis need daily mental and physical exercise or they are apt to be destructive. Coat care is minimal, consisting of only occasional brushing to remove dead hair.

HEALTH   Concerns: Fanconi syndrome, Basenji enteropathy, PRA
Suggested tests: Eye
Life span: 12–14 years

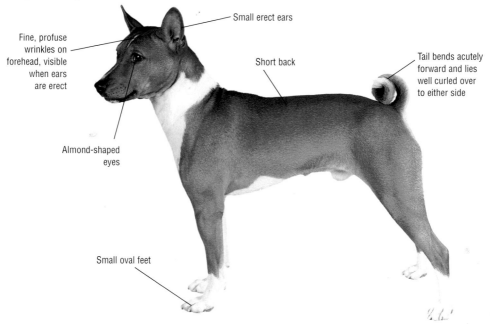

Small erect ears

Fine, profuse wrinkles on forehead, visible when ears are erect

Short back

Tail bends acutely forward and lies well curled over to either side

Almond-shaped eyes

Small oval feet

Basset Hound

Area of Origin: France
Original Function: Trailing rabbits and hare
Coat: Hard, smooth, short
Color: Any recognized hound color
Height: Preferably not over 14″
Weight: 40–60 lb

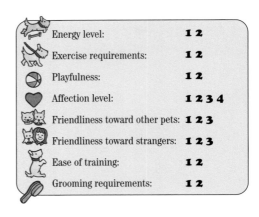

Energy level:	**1 2**
Exercise requirements:	**1 2**
Playfulness:	**1 2**
Affection level:	**1 2 3 4**
Friendliness toward other pets:	**1 2 3**
Friendliness toward strangers:	**1 2 3**
Ease of training:	**1 2**
Grooming requirements:	**1 2**

HISTORY The word Basset is derived from the French *bas* meaning "low thing." Dwarfed short-legged specimens occur in many breeds and have been known since ancient times, but it is difficult to know at what point such dogs were purposefully bred and which ones led to the present Basset Hound. After the French Revolution, greater numbers of commoners took up hunting. They needed a good scenting hound they could follow on foot, and that wouldn't scare the quarry out of gun range. The dogs were especially suited for rabbits. Four different versions of short-legged hounds were created, with the Basset Artesien Normand most closely resembling today's Basset. The first Bassets were brought to England and America in the late 1800s. By the mid-1900s, the Basset's droll expression had won it a place in advertising and homes.

TEMPERAMENT Basset Hounds are good-natured and easygoing, amiable with all. They are slow, can be stubborn, and may not be playful enough for active children. They enjoy sniffing and trailing, and are not easily called off a scent. They can bay loudly.

UPKEEP Bassets need regular, but unhurried, exercise. The coat needs only minimal grooming, but the face may need regular cleaning around the mouth and wrinkles. Bassets tend to drool.

HEALTH Concerns: Elbow dysplasia, ear problems, eyelid problems, glaucoma, gastric torsion, hip dysplasia, vWD
Suggested tests: Eye, hip, vWD
Life span: 8-12 years

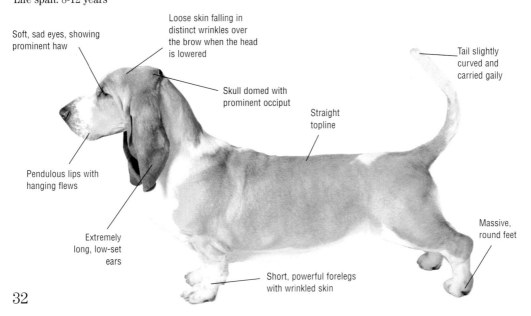

Soft, sad eyes, showing prominent haw

Loose skin falling in distinct wrinkles over the brow when the head is lowered

Skull domed with prominent occiput

Straight topline

Tail slightly curved and carried gaily

Pendulous lips with hanging flews

Extremely long, low-set ears

Short, powerful forelegs with wrinkled skin

Massive, round feet

Beagle

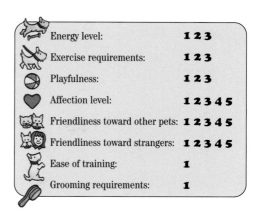

Energy level:	**1 2 3**
Exercise requirements:	**1 2 3**
Playfulness:	**1 2 3**
Affection level:	**1 2 3 4 5**
Friendliness toward other pets:	**1 2 3 4 5**
Friendliness toward strangers:	**1 2 3 4 5**
Ease of training:	**1**
Grooming requirements:	**1**

Area of Origin: England
Original Function: Trailing rabbits
Coat: Hard, smooth, short
Color: Any true hound color
Height: 13″ variety: not exceeding 13″; 15″ variety: over 13″, but not exceeding 15″
Weight: 18–30 lb

HISTORY Beagle-type dogs were probably used in England by the 14th century for hare hunting, although the word Beagle was not used until 1475. Frequent references to Beagles can be found from the 16th century on. Hunters could follow these dogs on foot, and could even carry one in a pocket if the need arose. By the 1800s Beagles existed in several sizes, but the smaller "pocket-size" dogs were particularly popular. One of the special appeals of the smaller Beagles was that the hunt could be followed even by "ladies, the aged, or the infirm," as they slowly followed the winding path of the hare. The first mention of the Beagle in America was in 1642. By the end of the 19th century Beagles were popular competitors in both field and conformation exhibitions. They eventually became one of America's all-time favorite breeds.

TEMPERAMENT Amiable pack hounds, Beagles get along well with all. They are gentle, tolerant, and always ready to join in a game or adventure. They are independent, however, and may run off if a trail beckons. They tend to bark and howl.

UPKEEP Beagles needs daily exercise, either a long walk on leash or a romp in a safe area. Their coat needs brushing once a week.

HEALTH Concerns: Intervertebral disk disease, hip dysplasia
Suggested tests: Hip
Life span: 12–15 years

Gentle pleading expression

Stop moderately defined

Slightly curved tail, carried gaily

Short back

Square muzzle

Rounded ears

Round feet

Black and Tan Coonhound

Area of Origin: United States
Original Function: Hunting raccoons
Coat: Smooth, short
Color: Black and tan
Height: Male: 25–27″; Female: 23–25″
Weight: 55–75 lb

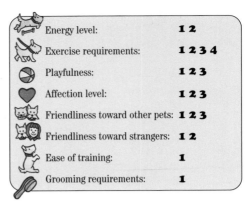

Energy level:	**1 2**
Exercise requirements:	**1 2 3 4**
Playfulness:	**1 2 3**
Affection level:	**1 2 3**
Friendliness toward other pets:	**1 2 3**
Friendliness toward strangers:	**1 2**
Ease of training:	**1**
Grooming requirements:	**1**

HISTORY Black and Tan Coonhounds probably originated from crosses of Bloodhounds and Foxhounds, particularly the Black and Tan Virginia Foxhound. Their development occurred mostly in the Appalachian, Blue Ridge, Ozark, and Smokey mountains, where they were used to hunt raccoons and bears over fairly rugged terrain. These dogs, as well as other coonhounds, trailed in the fashion of their Bloodhound ancestors, with nose to ground but at a somewhat swifter pace. Although they will trail any mammal, they specialize in raccoons and opossums, often trailing at night. When the quarry is treed, the dogs bay until the hunter arrives and shoots the animal. The AKC recognized the breed in 1945, but it has always been much more popular as a hunting dog than as a show dog or pet.

TEMPERAMENT Black and Tan Coonhounds are mellow, amiable, calm, and unobtrusive indoors. Outdoors, their strong hunting instincts take over and they are difficult to turn from a scent. They are gentle and tolerant with children, but are also strong, independent, and stubborn. They bay and howl.

UPKEEP Black and Tans can run for miles, but can be content with a moderate jog or long walk daily. The coat needs only occasional brushing. They tend to drool, and the face may need regular wiping.

HEALTH Concerns: Hip dysplasia, ectropion
Suggested tests: Hip, eye
Life span: 10–12 years

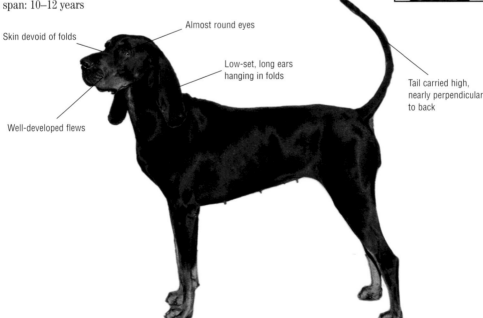

Skin devoid of folds

Almost round eyes

Low-set, long ears
hanging in folds

Well-developed flews

Tail carried high,
nearly perpendicular
to back

Bloodhound

Area of Origin: Belgium, England
Original Function: Trailing
Coat: Smooth, short
Color: Black and tan, liver and tan, and red
Height: Male: 25–27"; Female: 23–25"
Weight: Male: average 90 lb, up to 110 lb; Female: average 80 lb, up to 100 lb (Note: Most Bloodhounds are actually heavier than this.)

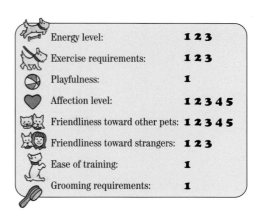

Energy level:	**1 2 3**
Exercise requirements:	**1 2 3**
Playfulness:	**1**
Affection level:	**1 2 3 4 5**
Friendliness toward other pets:	**1 2 3 4 5**
Friendliness toward strangers:	**1 2 3**
Ease of training:	**1**
Grooming requirements:	**1**

HISTORY The Bloodhound's roots trace to ancient times. Their earliest ancestors were the black Saint Hubert hounds documented in Europe by the 8th century. In the 12th century, many Church dignitaries were interested in hunting with these dogs, and most monasteries kept carefully bred packs. So highly bred were these dogs that they came to be known as "blooded hounds," referring to their pure blood and noble breeding. Bloodhounds have been known in America since the mid-1800s. The Bloodhound has since proven itself to be one of the most useful of breeds, using its unrivaled sense of smell to trail lost persons and criminals alike. Bloodhounds hold many trailing records (for both length and age of trail), and at one time were the only breed of dog whose identifications were accepted in a court of law.

TEMPERAMENT Bloodhounds are quiet at home, but tireless trailers once on the track. Once on a trail, they cannot be called off. They are tough, stubborn, and independent, yet gentle and placid. They are reserved with strangers.

UPKEEP Bloodhounds need daily long walks. Bloodhounds drool a lot, so their facial wrinkles require daily cleaning. The ear tips drag in food and must also be kept clean. The coat needs only occasional brushing.

HEALTH Concerns: Eyelid problems, gastric torsion, ear problems, skin-fold dermatitis, hip dysplasia, elbow dysplasia
Suggested tests: Hip, eye
Life span: 7–10 years

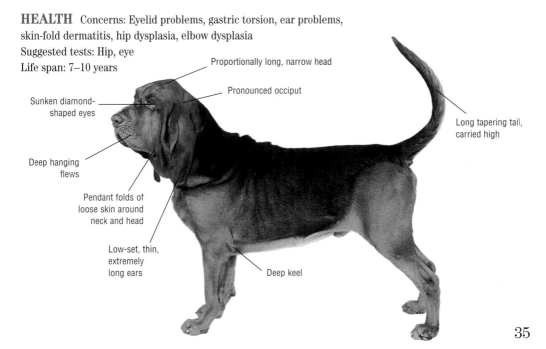

Proportionally long, narrow head

Pronounced occiput

Sunken diamond-shaped eyes

Long tapering tail, carried high

Deep hanging flews

Pendant folds of loose skin around neck and head

Low-set, thin, extremely long ears

Deep keel

Borzoi

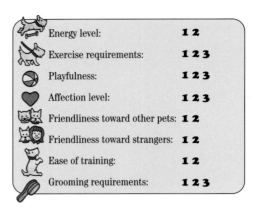

Energy level:	**1 2**	
Exercise requirements:	**1 2 3**	
Playfulness:	**1 2 3**	
Affection level:	**1 2 3**	
Friendliness toward other pets:	**1 2**	
Friendliness toward strangers:	**1 2**	
Ease of training:	**1 2**	
Grooming requirements:	**1 2 3**	

Area of Origin: Russia
Original Function: Coursing wolves
Coat: Long, silky, either flat, wavy, or rather curly
Color: Any
Height: Male: at least 28″ (30″ average); Female: at least 26″
   (28″ average)
Weight: Male: 75–105 lb; Female: 60–85 lb

HISTORY Borzoi were bred by the Russian aristocracy for hundreds of years, with the first standard written in the 1600s in a book about hunting with Borzoi. Borzoi hunts were grand events. A pair or trio of matched Borzoi would be unleashed when a wolf was sighted. The dogs would strike at the same time, forcing the wolf down and holding it until the hunter arrived to bind the wolf—and then, often, set it free. After the Russian Revolution, the days of the nobility were over, and many Borzoi were killed. The fate of the breed was left in the hands of foreign royalty who had been given Borzoi, and of a few remaining Borzoi kennels. In America, the Borzoi soon gained the reputation as the ultimate glamour dog, often seen at the side of movie stars and models.

TEMPERAMENT Borzoi are quiet indoors and lively outdoors. They are independent but very sensitive, and are reserved with strangers. They tend to chase small animals.

UPKEEP Borzoi need daily exercise, plus a chance to run a few times a week. The coat, which is characteristically fuller on males, needs brushing or combing two or three times week; at times it sheds a lot.

HEALTH Concerns: Gastric torsion, heart problems
Suggested tests: Heart
Life span: 10–12 years

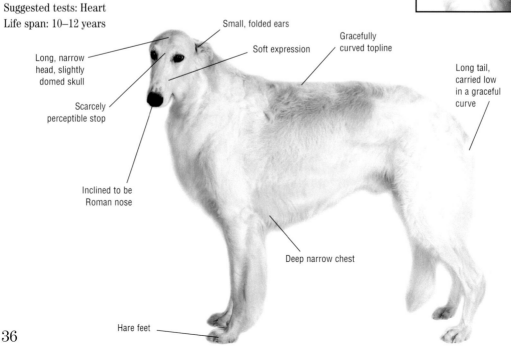

Small, folded ears

Soft expression

Gracefully curved topline

Long, narrow head, slightly domed skull

Scarcely perceptible stop

Inclined to be Roman nose

Long tail, carried low in a graceful curve

Deep narrow chest

Hare feet

Dachshund

Energy level:	**1 2 3 4**	
Exercise requirements:	**1 2**	
Playfulness:	**1 2 3**	
Affection level:	**1 2 3**	
Friendliness toward other pets:	**1 2**	
Friendliness toward strangers:	**1**	
Ease of training:	**1 2**	
Grooming requirements:	**1 2 3**	

Area of Origin: Germany

Original Function: Flushing badgers

Coat: Longhaired: straight or slightly wavy, long; Smooth: smooth, short; Wirehaired: rough, medium length

Color: Solid red, sable, or cream; black and tan, chocolate and tan, wild boar and tan, gray and tan, or fawn and tan; single dapple (lighter color set on darker background, as in a merle); double dapple (white in addition to dapple); brindle

Height: Miniature: 5–6″; Standard: 8–9″

Weight: Miniature: 11 lb and under; Standard: over 11 lb (usually 16–32 lb)

HISTORY Short-legged dogs have been known since antiquity, but definitive evidence of the Dachshund as a breed isn't found until the 16th century, when reference was made to a "low crooked legged" dog called a Little Burrow Dog, Dacksel, or Badger Dog. In fact, the modern name "Dachshund" means simply Badger (*dachs*) Dog (*hund*) in German, although the breed is called the "Teckel" in its native land. These tenacious hunters would follow their quarry, enter its burrow, pull it out, and kill it. The Dachshund comes in three coat varieties (longhaired, smooth, and wirehaired) and two sizes (standard and miniature) in the United States. Each coat type was best suited for hunting in slightly different terrain and under different climatic conditions, but all were tough, strong dogs capable of dispatching badger, fox, and other small mammals. The Dachshund has since become a popular family dog.

TEMPERAMENT Dachshunds are bold, curious, and always up for adventure. They enjoy hunting, digging, tracking, and going to ground after game. Though independent, they gladly join in family fun. They are one-family dogs, and don't take to strangers. Some bark.

UPKEEP Dachshunds need daily romps or short walks. The Smooth coat requires weekly brushing, the Long coat twice weekly. The Wire coat requires weekly brushing plus stripping to remove dead hair twice yearly.

HEALTH Concerns: Intervertebral disk disease, dry eye

Suggested tests: Eye

Life span: 12–14 years

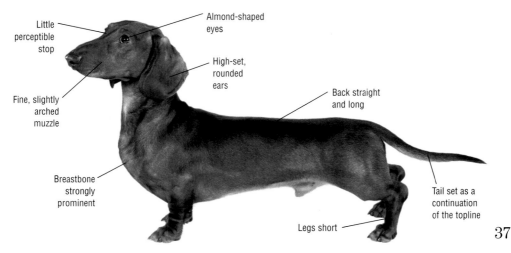

Little perceptible stop

Almond-shaped eyes

High-set, rounded ears

Back straight and long

Fine, slightly arched muzzle

Breastbone strongly prominent

Tail set as a continuation of the topline

Legs short

Foxhound (American)

Area of Origin: United States
Original Function: Trailing fox
Coat: Smooth, short
Color: Any
Height: Male: 22–25″; Female: 21–24″
Weight: 40–65 lb

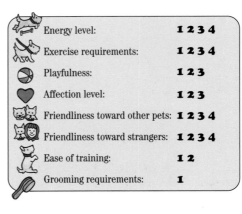

Energy level:		**1 2 3 4**
Exercise requirements:		**1 2 3 4**
Playfulness:		**1 2 3**
Affection level:		**1 2 3**
Friendliness toward other pets:	**1 2 3 4**
Friendliness toward strangers:	**1 2 3 4**
Ease of training:		**1 2**
Grooming requirements:		**1**

HISTORY By the 1700s riding to foxhounds had become extremely popular with the upper class in the northeastern United States. When the sport spread to the South, hunters preferred a faster dog with the ability to start, chase, and kill a fox alone, and to also give chase to deer. The dogs became more streamlined and eventually became specialized for competitive field trials, hunting foxes with guns, racing after a dragged lure, and hunting in packs. It is the pack type that is generally considered the prototypical Foxhound. These dogs combine great speed, endurance, and jumping ability with a strong nose and willingness to give chase as a pack member. Most Foxhounds are registered with Foxhound specialty studbooks, most notably the International Foxhunter's Studbook, rather than the AKC.

TEMPERAMENT Foxhounds are tolerant, amiable, and gentle, though not very demonstrative. Most are reserved with strangers. They are first of all hunters, ready to follow a trail. Once on a scent, they will follow gleefully, heedless of commands. They bay.

UPKEEP Foxhounds need a long walk or jog daily. They are highly sociable and should never be expected to live alone. The coat requires weekly brushing.

HEALTH Concerns: Blood platelet abnormality
Suggested tests: Blood
Life span: 11–13 years

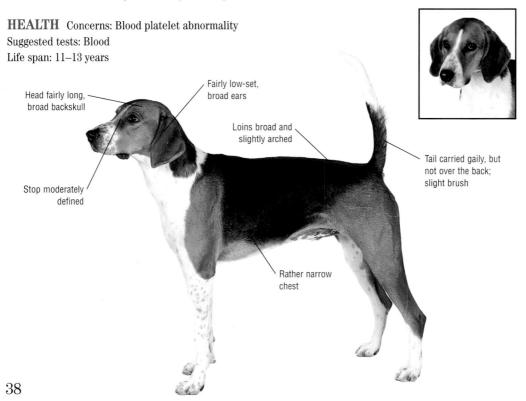

Head fairly long, broad backskull

Fairly low-set, broad ears

Loins broad and slightly arched

Tail carried gaily, but not over the back; slight brush

Stop moderately defined

Rather narrow chest

38

Foxhound (English)

Area of Origin: Great Britain
Original Function: Trailing fox
Coat: Smooth, short
Color: Any good hound color
Height: 23–27″
Weight: 55–75 lb

Energy level:	**1 2 3 4**	
Exercise requirements:	**1 2 3 4**	
Playfulness:	**1 2 3**	
Affection level:	**1 2 3**	
Friendliness toward other pets:	**1 2 3**	
Friendliness toward strangers:	**1 2 3 4**	
Ease of training:	**1 2**	
Grooming requirements:	**1**	

HISTORY Around 1750 a few men envisioned hunting foxes with swift horses and hounds. The hounds would have to be able to track a faint scent while on the run and to maintain their chase for hours. Foxhunting gained its appeal as a pastime of the wealthy, and riding to the hounds became an affair steeped in ceremony. As the esthetic aspects of the hunt increased in significance, care was taken to produce dogs that not only looked good individually, but as a pack. Thus, pack members would usually share the same coat coloration, most often the black saddle over a tan body with white points. The American Foxhound has since surpassed the English Foxhound in popularity in America, although neither is popular as a pet. The English Foxhound is still the first choice of hunters wishing a traditional outing on horseback.

TEMPERAMENT English Foxhounds get along well with horses, dogs, children, and other pets. They are tolerant, amiable, and gentle dogs, though not very demonstrative. Most are reserved with strangers. They are avid sniffers and enjoy baying when on scent.

UPKEEP Foxhounds were bred to run for miles, so they need long daily walks at minimum. The coat needs only occasional brushing to remove dead hair.

HEALTH Concerns: None noted
Suggested tests: Hip
Life span: 10–13 years

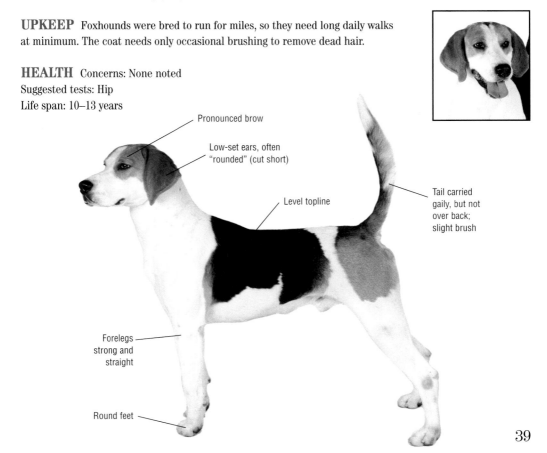

Pronounced brow

Low-set ears, often "rounded" (cut short)

Level topline

Tail carried gaily, but not over back; slight brush

Forelegs strong and straight

Round feet

Greyhound

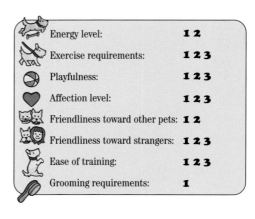

	Energy level:	**1 2**
	Exercise requirements:	**1 2 3**
	Playfulness:	**1 2 3**
	Affection level:	**1 2 3**
	Friendliness toward other pets:	**1 2**
	Friendliness toward strangers:	**1 2 3**
	Ease of training:	**1 2 3**
	Grooming requirements:	**1**

Area of Origin: Great Britain
Original Function: Coursing hares
Coat: Smooth, short
Color: Immaterial (includes black, gray, red, fawn, either solid or brindled, either whole colored or spotted)
Height: Male: 27–29″; Female 26–28″
Weight: Male: 65–70 lb; Female: 60–65 lb

HISTORY Greyhound-like dogs have been depicted since ancient Egyptian, Greek, and Roman times. The name Greyhound may come from *Graius*, meaning Greek, or from the Latin *gradus*, denoting high grade. By Saxon time Greyhounds were well established in Britain and were valued both by commoners for their ability to put food on the table and nobility for the sport of the chase. In the 1800s coursing hare for sport became a consuming pastime of the upper class. When racing was made available to the masses by staging it on tracks after a mechanical lure, the sport proved so popular that dogs were bred specifically for short bursts of speed. Greyhounds bred for the track are the fastest type of dog, but diverged from non-track Greyhounds, which are now registered in America by the National Greyhound Association. Retired racers are popular as pets.

TEMPERAMENT Greyhounds are quiet and calm indoors. Despite their independent nature, they are sensitive and eager to please. They are amiable with other dogs, but tend to chase small animals when outdoors.

UPKEEP Greyhounds' exercise needs are best met with sprints or long walks. Their great speed demands running in only the safest areas. They need soft bedding and warmth. The coat needs weekly brushing.

HEALTH Concerns: Gastric torsion, bone cancer
Suggested tests: None
Life span: 10–13 years

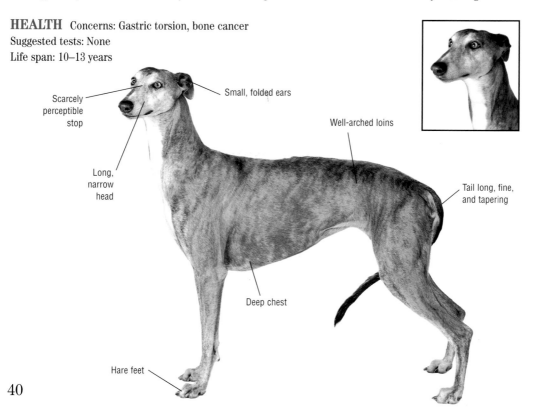

Scarcely perceptible stop

Small, folded ears

Well-arched loins

Long, narrow head

Tail long, fine, and tapering

Deep chest

Hare feet

Harrier

Area of Origin: Great Britain
Original Function: Trailing hares
Coat: Smooth, short
Color: Any
Height: 19–21″
Weight: Male: 45–60 lb; Female 35–45 lb

Energy level:	**1 2 3 4**
Exercise requirements:	**1 2 3 4**
Playfulness:	**1 2 3**
Affection level:	**1 2 3**
Friendliness toward other pets:	**1 2 3**
Friendliness toward strangers:	**1 2 3 4**
Ease of training:	**1 2**
Grooming requirements:	**1**

HISTORY The Harrier may be one of the older scent hounds still in existence today, with references dating to 13th-century England. Although Harrier packs were kept by the gentry, poorer hunters without horses could also hunt with Harriers on foot, often combining the few dogs each individual had to form an impromptu pack. Smaller English Foxhounds may have been bred with these dogs in the early 1800s to develop a longer-legged, faster dog also capable of running with mounted hunters. The Harrier has been known in America since colonial times. Despite its classic proportions and handy size, it has never been popular as a show dog or pet.

TEMPERAMENT Harriers are amiable, tolerant, and good with children, more playful and outgoing than Foxhounds, but less so than Beagles. Its first love is for the hunt. It tends to bay.

UPKEEP Harriers need a long walk or jog or a vigorous romp daily. The coat is easily cared for, needing only occasional brushing to remove dead hair.

HEALTH Concerns: Hip dysplasia
Suggested tests: Hip
Life span: 12–14 years

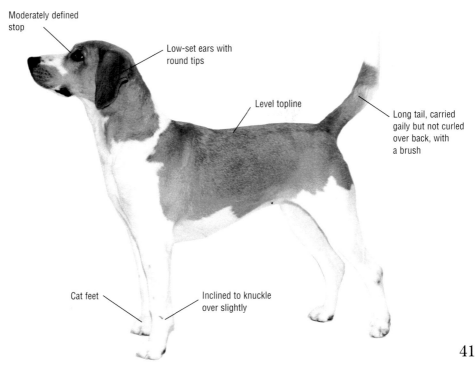

Moderately defined stop

Low-set ears with round tips

Level topline

Long tail, carried gaily but not curled over back, with a brush

Cat feet

Inclined to knuckle over slightly

41

Hound Group

	Energy level:	**1 2 3**
	Exercise requirements:	**1 2 3**
	Playfulness:	**1 2 3**
	Affection level:	**1 2**
	Friendliness toward other pets:	**1 2 3**
	Friendliness toward strangers:	**1 2 3**
	Ease of training:	**1 2**
	Grooming requirements:	**1 2 3**

Ibizan Hound

Area of Origin: Ibiza (Balaeric Islands)
Original Function: Hunting rabbits
Coat: Short: hard, smooth, short; Wire-haired: harsh, short to medium length
Color: White or red (from light yellowish red to deep red), solid or in any combination
Height: Male: 23.5–27.5″; Female: 22.5–26″
Weight: Male: 50 lb; Female: 45 lb

HISTORY The Ibizan Hound probably shares the same roots as the Pharaoh Hound, bearing an uncanny resemblance to the dogs depicted on Egyptian tombs and to the jackal god *Anubis*. Phoenician sea traders may have taken the dogs to the island of Ibiza in ancient times, where they remained in relative seclusion. The hard conditions on the island imposed stringent selection by islanders, as only the best rabbit hunters could be allowed to procreate, or for that matter, survive. These factors produced a hardy, true-breeding dog little changed from its ancestral stock. The first Ibizan Hounds came to America in the 1950s. Their striking appearance aroused much attention but the breed has failed to attract a great number of pet owners. They gradually gained enough popularity to warrant AKC recognition in 1979.

TEMPERAMENT Ibizan Hounds are gentle, mild-mannered, even-tempered, and loyal. They retain great hunting instinct, using acute hearing and smell to locate small animals, and relishing the opportunity to chase anything that moves. They bark when chasing.

UPKEEP Ibizan Hounds need to run or jog daily, although a long walk will do. They appreciate soft bedding. They are gifted jumpers, and need a high fence. Both coat types need weekly brushing.

HEALTH Concerns: Allergies
Suggested tests: Eye
Life span: 12–14 years

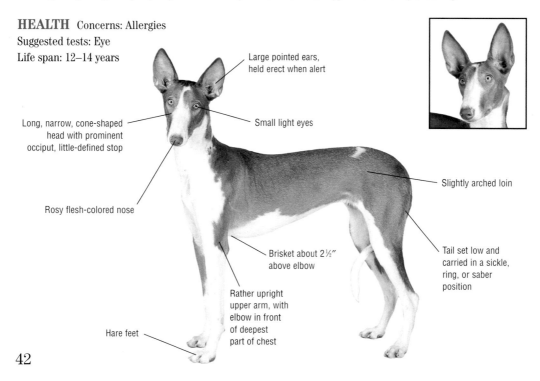

Large pointed ears, held erect when alert

Small light eyes

Long, narrow, cone-shaped head with prominent occiput, little-defined stop

Rosy flesh-colored nose

Slightly arched loin

Brisket about 2 ½″ above elbow

Tail set low and carried in a sickle, ring, or saber position

Rather upright upper arm, with elbow in front of deepest part of chest

Hare feet

Irish Wolfhound

Area of Origin: Ireland
Original Function: Coursing wolves
Coat: Rough, medium length
Color: Gray, brindle, red, black, white, or fawn
Height: Male: at least 32″; Female: at least 30″
Weight: Male: at least 120 lb; Female: at least 105 lb

Energy level:	1
Exercise requirements:	1 2 3
Playfulness:	1
Affection level:	1 2 3
Friendliness toward other pets:	1 2 3
Friendliness toward strangers:	1 2 3
Ease of training:	1 2
Grooming requirements:	1 2 3

HISTORY The first definite mention of the Irish Wolfhound occurred in Rome in 391 A.D. Later favored by Irish chieftains for the hunt, it gained a reputation as an unparalleled hunter of wolves and Irish elk. Illustrations of these dogs from the 17th century look very similar to modern Irish Wolfhounds. The practice of giving Wolfhounds to visiting nobility, along with the extinction of the wolf in Ireland in the 18th century, contributed to the decline of the breed's numbers. By the 19th century Irish Wolfhounds were almost extinct in Ireland, and the famine of 1845 virtually decimated the breed. In 1869 Captain G. A. Graham resurrected the breed by crossing the few existing Wolfhounds with Scottish Deerhounds and other breeds. When first exhibited at a dog show in the 1870s, the reborn Wolfhound created a sensation—the same reaction it inspires today.

TEMPERAMENT Irish Wolfhounds are gentle, calm, easygoing, sensitive, and sweet. Despite their great size, they are good with children, pets, and other dogs. They are reserved with strangers, and courageous when the need arises.

UPKEEP Wolfhounds need daily walks, plus a lot of room at home. They can develop calluses from lying on hard surfaces. The coat should be combed twice weekly, plus stripped twice yearly.

HEALTH Concerns: Gastric torsion, elbow dysplasia, hip dysplasia, heart problems, bone cancer
Suggested tests:
Hip, heart
Life span: 5–7 years

Small, folded ears

Rather long back
with arched loins

Long head
and muzzle

Very deep chest

Large round feet

43

Norwegian Elkhound

Area of Origin: Norway
Original Function: Hunting moose, bear, other big game
Coat: Double coat; outer coat coarse, straight, standing off, medium length
Color: Gray, with lighter undercoat and undersides. Muzzle, ears, and tail tip are black
Height: Male: 20.5″; Female: 19.5″
Weight: Male: 55 lb; Female: 48 lb

Energy level:	**1 2 3 4**	
Exercise requirements:	**1 2 3**	
Playfulness:	**1 2 3 4**	
Affection level:	**1 2 3**	
Friendliness toward other pets:	**1 2**	
Friendliness toward strangers:	**1 2 3 4**	
Ease of training:	**1 2 3**	
Grooming requirements:	**1 2**	

HISTORY The Norwegian Elkhound has served humans as a hunter, guardian, herder, and defender at least since the time of the Vikings. In a land of sub-zero temperatures, deep snow, thick forests, and rugged mountains, only the hardiest of breeds could evolve to perform the variety of jobs at which the Elkhound excels. It is an unusual hound because its roots lie in the spitz breeds, which it still closely resembles. Its placement in the Hound Group reflects its hunting ability, as the breed hunts like a hound. Of all its roles, hunting elk (actually, moose) is this breed's forte. The Elkhound's job is not to kill the elk, but to locate it and hold it at bay until the hunter can shoot it. The AKC recognized the breed around 1930, and it has enjoyed moderate popularity since then.

TEMPERAMENT Elkhounds are bold, playful, independent, alert, boisterous, and even protective. They are friendly with strangers, but may quarrel with strange dogs. They tend to pull when on leash unless trained, and may bark a lot.

UPKEEP Norwegian Elkhounds need a good jog, a very long walk, or an invigorating play session daily. They enjoy cold weather. The double coat needs brushing twice weekly, and daily when shedding.

HEALTH Concerns: Hip dysplasia, hot spots, kidney disease
Suggested tests: Hip
Life span: 10–12 years

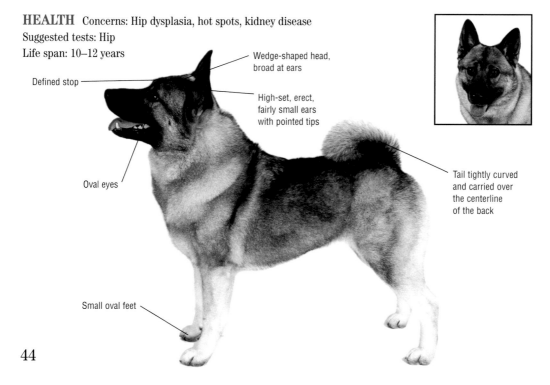

Wedge-shaped head, broad at ears

Defined stop

High-set, erect, fairly small ears with pointed tips

Oval eyes

Tail tightly curved and carried over the centerline of the back

Small oval feet

44

Otterhound

Area of Origin: England
Original Function: Hunting otters
Coat: Rough, crisp, medium length
Color: Any
Height: Male: 27″; Female: 24″
Weight: Male: 115 lb; Female: 80 lb

	Energy level:	1 2
	Exercise requirements:	1 2 3
	Playfulness:	1 2 3
	Affection level:	1 2 3 4 5
	Friendliness toward other pets:	1 2 3
	Friendliness toward strangers:	1 2 3 4 5
	Ease of training:	1 2
	Grooming requirements:	1 2 3

HISTORY Otterhounds may have originated in France, as they closely resemble the old French Vendeen hound. They are most associated with England, where they served to hunt otters that depleted fish in local streams. They would trail the otter to its den and bay when locating it. Otterhunting was never among the most popular of sports, lacking the formal trappings of foxhunting and taking place in wet and uncomfortable conditions. The sport reached its peak during the latter half of the 19th century, but essentially died out after the World War II. The first Otterhounds came to America at the beginning of the 20th century. Despite the fact that the Otterhound is one of the most ancient of the English breeds, it is one of the rarest of English Kennel Club or AKC-recognized breeds, verging perilously close to extinction.

TEMPERAMENT Otterhounds are boisterous, amiable, and easygoing (though stubborn), affectionate with their family, and good with other dogs. They love to hunt, swim, and follow scent trails. They are not among the most responsive of breeds. They have a loud, melodious bark.

UPKEEP Otterhounds needs moderate exercise every day. The coat requires only weekly brushing or combing. The hairy feet track in dirt, and the beard can hold water and food.

HEALTH Major concerns: Hip dysplasia, gastric torsion, elbow dysplasia, blood platelet abnormality
Suggested tests: Hip
Life span: 10-13 years

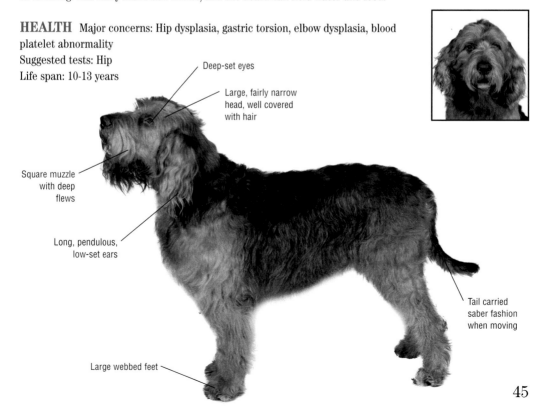

Deep-set eyes

Large, fairly narrow head, well covered with hair

Square muzzle with deep flews

Long, pendulous, low-set ears

Tail carried saber fashion when moving

Large webbed feet

45

Petit Basset Griffon Vendéen

Area of Origin: France
Original Function: Trailing hare
Coat: Rough, harsh, medium length
Color: White with any combination of lemon, orange, tricolor, or grizzle marking
Height: 13–15″
Weight: 25–35 lb

Energy level:	**1 2 3 4**
Exercise requirements:	**1 2 3**
Playfulness:	**1 2 3 4**
Affection level:	**1 2 3 4 5**
Friendliness toward other pets:	**1 2**
Friendliness toward strangers:	**1 2 3 4**
Ease of training:	**1**
Grooming requirements:	**1 2**

HISTORY The PBGV, as it is affectionately known, is an ancient breed with roots in 16th century Europe. The long French name provides an accurate description of the breed: *Petit* (small) *Basset* (low) *Griffon* (rough-coated) Vendéen (its area of origin in France). Hunting rabbits in this rocky terrain demanded a dog that had a coat that could withstand brambles, short legs that could enable it to wind its way through the underbrush, and nimbleness that allowed it to run over rocks without tiring. In England in the mid-1800s, PBGVs were shown with Basset Hounds as a wire-coated variety, but the PBGV is a longer-legged, more nimble hound. In France, the Griffon Vendéen was considered to be one breed with two sizes until the 1950s. The two sizes were still interbred until the 1970s. The AKC recognized the PBGV in 1990.

TEMPERAMENT PBGVs are merry, inquisitive, tough, and busy, but also stubborn and independent. They love to sniff, explore, trail, and dig. They are good with children, other dogs, and pets, and friendly toward strangers. They tend to bark.

UPKEEP PBGVs need a good walk on leash or vigorous romp in the yard every day. The coat needs weekly brushing and occasional tidying of straggling hairs.

HEALTH Concerns: Ear problems
Suggested tests: Hip, eye
Life span: 11–14 years

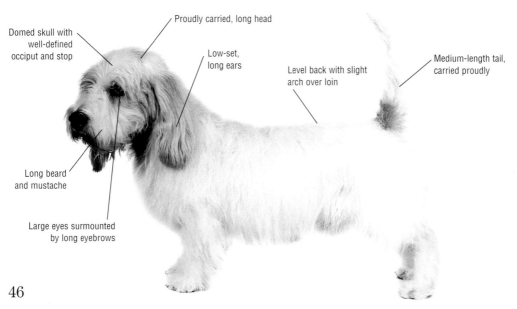

Domed skull with well-defined occiput and stop

Proudly carried, long head

Low-set, long ears

Level back with slight arch over loin

Medium-length tail, carried proudly

Long beard and mustache

Large eyes surmounted by long eyebrows

Pharaoh Hound

Area of Origin: Malta
Original Function: Hunting rabbits
Coat: Smooth, short
Color: Tan or chestnut, with a white tail tip desired
Height: Male: 23–25″; Female: 21–24″
Weight: 45–55 lb

Energy level:	**123**
Exercise requirements:	**1234**
Playfulness:	**123**
Affection level:	**123**
Friendliness toward other pets:	**12**
Friendliness toward strangers:	**12**
Ease of training:	**123**
Grooming requirements:	**1**

HISTORY A hunting account from the XIX Egyptian dynasty describes a "red, long-tailed dog" whose "face glows like a God." Even today, the Pharaoh Hound is noted for "blushing": the tendency of its nose and ears to flush with blood and "glow" when excited. Phoenician traders may have introduced the dogs from Greece and North Africa to the islands of Malta and Gozo, where they became secluded from the rest of the world. Here they flourished as rabbit dogs, or *Kelb-tal-Fewek*. Several hounds would be released to find the scent of a rabbit; barking once the rabbit went to ground (usually in a stone wall or rocky crevice). A belled ferret was then sent after the rabbit, flushing it to be caught by the dog. In the 1960s the breed was rediscovered and imported to England and later America.

TEMPERAMENT Pharaoh Hounds are calm indoors but love to run and hunt outdoors. They are sensitive, loving, gentle, good with children and other dogs, but may chase small animals. They are independent but willing to please.

UPKEEP Pharaoh Hounds need long daily walks and occasional sprints. They appreciate soft bedding and warmth. The coat requires only occasional brushing.

HEALTH Concerns: None noted
Suggested tests: None
Life span: 11–14 years

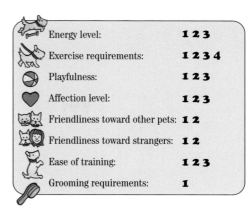

Long chiseled head

Slight stop

Flesh-covered nose

Amber-colored eyes

Large ears, carried erect when alert

Whiplike tail

47

Plott

Energy level:	**1 2 3**	
Exercise requirements:	**1 2 3**	
Playfulness:	**1 2 3**	
Affection level:	**1 2 3**	
Friendliness toward other pets:	**1 2**	
Friendliness toward strangers:	**1 2**	
Ease of training:	**1 2**	
Grooming requirements:	**1**	

Area of Origin: United States
Original Function: Cold trailing, bear hunting
Coat: Smooth, short
Color: Any shade of brindle, including blue; solid black,
   brindle with black saddle, black with brindle trim,
   buckskin; some white permissible on chest or feet only
Height: Male: 20–25″; Female: 20–23″
Weight: Male 50–60 lb; Female: 40–55 lb

HISTORY In 1750, 16-year-old Joahnnes Georg Plott brought five Hanoverian Schweisshunds from Germany to his new home in the Great Smoky Mountains. The dogs and their descendants proved themselves to be great cold trailers of large animals, especially bear. In the early 1900s crosses with other lines were made to improve the Plott strain. This introduced the black-saddled brindle pattern into the breed. Although used primarily for bear, boar, and mountain lions, many Plotts were also adept at treeing raccoons, and coonhunters—far more populous than bear hunters—found them ideal for their needs. In 1946 the breed finally received the official name of Plott Hound when it was recognized by the United Kennel Club. The AKC admitted the Plott into the Hound Group in 2007.

TEMPERAMENT Plotts are eager to please, loyal, and courageous, but also headstrong and independent. They can be wary of strangers, but generally warm up quickly. They are not as gregarious with other dogs as some hounds.

UPKEEP Plotts need a long walk or outing every day. They enjoy swimming. The coat needs weekly brushing.

HEALTH Concerns: None noted
Suggested tests: Hip
Life span: 11–13 years

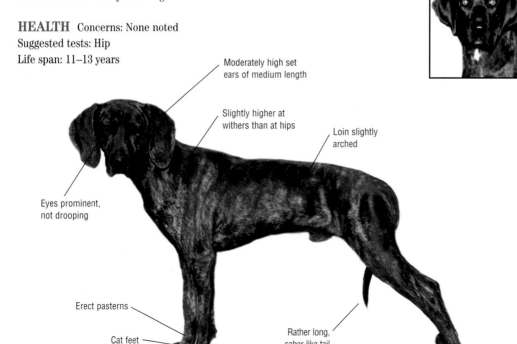

Moderately high set
ears of medium length

Slightly higher at
withers than at hips

Loin slightly
arched

Eyes prominent,
not drooping

Erect pasterns

Cat feet

Rather long,
saber-like tail

Rhodesian Ridgeback

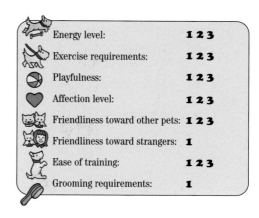

Energy level:		**1 2 3**
Exercise requirements:		**1 2 3**
Playfulness:		**1 2 3**
Affection level:		**1 2 3**
Friendliness toward other pets:		**1 2 3**
Friendliness toward strangers:		**1**
Ease of training:		**1 2 3**
Grooming requirements:		**1**

Area of Origin: South Africa
Original Function: Large game (including lion) hunting, guardian
Coat: Smooth, short, with ridge of hair growing in reverse direction on back.
Color: Light wheaten to red wheaten; nose can be black, brown, or liver
Height: Male: 25–27″; Female: 24–26″
Weight: Male: 85 lb; Female: 70 lb

HISTORY When European Boer settlers arrived in South Africa in the 16th and 17th centuries, they crossed European dogs with native Hottentot tribal hunting dogs (which were distinguished by a ridge of hair growing in the opposite direction along the top of their back). These dogs hunted by both sight and scent, and were devoted protectors of the entire family. In the 1870s several of these dogs were taken to Rhodesia to hunt lions from horseback, chasing and harassing the lion until the hunter could shoot it. The dogs were so successful that these "Lion Dogs" became popular, their distinctive ridge becoming a trademark of quality. By the 1920s a standard of desirable points was written, and dogs meeting it were called Rhodesian Ridgebacks. The breed was introduced into England in the 1930s, and to America soon after.

TEMPERAMENT Rhodesian Ridgebacks are strong-willed and powerful, protective of family. They are keen hunters, and can be aggressive toward strange dogs and animals. Some can become domineering.

UPKEEP Ridgebacks need daily jogs or long walks. Coat care is minimal, consisting only of occasional brushing to remove dead hair.

HEALTH Concerns: Hip dysplasia, elbow dysplasia, dermoid sinus
Suggested tests: Hip, check puppies for dermoid sinus
Life span: 10–12 years

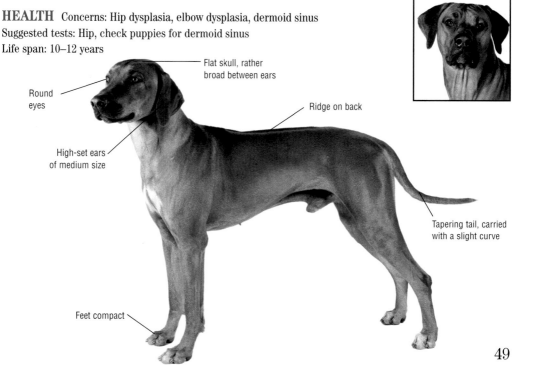

Flat skull, rather broad between ears

Round eyes

High-set ears of medium size

Ridge on back

Tapering tail, carried with a slight curve

Feet compact

Saluki

Area of Origin: Middle East

Original Function: Coursing hare and gazelles

Coat: Feathered: smooth, short, with long hair on ears, tail, feet; Smooth: smooth, short

Color: White, cream, fawn, golden, red, grizzle, black and tan, tricolor, or any of these on a white background

Height: Male: 23–28″; Female: may be considerably smaller

Weight: 35–65 lb

Energy level:	**1 2**	
Exercise requirements:	**1 2 3**	
Playfulness:	**1 2 3**	
Affection level:	**1 2 3**	
Friendliness toward other pets:	**1 2 3**	
Friendliness toward strangers:	**1**	
Ease of training:	**1 2 3**	
Grooming requirements:	**1 2**	

HISTORY The name Saluki may come from the ancient civilization of Seleucia. Arab nomads used Salukis to run down gazelles, foxes, and hares in the desert, often with the aid of falcons. Although the Muslim religion considered the dog to be unclean, an exception was made for the Saluki, which was referred to as "*el hor*: the noble one." Unlike other dogs, the Saluki was allowed to sleep in the tents, and enjoy the tender attention of its Bedouin master. Salukis were not allowed to breed with non-Salukis, accounting for their purity throughout the centuries. Because they ranged with their nomadic owners over a wide area of the Middle East, Salukis became widely distributed with great local variation, accounting for the breed's variability today. They came to the attention of the western world after World War I, and were recognized by the AKC in 1928.

TEMPERAMENT Salukis are sensitive and reserved, especially aloof with strangers. Though gentle, they may not be playful enough to satisfy children. They are sedate inside, and enjoy running, and especially chasing, outside. They may not come when called.

UPKEEP Salukis need long walks or short vigorous runs daily. They enjoy warmth and soft bedding. The smooth coat needs only occasional brushing, but the longer feathering needs combing twice weekly to prevent matting.

HEALTH Concerns: Hemangiosarcoma, heart problems

Suggested tests: Heart

Life span: 12–14 years

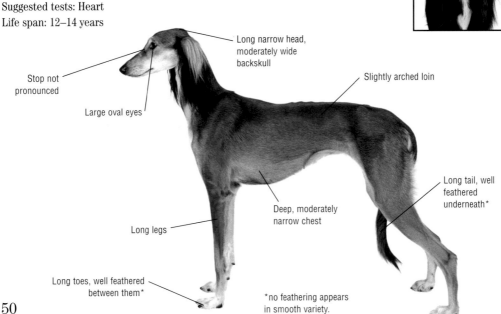

Long narrow head, moderately wide backskull

Stop not pronounced

Large oval eyes

Slightly arched loin

Long tail, well feathered underneath*

Deep, moderately narrow chest

Long legs

Long toes, well feathered between them*

*no feathering appears in smooth variety.

50

Scottish Deerhound

Area of Origin: Scotland
Original Function: Coursing stag
Coat: Harsh, wiry, medium length
Color: All shades of gray and gray brindle, with dark blue-gray preferred; yellow, red, and fawn are permitted but not seen today
Height: Male: 30–32″ (average 32″); Female: at least 28″ (average 30″)
Weight: Male: 85–110 lb; Female: 75–95 lb

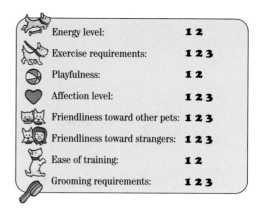

Energy level:	**1 2**
Exercise requirements:	**1 2 3**
Playfulness:	**1 2**
Affection level:	**1 2 3**
Friendliness toward other pets:	**1 2 3**
Friendliness toward strangers:	**1 2 3**
Ease of training:	**1 2**
Grooming requirements:	**1 2 3**

HISTORY The Scottish Deerhound was valued by nobility for deer coursing at least since the 16th century. These large, rough-coated dogs suited for hunting stag in the Scottish Highlands were hoarded by highland chieftains. This hoarding resulted in the decline of the breed in the mid-1700s following the collapse of the clan system of Culloden. Further decline occurred with the advent of breech-loading rifles in the 1800s, as hunting deer with guns supplanted coursing in popularity. By the mid-1800s a concerted effort to restore the breed was successful. World War I again decimated the breed's numbers, as most of the dogs had been the property of a limited number of large estates, most of which did not survive the war intact. The Deerhound has since remained low in number.

TEMPERAMENT Scottish Deerhounds are mellow and easygoing, and well mannered in the home. They are independent, but willing to please, and are very sensitive. They are good with other dogs, and usually other pets although they may give chase to small animals.

UPKEEP Deerhounds need a moderate walk daily. Inside, they need room to stretch out on soft bedding. The wiry coat needs combing once or twice weekly. Dead hair must be stripped twice yearly.

HEALTH Concerns: Gastric torsion, heart problems, bone cancer
Suggested tests: Heart
Life span: 7–9 years

Long head with flat skull

Small, folded ears, dark in color

Arched loin drooping to the tail

Wide, drooping hindquarters

Good mustache and beard of silky hair

Deep chest

Long, tapering tail

Compact feet

51

Whippet

Area of Origin: England
Original Function: Racing, rabbit coursing
Coat: Smooth, short
Color: Immaterial
Height: Male: 19–22″; Female: 18–21″
Weight: 20–40 lb

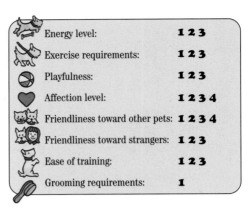

Energy level:	**1 2 3**
Exercise requirements:	**1 2 3**
Playfulness:	**1 2 3**
Affection level:	**1 2 3 4**
Friendliness toward other pets:	**1 2 3 4**
Friendliness toward strangers:	**1 2 3**
Ease of training:	**1 2 3**
Grooming requirements:	**1**

HISTORY Whippets were used by peasants for poaching rabbits and other small game in the 18th century. The peasants also found entertainment in "snap dog" contests, in which bets were made on which dog could "snap up" as many rabbits as possible before they escaped from a circle. It was the advent of the Industrial Revolution, however, that spurred the development of the true Whippet breed. Masses of rural workers moved to industrialized areas, bringing with them their snap dogs and a need for entertainment. Without a supply of rabbits, they found their dogs would just as readily race toward a waving rag. Rag racing became the sport of coal miners; in fact, the Whippet was dubbed the "poor man's race horse." After Whippets were officially recognized in 1888, they began to be appreciated for their aesthetic appeal and companionship qualities.

TEMPERAMENT Whippets are the most demonstrative and obedient of the sighthounds. They are calm inside, gentle with children, and good with other pets. They are playful but very sensitive.

UPKEEP Whippets need a long walk or short run daily. They must have a warm, soft bed, and may need a coat for cold weather. The short coat needs only occasional brushing.

HEALTH Concerns: None noted
Suggested tests: None
Life span: 12–15 years

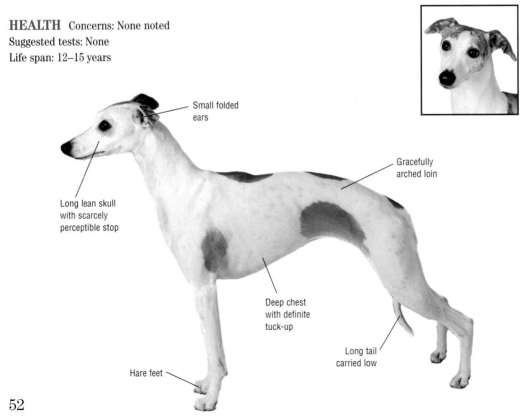

Small folded
ears

Long lean skull
with scarcely
perceptible stop

Gracefully
arched loin

Deep chest
with definite
tuck-up

Long tail
carried low

Hare feet

WORKING

Energy level:	**1 2 3**	
Exercise requirements:	**1 2 3**	
Playfulness:	**1 2 3**	
Affection level:	**1 2 3**	
Friendliness toward other pets:	**1 2**	
Friendliness toward strangers:	**1**	
Ease of training:	**1 2 3**	
Grooming requirements:	**1 2**	

Akita

Area of Origin: Japan
Original Function: Large game hunting, dog fighting, guardian
Coat: Straight, harsh, medium length
Color: Any color, including white, pinto, or brindle
Height: Male: 25–28″; Female: 23–26″
Weight: Male: 85–115 lb; Female: 65–90 lb

HISTORY The Akita was perfected in the Akita Prefecture of the island of Honshu, a rugged area with intensely cold winters. These dogs distinguished themselves hunting bear, deer, and wild boar, holding the game at bay for the hunter. These Akita forebears were called *matagi-inu*, or "hunting dog." In the late 1800s the Akita was used as a fighting dog. In 1927, the Akita-inu Hozankai Society of Japan was formed to preserve the original Akita, and in 1931 the Akita was designated as one of Japan's natural treasures. The first Akita arrived in America in 1937, when Helen Keller returned from Japan with one. Following World War II, U.S. servicemen also returned home with Akitas from Japan. The breed's popularity grew slowly until it received AKC recognition in 1972.

TEMPERAMENT Akitas are bold, independent, stubborn, and tenacious. Demonstrative and devoted to their family, they are reserved with strangers and can be aggressive toward other dogs. They can be domineering.

UPKEEP Akitas need a long walk or good run daily. The coat needs brushing about once a week to remove dead hair, more often when shedding.

HEALTH Concerns: Hip dysplasia, PRA, elbow dysplasia, pemphigus, gastric torsion
Suggested tests: Hip, elbow, eye
Life span: 10–12 years

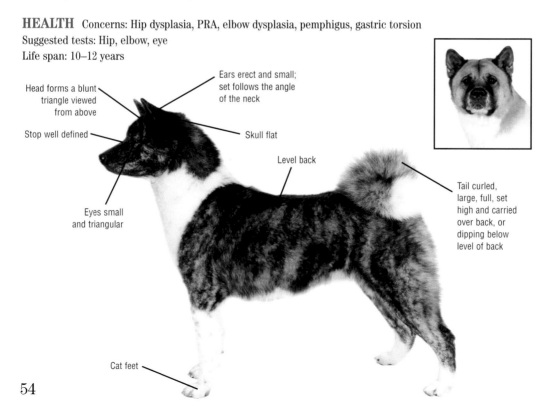

Ears erect and small; set follows the angle of the neck

Head forms a blunt triangle viewed from above

Stop well defined

Skull flat

Level back

Tail curled, large, full, set high and carried over back, or dipping below level of back

Eyes small and triangular

Cat feet

Alaskan Malamute

Area of Origin: Alaska
Original Function: Heavy sled pulling, large game hunting
Coat: Thick, coarse, medium length
Color: Light gray through to black, with white shading and a white mask or cap; also shades of sable or red with shading, or all white
Height: Male: 25″; Female: 23″
Weight: Male: 85 lb; Female 75 lb

Energy level:	1 2 3
Exercise requirements:	1 2 3 4
Playfulness:	1 2 3
Affection level:	1 2 3 4 5
Friendliness toward other pets:	1
Friendliness toward strangers:	1 2 3 4
Ease of training:	1
Grooming requirements:	1 2 3

HISTORY The Alaskan Malamute was first described living among the native Inuit people known as the Mahlemuts, who lived along Norton Sound on Alaska's northwest coast. They helped hunt and haul seals and polar bears. They were an essential cog in the Inuits' lives and were treated almost as part of the family. With the discovery of gold in 1896, a flood of outsiders came to Alaska. As the breed's reputation grew, some were chosen to help Admiral Byrd in his 1933 trek to the South Pole. During World War II, Malamutes were once again called into service, this time to serve as freight haulers, pack animals, and search-and-rescue dogs. In 1935 the breed received AKC recognition.

TEMPERAMENT Alaskan Malamutes are powerful, independent, strong-willed and fun-loving. They love to pull, run and roam. They are friendly toward people, but may be aggressive toward strange dogs. Some can be domineering. They tend to dig and howl.

UPKEEP Malamutes need a long walk or the opportunity to run or mush. The coat needs brushing once or twice a week—more often when shedding.

HEALTH Concerns: Hip dysplasia, cataracts, chondrodysplasia
Suggested tests: Hip, eye, chondrodysplasia clear rating
Life span: 10–12 years

Head broad and powerful

Ears medium sized, triangular, slightly rounded at tips

Straight back

Tail carried over back

Muzzle large

Eyes almond shaped, moderately large

Large feet

Anatolian Shepherd

Area of Origin: Turkey
Original Function: Flock guard
Coat: Short to rough (medium length)
Color: Any, most common is fawn with black mask
Height: Male: from 29″ up; Female: from 27″ up
Weight: Male: 110–150 lb; Female: 80–120 lb

Energy level:	**1 2**	
Exercise requirements:	**1 2 3**	
Playfulness:	**1 2 3**	
Affection level:	**1 2 3**	
Friendliness toward other pets:	**1 2 3**	
Friendliness toward strangers:	**1**	
Ease of training:	**1 2 3**	
Grooming requirements:	**1 2**	

HISTORY The Anatolian Shepherd is an ancient guardian breed probably descended from Roman war dogs that came to Turkey more than 4,000 years ago. Here Anatolian shepherds proved invaluable as staunch defenders of livestock against formidable predators, including wolves and bears. They accompanied the nomadic shepherds and became widespread over a large geographical region, accounting for the Anatolian's great variation in size, coat type, and color. Its Turkish name, *koban copek*, means "shepherd's dog." The first of the breed did not come to America until the 1950s. In 1996 the Anatolian Shepherd was accepted in the AKC Miscellaneous Class; soon afterward it became a member of the Working Group.

TEMPERAMENT Anatolian Shepherds are laid back and easygoing. They are devoted to family and suspicious of strangers. They are not good with strange dogs. Anatolians are serious when it comes to guardian duty.

UPKEEP Anatolians need a moderate walk or brisk run daily. Coat care consists only of brushing once or twice weekly to remove dead hair.

HEALTH Concerns: Hip dysplasia, entropion
Suggested tests: Hip
Life span: 10–13 years

Eyes almond-shaped

V-shaped ears with rounded apex

Gradual arch over loin

Tail long, highset, with a curl in the end; carried in a wheel when alert

Dewlap not excessive

Oval feet

Double dewclaws optional on rear feet

Bernese Mountain Dog

Area of Origin: Switzerland
Original Function: Draft
Coat: Straight or slightly wavy, thick, moderately long
Color: Tricolored; black with tan markings and white flashings
Height: Male: 25–27.5″; Female: 23–26″
Weight: Male: 90–120 lb; Female: 70–100 lb

Energy level:	1 2	
Exercise requirements:	1 2 3	
Playfulness:	1 2	
Affection level:	1 2 3	
Friendliness toward other pets:	1 2 3 4	
Friendliness toward strangers:	1 2 3	
Ease of training:	1 2 3 4	
Grooming requirements:	1 2 3	

HISTORY The Bernese Mountain Dog is the best known of the *sennehunde*, or "Swiss mountain dogs." Some experts believe its history traces back to the Roman invasion of Switzerland, when the Roman mastiffs were crossed with native flock-guarding dogs, producing a strong cold-resistant dog that could serve as draft dog, flock guard, drover, herder, and general farm dog. Despite the utility of these dogs, little attempt was made to perpetuate them as a breed, and they were almost lost by the late 1800s. A study of Swiss dogs identified Bernese Mountain Dogs as one of the existing types, found only in the valleys of the lower Alps. They were promoted throughout Switzerland and even Europe. The first Bernese came to America in 1926; official AKC recognition was granted in 1937.

TEMPERAMENT Bernese Mountain Dogs are easygoing, calm, sensitive, loyal, and extremely devoted. They are often reserved with strangers, but generally get along well with other dogs and pets.

UPKEEP Bernese Mountain Dogs need a moderate walk daily. They enjoy cold weather. The coat needs brushing once or twice weekly, much more often when shedding.

HEALTH Concerns: Hip dysplasia, elbow dysplasia, mast cell tumor, gastric torsion
Suggested tests: Hip, elbow, eye
Life span: 6–9 years

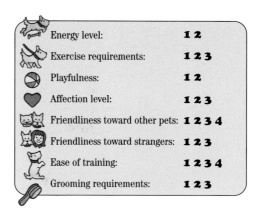

Skull flat

Well-defined stop

Ears medium sized, triangular with rounded tips, hanging close to head

Tail bushy, carried low

Feet round

Black Russian Terrier

Area of Origin: The former Soviet Union
Original Function: Military
Coat: Coarse, tousled, medium length
Color: Black or black with a few gray hairs
Height: Male: 27–30″; Female: 26–29″
Weight: 80–145 lb

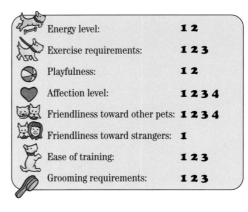

Energy level:		1 2
Exercise requirements:		1 2 3
Playfulness:		1 2
Affection level:		1 2 3 4
Friendliness toward other pets:		1 2 3 4
Friendliness toward strangers:		1
Ease of training:		1 2 3
Grooming requirements:		1 2 3

HISTORY In the 1940s the Soviets imported breeds from their occupied countries, mainly German breeds, into their state-owned Red Star Kennels in order to produce military dogs. One strain descended predominantly from a Giant Schnauzer sire, and these were distinguished from the others as the "Black Terrier" group. Besides sharing border guard duty with soldiers, military tasks included detecting mines and explosives, transporting supplies, pulling sleighs, and finding wounded soldiers, all done independently and in the harshest of climates. Black Russian Terriers served in military operations in Afghanistan and Bosnia. In 1968 a breed standard was registered. In 2004 the Black Russian Terrier obtained AKC recognition.

TEMPERAMENT Black Russian Terriers are calm, confident, and courageous. They are reserved with strangers, but devoted to and protective of family. They are affectionate and gentle. They may not be good with strange or dominant dogs, but are fine with other pets and smaller canine housemates.

UPKEEP Black Russian Terriers need a long walk or active play session daily. The coat needs thorough combing once or twice a week, and trimming every six to eight weeks.

HEALTH Concerns: Hip dysplasia, elbow dysplasia
Suggested tests: Hip, elbow
Life span: 10–11 years

High-set triangular ears, rather small

Dark oval eyes

Powerful head

Straight level topline

Thick, high-set tail, docked to 3 to 5 vertebra

Large round feet

Boxer

Area of Origin: Germany
Original Function: Bull baiting, guardian
Coat: Smooth, short
Color: Fawn and brindle, both with or without white flashing and black mask
Height: Male: 22.5–25″; Female: 21–23.5″
Weight: Male: 65–80 lb; Female: 50–65 lb

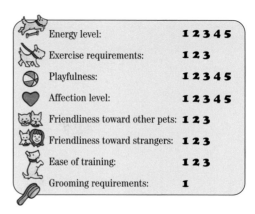

Energy level:	**1 2 3 4 5**
Exercise requirements:	**1 2 3**
Playfulness:	**1 2 3 4 5**
Affection level:	**1 2 3 4 5**
Friendliness toward other pets:	**1 2 3**
Friendliness toward strangers:	**1 2 3**
Ease of training:	**1 2 3**
Grooming requirements:	**1**

HISTORY In the 1830s German hunters began a concerted effort to create a new breed, crossing their bull baiting dogs with mastiff-type dogs for size and with terriers for tenacity. The result was a tough agile dog with a streamlined body and strong grip. When bull-baiting was outlawed, the dogs were mostly used as butchers' dogs in Germany, controlling cattle in slaughter yards. By 1895 an entirely new breed, the Boxer, had been established. Although the exact origin of the name Boxer is obscure, it may have been derived from the German *boxl*, as they were called in the slaughterhouses. The Boxer was one of the first breeds to be employed as a police and military dog in Germany.

TEMPERAMENT Boxers are playful, exuberant, inquisitive, attentive, demonstrative, devoted, and outgoing. They can be stubborn, but are sensitive and responsive to commands. They may be aggressive toward strange dogs, but are generally good with other household dogs and pets.

UPKEEP Boxers need a long walk or good run daily. They do not do well in hot weather. The coat needs only occasional brushing to remove dead hair.

HEALTH Concerns: Heart problems, hip dysplasia, gastric torsion, tumors
Suggested tests: Heart, hip
Life span: 8–10 years

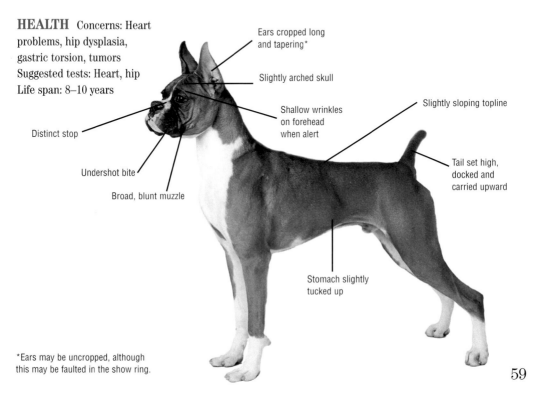

Ears cropped long and tapering*

Slightly arched skull

Shallow wrinkles on forehead when alert

Slightly sloping topline

Distinct stop

Undershot bite

Broad, blunt muzzle

Tail set high, docked and carried upward

Stomach slightly tucked up

*Ears may be uncropped, although this may be faulted in the show ring.

59

Bullmastiff

Area of Origin: England
Original Function: Estate guardian
Coat: Smooth, short
Color: Red, fawn, or brindle
Height: Male: 25–27″; Female: 24–26″
Weight: Male: 110–130 lb; female: 100–120 lb

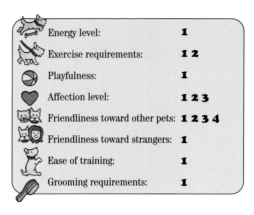

Energy level:	**1**	
Exercise requirements:	**1 2**	
Playfulness:	**1**	
Affection level:	**1 2 3**	
Friendliness toward other pets:	**1 2 3 4**	
Friendliness toward strangers:	**1**	
Ease of training:	**1**	
Grooming requirements:	**1**	

HISTORY The documented history of the Bullmastiff begins near the end of the 19th century, when poaching game from the large estates had become such a problem that the gamekeepers' lives were endangered. They needed a tough courageous dog that could wait silently as a poacher approached, attack on command, and subdue, but not maul the poacher. The Mastiff was not fast enough, and the Bulldog was not large enough, so they crossed the breeds in an attempt to create their perfect dog: the aptly named "gamekeeper's night dog." Breeders worked for an ideal animal that appeared to be 60 percent Mastiff and 40 percent Bulldog. AKC recognition came in 1933.

TEMPERAMENT Bullmastiffs are gentle and quiet. Not easily roused, once threatened they are fearless. Some can be aggressive toward strange dogs. They can be stubborn, and are not for fragile or timid owners.

UPKEEP Bullmastiffs need a moderate walk or short play session daily. They do not do well in hot weather. They drool; some snore. Coat care is minimal.

HEALTH Concerns: Gastric torsion, hip dysplasia, elbow dysplasia
Suggested tests: Hip, elbow
Life span: 8–10 years

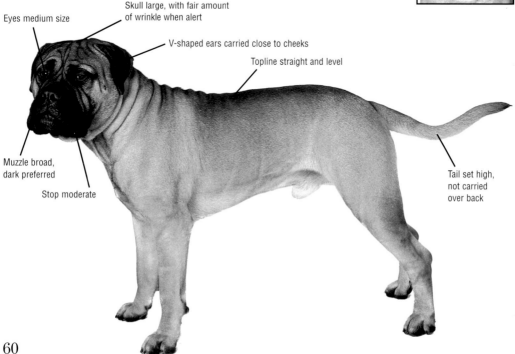

Eyes medium size

Skull large, with fair amount of wrinkle when alert

V-shaped ears carried close to cheeks

Topline straight and level

Muzzle broad, dark preferred

Stop moderate

Tail set high, not carried over back

Doberman Pinscher

Area of Origin: Germany
Original Function: Guardian
Coat: Smooth, short
Color: Black, red, blue, and fawn, all with tan markings
Height: Male: 26–28″; Female: 24–26″
Weight: 65–90 lb

Energy level:	**1 2 3 4**
Exercise requirements:	**1 2 3**
Playfulness:	**1 2 3**
Affection level:	**1 2 3**
Friendliness toward other pets:	**1 2 3**
Friendliness toward strangers:	**1**
Ease of training:	**1 2 3 4 5**
Grooming requirements:	**1**

HISTORY Louis Dobermann was a door-to-door tax collector who needed a watchful guard dog to accompany him on his rounds. In the late 1800s he set about to create an alert, streamlined guard dog. The original Dobermans were still somewhat heavy-boned and round-headed; subsequent breeders selected for a more racy-looking dog. The breed evolved in remarkable time; by 1899 the first breed club was formed. The breed continued to attract acclaim, and the first Doberman arrived in America in 1908. It soon found favor throughout Europe and America as a police and guard dog, and later as a war dog. As its fame grew, many families grew to appreciate the breed as a family pet, and the Doberman eventually rose to be the second-most popular breed in America in 1977.

TEMPERAMENT Doberman Pinschers are alert, loyal, protective, and adventurous. They are sensitive and very responsive to their family's wishes, though some can be domineering. They are generally reserved with strangers, and can be aggressive with strange dogs.

UPKEEP Dobermans need a long jog or walk, or a strenuous run, daily. The short coat should be brushed weekly.

HEALTH Concerns: Wobbler's syndrome, cardiomyopathy, vWD, gastric torsion, hip dysplasia
Suggested tests: Heart, vWD
Life span: 10–12 years

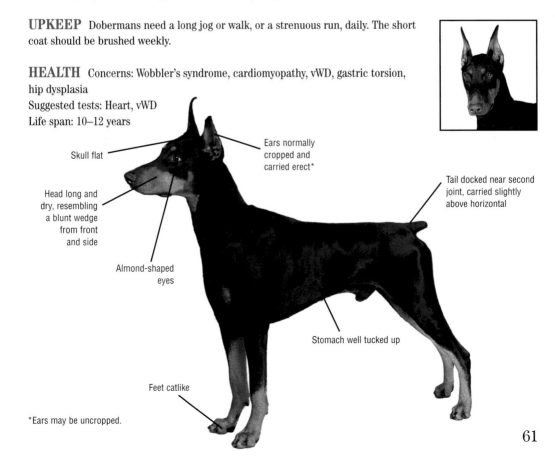

Skull flat

Ears normally cropped and carried erect*

Head long and dry, resembling a blunt wedge from front and side

Tail docked near second joint, carried slightly above horizontal

Almond-shaped eyes

Stomach well tucked up

Feet catlike

*Ears may be uncropped.

German Pinscher

Area of Origin: Germany
Original Function: Ratting
Coat: Smooth, short
Color: Isabella (fawn) to red to stag red; black and tan, blue and tan
Height: 17–20"
Weight: 25–35 lb

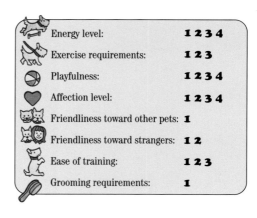

Energy level:	**1 2 3 4**
Exercise requirements:	**1 2 3**
Playfulness:	**1 2 3 4**
Affection level:	**1 2 3 4**
Friendliness toward other pets:	**1**
Friendliness toward strangers:	**1 2**
Ease of training:	**1 2 3**
Grooming requirements:	**1**

HISTORY The German Pinscher can trace back its history to the 1600s, when they were known as the *Rattenfanger*, a versatile working ratter and watchdog. The *Rattenfanger* became the Pinscher, and it remained a hardworking dog for several centuries, especially valued for its rodent-catching ability around the stables. The first Pinscher breed standard was drawn up in 1884. The breed didn't garner immediate favor with dog fanciers and numbers fell. After World War II the breed was on the verge of extinction. The breed had to be rescued by crosses to four oversized Miniature Pinschers. Almost all current German Pinschers descend from these dogs plus one female smuggled out of East Germany. German Pinschers began their presence in America in the late 1970s. In 2003 the breed joined the AKC Working Group.

TEMPERAMENT German Pinschers are vivacious, tenacious, and courageous. They are watchful, playful, and affectionate. They can be wary of strangers, and may not be good with small pets.

UPKEEP German Pinschers need a moderate walk plus lots of activity every day. Grooming is wash and wear; only occasional brushing is required.

HEALTH Concerns: None noted
Suggested tests: None
Life span: 12–15 years

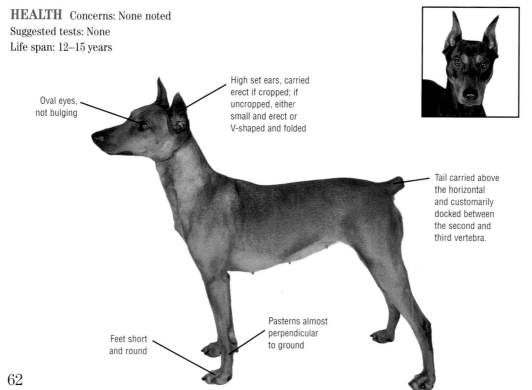

Oval eyes, not bulging

High set ears, carried erect if cropped; if uncropped, either small and erect or V-shaped and folded

Tail carried above the horizontal and customarily docked between the second and third vertebra.

Feet short and round

Pasterns almost perpendicular to ground

Giant Schnauzer

Area of Origin: Germany
Original function: Cattle herding, guardian
Coat: Hard, wiry, short to medium length
Color: Solid black or pepper and salt
Height: Male: 25.5–27.5″; Female: 23.5–25.5″
Weight: 65–90 lb

Energy level:		1 2 3
Exercise requirements:		1 2 3 4
Playfulness:		1 2 3 4
Affection level:		1
Friendliness toward other pets:		1 2
Friendliness toward strangers:		1
Ease of training:		1 2 3
Grooming requirements:		1 2 3

HISTORY Impressed by the smaller Standard Schnauzer, cattlemen in the countryside of Bavaria and Wurrtemburg sought to create a larger-scaled Schnauzer more suitable for driving cattle. Through a series of crosses they created a weather-resistant, smart-looking dog capable of handling cattle, then known as the *Munchener*. Giant Schnauzers later became more popular as butchers' or stockyard dogs, and even later, as brewery guard dogs. The dogs maintained a low profile, with little exposure until just before World War I, when it was suggested that they could be trained as police dogs. They excelled at their new assignment but have not been well accepted outside of Germany in that capacity.

TEMPERAMENT Playful and rambunctious, Giant Schnauzers are bold and protective of family. They are reserved with strangers and may be aggressive toward other dogs.

UPKEEP The Giant Schnauzer needs daily exercise and fun. Its exercise requirements can be met with vigorous games and long hikes or walks. It can live outside in temperate to cool climates, but it does best when allowed to divide its time between house and yard. Its harsh coat needs combing once or twice weekly, plus shaping two to four times yearly. Shaping is best done by professional scissoring and hand-stripping, but clipping is acceptable for pets.

HEALTH Concerns: Hip dysplasia, gastric torsion
Suggested tests: Hip
Life span: 10–12 years

Rectangular head

Oval deep-set eyes

Ears may be cropped or uncropped; when uncropped, ears are V-shaped

Short, straight back

Tail docked to second or third joint, carried high

Cat feet

Great Dane

Area of Origin: Germany
Original Function: Guardian, hunting large game
Coat: Smooth, short
Color: Brindle, black-masked fawn, blue, black, harlequin (white with irregular black patches), or mantle (black with white collar, muzzle, chest, and tail tip)
Height: Male: at least 30″, preferably 32″ or more (Note: most 32–35″); Female: at least 28″, preferably 30″ or more (Note: most 31–33″)
Weight: Male: 130–180 lb; Female 110–150 lb

Energy level:	**1 2**
Exercise requirements:	**1 2**
Playfulness:	**1 2**
Affection level:	**1 2 3 4**
Friendliness toward other pets:	**1 2**
Friendliness toward strangers:	**1 2 3 4**
Ease of training:	**1 2 3**
Grooming requirements:	**1**

HISTORY Dubbed the "Apollo of Dogs," the Great Dane's ancestors were used as war dogs and hunting dogs; thus, its ability as a fearless big-game hunter seemed only natural. By the 14th century these dogs were proving themselves as able hunters of wild boar in Germany. The noble dogs became popular with the landed gentry not only because of their hunting ability but also because of their imposing yet graceful appearance. Exactly when and why the breed was later dubbed the Great Dane is a mystery because, although undeniably great, it is not Danish. It is a German breed, and in 1880 German authorities declared that the dog should only be referred to as the *Deutsche Dogge*, the name by which it still goes in Germany. By the late 1800s the Great Dane had come to America.

TEMPERAMENT Great Danes are gentle, loving, easygoing, and sensitive. They are usually friendly toward other dogs and pets. Though powerful, they are sensitive and responsive to training.

UPKEEP Great Danes need daily moderate exercise. They need soft bedding and sufficient room to stretch out when sleeping. Some tend to drool. Coat care is minimal.

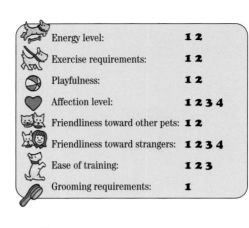

HEALTH Concerns: Gastric torsion, hip dysplasia, cardiomyopathy, elbow dysplasia, bone cancer
Suggested tests: Heart, elbow, hip
Life span: 7–10 years

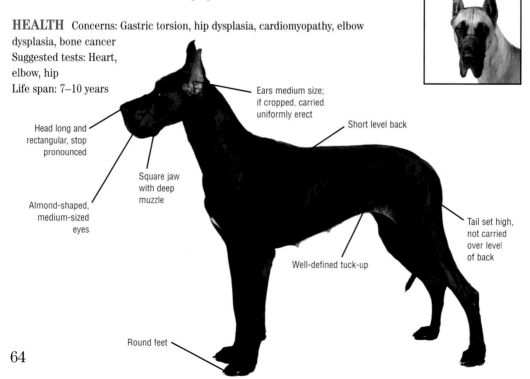

Ears medium size; if cropped, carried uniformly erect

Short level back

Head long and rectangular, stop pronounced

Square jaw with deep muzzle

Almond-shaped, medium-sized eyes

Tail set high, not carried over level of back

Well-defined tuck-up

Round feet

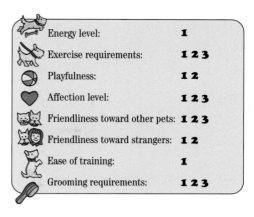

Energy level:	**1**	
Exercise requirements:	**1 2 3**	
Playfulness:	**1 2**	
Affection level:	**1 2 3**	
Friendliness toward other pets:	**1 2 3**	
Friendliness toward strangers:	**1 2**	
Ease of training:	**1**	
Grooming requirements:	**1 2 3**	

Great Pyrenees

Area of Origin: France
Original function: Sheep guardian
Coat: Dense wooly undercoat; long, flat, coarse outer coat
Color: White or white with markings of gray, badger, reddish brown, or tan
Height: Male: 27–32″; Female: 25–29″
Weight: Male: 115 lb; Female: 85–90 lb

HISTORY The Great Pyrenees was used from the earliest times to guard flocks. In medieval France, the Pyrenees became a formidable fortress guard, and eventually, a band of these imposing dogs was the pride of many large châteaus. In the late 1600s the breed caught the eye of the French nobility, and in 1675 the Great Pyrenees was decreed the "Royal Dog of France" by Louis XIV. The first documented Pyrenees came to America with General Lafayette in 1824. By the 1900s the breed had disappeared from French court life, and the remaining dogs were those found still working in the isolated Basque countryside. Serious importation of the breed to America occurred in the 1930s, and by 1933 the Great Pyrenees received AKC recognition.

TEMPERAMENT Great Pyrenees are capable guardians, devoted to family, and wary of strange people and dogs. They are calm, serious, independent, somewhat stubborn, and sometimes domineering. They tend to bark a lot.

UPKEEP Great Pyrenees need a moderate walk every day. They do not enjoy warm weather. The coat needs brushing once or twice weekly, daily when shedding. They may drool.

HEALTH Concerns: Hip dysplasia, patellar luxation, entropion, bone cancer
Suggested tests: Hip, knee
Life span: 10–12 years

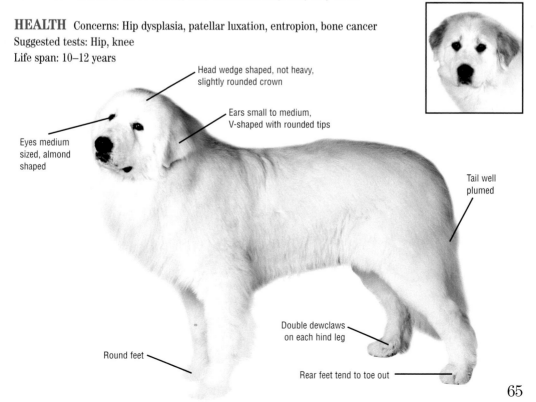

Head wedge shaped, not heavy, slightly rounded crown

Ears small to medium, V-shaped with rounded tips

Eyes medium sized, almond shaped

Tail well plumed

Double dewclaws on each hind leg

Round feet

Rear feet tend to toe out

Working Group

Greater Swiss Mountain Dog

Area of Origin: Switzerland
Original Function: Draft dog, guardian
Coat: Thick, fairly short
Color: Black and rust, with white feet, chest, tail tip, muzzle, blaze, and possibly collar; rust color present on legs between white and black
Height: Male: 25.5–28.5″; Female: 23.5–27″
Weight: Male: 105–140 lb; Female: 85–110 lb

Energy level:		**1 2**
Exercise requirements:		**1 2 3**
Playfulness:		**1 2**
Affection level:		**1 2 3**
Friendliness toward other pets:		**1 2 3 4**
Friendliness toward strangers:		**1 2**
Ease of training:		**1 2 3 4**
Grooming requirements:		**1**

HISTORY The Greater Swiss Mountain Dog is the oldest and largest of four varieties of Swiss mountain dogs; the other three are the Appenzeller, Entlebucher, and Bernese. They acted as guardians, herders, draft dogs, and sometimes, butchers' dogs. Until the late 1800s all these mountain dogs were assumed to be of one breed. Only when Professor Alfred Heim studied the native Swiss mountain breeds seriously did he discern consistent differences that allowed them to be categorized as four distinct breeds. In 1908 Heim spotted a dog that he dubbed the Greater Swiss because of its resemblance to the sturdy Swiss butchers' dogs. In 1968 the Greater Swiss come to America. It achieved full AKC recognition in 1995.

TEMPERAMENT Greater Swiss Mountain Dogs are sensitive, loyal, calm, and easygoing, but also territorial, alert, bold, and vigilant. They are devoted to family.

UPKEEP Swissies, as they are called, need a moderate walk or vigorous romp daily. The coat needs brushing once weekly, more often when shedding.

HEALTH Concerns: Hip dysplasia, gastric torsion, seizures
Suggested tests: Hip
Life span: 10–12 years

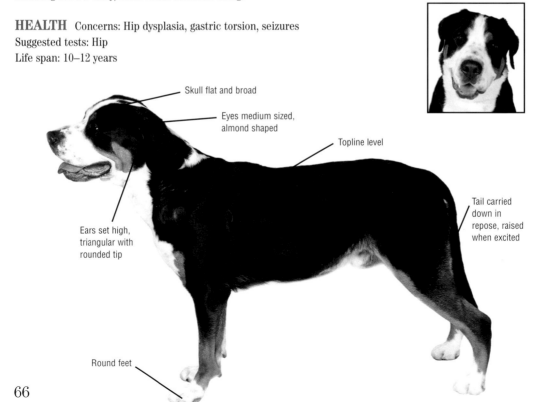

Skull flat and broad

Eyes medium sized, almond shaped

Topline level

Tail carried down in repose, raised when excited

Ears set high, triangular with rounded tip

Round feet

Komondor

Energy level:	1 2 3
Exercise requirements:	1 2 3
Playfulness:	1 2 3
Affection level:	1 2 3 4
Friendliness toward other pets:	1 2 3 4
Friendliness toward strangers:	1
Ease of training:	1 2 3
Grooming requirements:	1 2 3

Area of Origin: Hungary
Original Function: Sheep guardian
Coat: Wooly undercoat and coarse outercoat, wavy or curly, which form feltlike cords
Color: White
Height: Male: 27.5″ and up; Female: 25.5″ and up
Weight: Male: average 80 lb; Female: average 70 lb

HISTORY The earliest documentation of the Komondor dates back to 1555, although the breed is certain to have existed long before then. These dogs bore a close resemblance to the Magyar sheep, so they could mingle with them unseen by predators. It was so effective at protecting flocks that some claim it is responsible for wiping out the wolf in Hungary. The Komondor was still used as a guard into the 20th century. The first Komondor came to America in 1933, and the AKC recognized the breed in 1937. World War II almost decimated the breed in Europe, but through the concerted efforts of breeders, the Komondor was saved. Recent attempts to use the breed as a guardian of flocks in the western United States have yielded promising results.

TEMPERAMENT Komondorok are independent and can be stubborn, even domineering. They are reserved with strangers and possibly aggressive toward strange dogs. Although usually calm and quiet, they are protective and fearless when the need arises.

UPKEEP Komondorok need a moderate walk daily. The coat can be hard to keep clean, also hard to bathe and dry. The cords must be regularly separated or they will look like flat mats.

HEALTH Concerns: Hip dysplasia, gastric torsion, ear problems
Suggested tests: Hip
Life span: 10–12 years

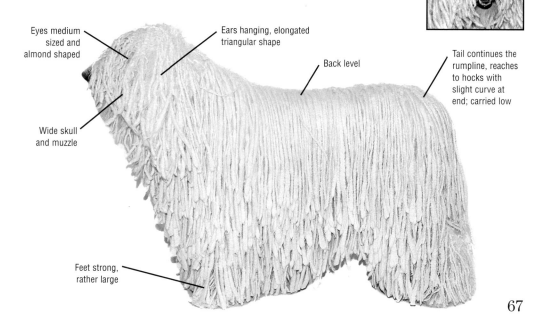

Eyes medium sized and almond shaped

Ears hanging, elongated triangular shape

Back level

Tail continues the rumpline, reaches to hocks with slight curve at end; carried low

Wide skull and muzzle

Feet strong, rather large

Kuvasz

Area of Origin: Hungary
Original Function: Guardian, hunting large game
Coat: Medium coarse, wavy to straight, medium length
Color: White
Height: Male: 28–30″; Female: 26–28″
Weight: Male: 100–115 lb; Female: 70–90 lb

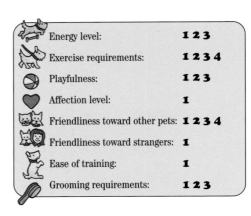

Energy level:	**1 2 3**
Exercise requirements:	**1 2 3 4**
Playfulness:	**1 2 3**
Affection level:	**1**
Friendliness toward other pets:	**1 2 3 4**
Friendliness toward strangers:	**1**
Ease of training:	**1**
Grooming requirements:	**1 2 3**

HISTORY In the latter 15th century the Kuvasz was held in the highest esteem. Breedings were carefully planned and recorded, and the dogs were a fixture of most large Hungarian estates. They served as both guard and hunting dogs, capable of defending the estate against marauders and of pulling down large game such as bear and wolf. King Matthias I was a special patron of the Kuvasz, keeping a large kennel and doing much to improve the quality of the breed. In the succeeding centuries, the Kuvasz gradually came into the hands of commoners, who found them to be capable livestock dogs. The breed seriously declined as a result of two world wars, but German stock formed a basis for the breed to continue through these hard times. The AKC recognized the Kuvasz in 1935.

TEMPERAMENT Kuvaszok are tough protectors. They are reserved with strangers and may be aggressive toward strange dogs. They are devoted and loyal but not very demonstrative. Some can be domineering.

UPKEEP Kuvaszok need a moderate to long walk daily. The coat needs brushing one or two times weekly, more often during heavy shedding periods.

HEALTH Concerns: Hip dysplasia
Suggested tests: Hip
Life span: 9–12 years

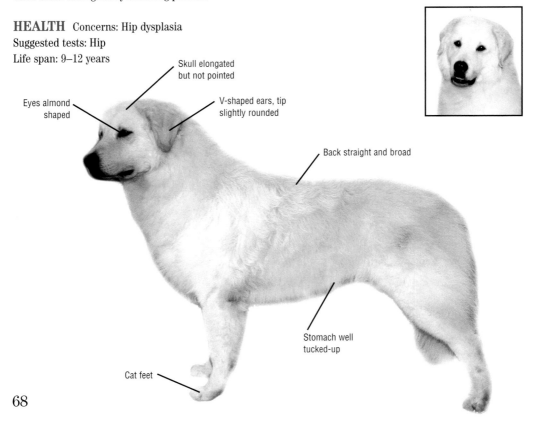

Skull elongated but not pointed

Eyes almond shaped

V-shaped ears, tip slightly rounded

Back straight and broad

Stomach well tucked-up

Cat feet

Mastiff

Area of Origin: England
Original Function: Guardian
Coat: Coarse, smooth, short
Color: Fawn, apricot, or brindle, all with dark muzzle, ears, and nose
Height: Male: minimum 30″; Female: minimum 27.5″
Weight: 175–190 lb

Energy level:	1
Exercise requirements:	1 2
Playfulness:	1
Affection level:	1 2 3 4
Friendliness toward other pets:	1 2 3 4
Friendliness toward strangers:	1 2
Ease of training:	1 2 3
Grooming requirements:	1

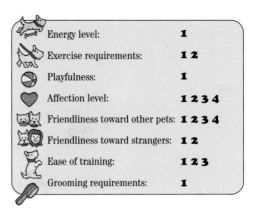

HISTORY By the time of Caesar, Mastiffs were used as war dogs and gladiators. In medieval times, they were used as guard dogs and hunting dogs, and later, for dog fighting, bull baiting, and bear baiting. The modern Mastiff descends not only from these pit dogs but also from more noble lines, being descendants of one of the most famous Mastiffs of all time: the Mastiff of Sir Peers Legh. When Legh was wounded in the battle of Agincourt, his Mastiff stood over him and protected him for many hours through the battle. Although Legh later died, the Mastiff returned to his home and was the foundation of the Lyme Hall Mastiffs. Five centuries later the Lyme Hall Mastiffs figured prominently in founding the modern breed. The breed's documented entry to America did not occur until the late 1800s.

TEMPERAMENT Mastiffs are calm, easygoing, and surprisingly gentle. They are very loyal though not excessively demonstrative.

UPKEEP Mastiffs need a good walk or play session every day. They tend to drool. Coat care is minimal.

HEALTH Concerns: Hip dysplasia, gastric torsion, elbow dysplasia, bone cancer
Suggested tests: Hip, elbow
Life span: 9–11 years

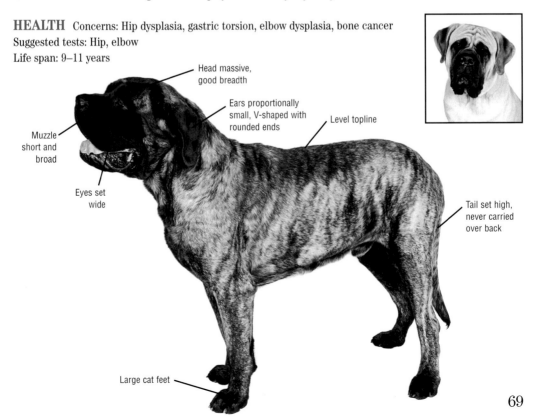

Head massive, good breadth

Ears proportionally small, V-shaped with rounded ends

Level topline

Muzzle short and broad

Eyes set wide

Tail set high, never carried over back

Large cat feet

Neapolitan Mastiff

Energy level:	**1 2**	
Exercise requirements:	**1**	
Playfulness:	**1**	
Affection level:	**1 2 3 4**	
Friendliness toward other pets:	**1 2**	
Friendliness toward strangers:	**1**	
Ease of training:	**1 2**	
Grooming requirements:	**1 2**	

Area of Origin: Italy

Original Function: Guardian

Coat: Smooth, short

Color: Gray, black, mahogany, tawny, with or without tan brindling; white allowed on underside, chest, throat, toes, and backs of pasterns

Height: Male: 26–31″; Female: 24–29″

Weight: Male: 150 lb; Female: 110 lb (Note: Most Neapolitan Mastiffs are actually heavier than this.)

HISTORY In 55 B.C. the Romans invaded Britain, where they admired and appropriated fierce British mastiff dogs that fought valiantly in defending Britain. These British mastiffs were bred with the Roman Molossus dogs to produce an unsurpassed strain of giant gladiators and war dogs. They were perfected over the next centuries for guarding estates and homes in the Neapolitan area in the south of Italy. The breed remained virtually unknown to the rest of the world until a chance sighting at a Naples dog show in 1946. Fanciers petitioned the Italian Kennel Club to recognize them under the name *Mastino Napoletano*. The first Neapolitans came to the United States in the 1970s. They entered the AKC Working Group in 2004.

TEMPERAMENT Neapolitan Mastiffs are loyal and devoted to family, watchful and suspicious of strangers, and tolerant of acquaintances. They may not get along well with other dogs, especially domineering-type dogs.

UPKEEP Neapolitans don't need a lot of exercise, but they do need a lot of living space. They drool and can leave a trail of food and water leading from their bowls. Coat care is minimal.

HEALTH Concerns: Hip dysplasia, cardiomyopathy, demodicosis, elbow dysplasia
Suggested tests: Hip, elbow, heart
Life span: 8–10 years

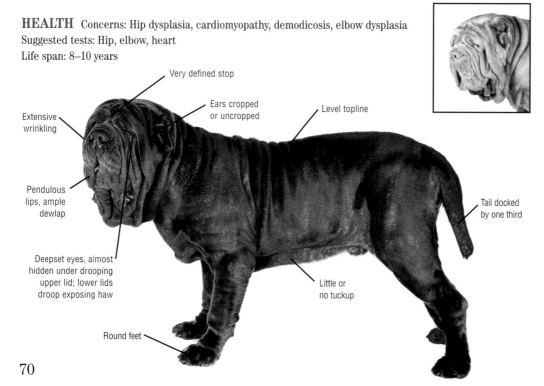

Very defined stop

Ears cropped or uncropped

Level topline

Extensive wrinkling

Pendulous lips, ample dewlap

Deepset eyes, almost hidden under drooping upper lid; lower lids droop exposing haw

Little or no tuckup

Tail docked by one third

Round feet

Newfoundland

Area of Origin: Canada
Original Function: All-purpose water dog and fishing aid, draft
Coat: Coarse, straight or wavy, medium length
Color: Solid black, brown, or gray, may have white on chin, chest, toes, and tail tip; or white base color with black markings ("Landseer")
Height: Male: 28″ average; Female: 26″ average
Weight: Male: 130–150 lb; Female: 100–120 lb

Energy level:	**1 2**	
Exercise requirements:	**1 2**	
Playfulness:	**1 2 3**	
Affection level:	**1 2 3 4 5**	
Friendliness toward other pets:	**1 2 3 4 5**	
Friendliness toward strangers:	**1 2 3 4 5**	
Ease of training:	**1 2 3**	
Grooming requirements:	**1 2 3**	

HISTORY The Newfoundland was developed on the coast of Newfoundland, Canada, as an all-purpose water dog, hauling heavy fishing nets through the cold water and saving many people from watery graves. Its work didn't stop on dry land; it also served as a draft dog and pack animal. They were massive water-loving, cold-resistant dogs found in either a solid black or black and white coloration. European visitors were so impressed that they returned to Europe with many specimens, and it is here that the breed first entered the show ring. The export of dogs from Newfoundland, along with laws forbidding ownership of more than one dog, drove the breed's numbers down in its place of origin. The breed's stronghold switched to England. After World War II, the tables turned, and American Newfoundlands were responsible for reviving the decimated English stock.

TEMPERAMENT Newfoundlands are sweet, calm, patient, easygoing, gentle, and amiable. They are also protective of family.

UPKEEP Newfoundlands need a moderate walk or short romp daily. They love to swim and pull, especially in cold weather. Their coat needs combing twice weekly—more frequently when shedding. Newfoundlands do drool and also tend to be messy drinkers.

HEALTH Concerns: Heart problems, elbow dysplasia, hip dysplasia, gastric torsion
Suggested tests: Hip, elbow, heart
Life span: 8–10 years

Proud head carriage

Ears relatively small, triangular with rounded tips

Broad skull

Eyes relatively small and deep set

Tail held down when relaxed; never carried over the back

Cat feet, webbed

71

Portuguese Water Dog

Area of Origin: Portugal
Original Function: Fishing aid
Coat: Curly or wavy, long
Color: Black, white, brown, or combinations of black
  or brown with white
Height: Male: 20–23"; Female: 17–21"
Weight: Male: 42–60 lb; Female: 35–50 lb

Energy level:	**1 2 3 4**
Exercise requirements:	**1 2 3 4**
Playfulness:	**1 2 3 4**
Affection level:	**1 2 3 4**
Friendliness toward other pets:	**1 2 3 4**
Friendliness toward strangers:	**1 2 3**
Ease of training:	**1 2 3**
Grooming requirements:	**1 2 3 4 5**

HISTORY The Portuguese Water Dog herded fish into nets, retrieved lost nets or equipment, and served as a boat-to-boat or boat-to-shore courier on the coast of Portugal. Later these dogs were part of trawler crews fishing the waters from Portugal to Iceland. The breed is known in its native land as *cao de agua* (pronounced kown-d'ahgwa), which means "dog of water." With the demise of traditional fishing methods, Portuguese fishermen and their dogs began to disappear from the coast in the early 20th century. The breed was saved largely through the attempts of a wealthy shipping magnate. After a brief appearance in England in the 1950s, the breed virtually died out there. Around this time, the first Portuguese Water Dogs came to America, where they slowly gained a following. The AKC officially recognized the breed in 1984.

TEMPERAMENT Portuguese Water Dogs are fun-loving, family-loving, and water-loving. They are good with other dogs and pets. They are sensitive and respond well to direction.

UPKEEP Portuguese Water Dogs need a long walk or jog or a vigorous romp daily. The coat needs combing every other day, plus monthly clipping or scissoring.

HEALTH Concerns: PRA, hip dysplasia, glycogen storage disease
Suggested tests: Eye, hip
Life span: 10–14 years

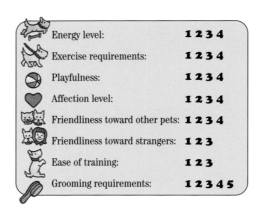

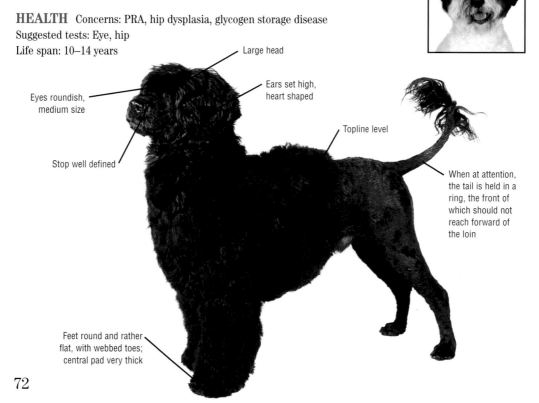

Large head

Ears set high, heart shaped

Eyes roundish, medium size

Topline level

Stop well defined

When at attention, the tail is held in a ring, the front of which should not reach forward of the loin

Feet round and rather flat, with webbed toes; central pad very thick

Rottweiler

Area of Origin: Germany
Original Function: Cattle drover, guardian, draft
Coat: Coarse, smooth, short
Color: Black with tan markings
Height: Male: 24–27″; Female: 22–25″
Weight: Male: 85–135 lb; Female: 80–100 lb

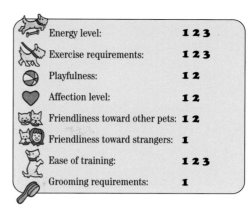

Energy level:	**1 2 3**
Exercise requirements:	**1 2 3**
Playfulness:	**1 2**
Affection level:	**1 2**
Friendliness toward other pets:	**1 2**
Friendliness toward strangers:	**1**
Ease of training:	**1 2 3**
Grooming requirements:	**1**

HISTORY Roman troops on long marches probably left behind Roman drover dogs in southern Germany. Throughout the succeeding centuries, the dogs continued to play a vital role as cattle drovers around what was to become the town of Rottweil and a center of cattle commerce. Their dogs drove and guarded cattle, guarded the money earned by the cattle sales, and served as draft animals. In the mid-19th century, cattle driving was outlawed, and dog carting was replaced by donkey carts and railroads. With little need for this once vital breed, the Rottweiler fell into such decline that it was nearly lost. Dog fanciers set about to revive it around 1900. By the 1930s it was competing in AKC competitions. At one time it was the second-most popular breed in America.

TEMPERAMENT Rottweilers are confident, bold, alert, and imposing, but also headstrong, stubborn and often domineering. They are protective of family and reserved, often wary, toward strangers.

UPKEEP Rottweilers need a long walk or jogs, or a vigorous play session daily. Coat care is minimal, consisting only of occasional brushing to remove dead hair.

HEALTH Concerns: Hip dysplasia, elbow dysplasia, heart problems, bone cancer, gastric torsion, vWD
Suggested tests: Hip, elbow, heart, vWD
Life span: 8–11 years

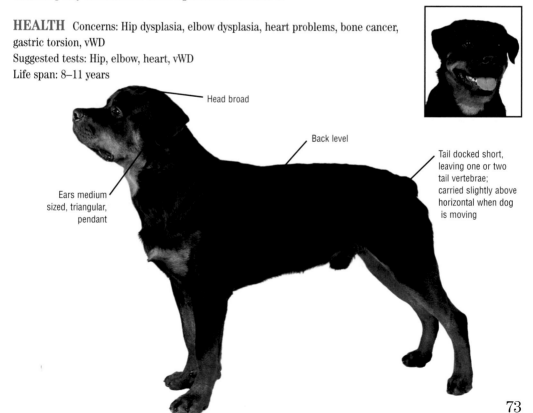

Head broad

Back level

Tail docked short, leaving one or two tail vertebrae; carried slightly above horizontal when dog is moving

Ears medium sized, triangular, pendant

Saint Bernard

Energy level:	**1 2**
Exercise requirements:	**1 2**
Playfulness:	**1 2 3**
Affection level:	**1 2 3 4**
Friendliness toward other pets:	**1 2 3 4**
Friendliness toward strangers:	**1 2 3**
Ease of training:	**1 2 3**
Grooming requirements:	**1 2 3**

Area of Origin: Switzerland

Original Function: Draft, search and rescue

Coat: Shorthaired: smooth, short; Longhaired: straight or slightly wavy, medium length

Color: White with red, red or brindle with white; white must appear on chest, feet, tail tip, noseband, and collar (or spot on nape); may have dark mask and ears

Height: Male: minimum 27.5″; Female: minimum 25″

Weight: 120–200 lb

HISTORY In the 1600s large dogs arrived at the St. Bernard Hospice, a refuge for travelers crossing between Switzerland and Italy. The dogs were originally used to pull carts and turn spits. The monks soon found they were adept at locating lost travelers, licking the person's face, lying beside them, and warming them. They served in this role for three centuries, saving more than 2,000 lives. The most famous of all Saint Bernards was Barry, who was credited with saving 40 lives. In the early 1800s many of the dogs were lost to severe weather, disease, and inbreeding. Some of the remaining dogs were crossed with Newfoundlands in 1830, creating the first long-coated Saints. The first Saint Bernards came to England around 1810, and to America around 1880.

TEMPERAMENT The calm, easygoing Saint Bernard is gentle and patient, but not particularly playful. They are devoted to family and are willing to please, but they can be stubborn.

UPKEEP Saint Bernards need a short to moderate walk every day. The coat, whether long or short, needs weekly brushing, more so when shedding. All Saint Bernards drool.

HEALTH Concerns: Hip dysplasia, gastric torsion, eyelid problems, elbow dysplasia, bone cancer, heart problems, diabetes

Suggested tests: Hip, elbow, heart, eye

Life span: 8–10 years

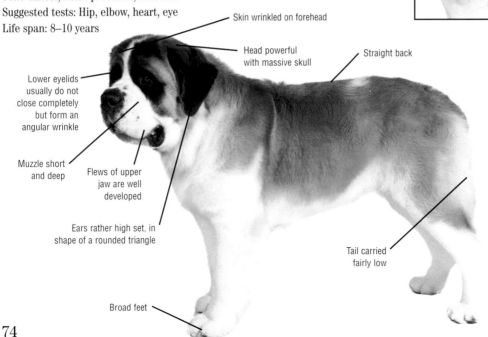

Skin wrinkled on forehead

Head powerful with massive skull

Straight back

Lower eyelids usually do not close completely but form an angular wrinkle

Muzzle short and deep

Flews of upper jaw are well developed

Ears rather high set, in shape of a rounded triangle

Tail carried fairly low

Broad feet

Working Group

Samoyed

Area of Origin: Russia (Siberia)
Original Function: Herding reindeer, guardian, draft
Coat: Wooly undercoat; straight, harsh outercoat, medium to long length, standing off body
Color: White, white and biscuit, cream, or all biscuit
Height: Male: 21–23.5″; Female: 19–21″
Weight: Male: 45–65 lb; Female: 35–50 lb

Energy level:	**1 2 3**	
Exercise requirements:	**1 2 3**	
Playfulness:	**1 2 3 4**	
Affection level:	**1 2 3 4**	
Friendliness toward other pets:	**1 2 3 4 5**	
Friendliness toward strangers:	**1 2 3 4**	
Ease of training:	**1 2**	
Grooming requirements:	**1 2 3**	

HISTORY The Samoyed herded and guarded reindeer herds kept for food by nomadic Samoyed people in northwestern Siberia from central Asia. The dogs occasionally helped to hunt bears and tow boats and sleighs. The first Samoyeds came to England in the late 1800s. One of these dogs was presented to Queen Alexandria, who did much to promote the breed. Descendants of the queen's dogs can still be found in modern pedigrees. In 1906 the first Samoyed came to America, originally a gift of Russia's Grand Duke Nicholas. Meanwhile, the breed was becoming a popular sled dog because it was more tractable than other sledding breeds. In the early 1900s Samoyeds formed part of the sled teams on expeditions to Antarctica, and shared in the triumph of reaching the South Pole.

TEMPERAMENT Samoyeds are gentle and playful, amiable with strangers and usually, other dogs. They are calm indoors, but can be mischievous. They are independent and often stubborn, but are willing to please.

UPKEEP Samoyeds need a long walk or jog or a vigorous play session daily. The thick coat needs brushing and combing two to three times a week, daily when shedding.

HEALTH Concerns: Hip dysplasia, gastric torsion
Suggested tests: Hip
Life span: 10–12 years

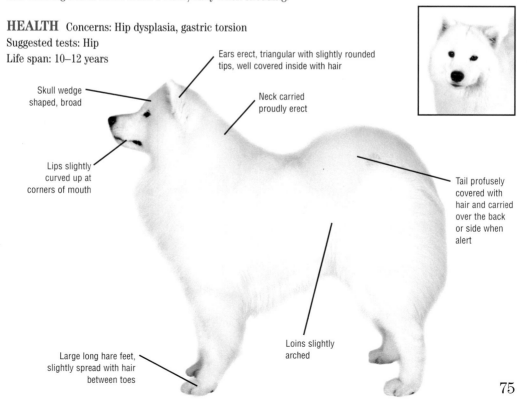

Ears erect, triangular with slightly rounded tips, well covered inside with hair

Skull wedge shaped, broad

Neck carried proudly erect

Lips slightly curved up at corners of mouth

Tail profusely covered with hair and carried over the back or side when alert

Large long hare feet, slightly spread with hair between toes

Loins slightly arched

Siberian Husky

Area of Origin: Russia (Siberia)
Original Function: Sled pulling
Coat: Dense undercoat; straight outercoat, medium length
Color: All colors from black to pure white
Height: Male: 21–23.5″; Female: 20–22″
Weight: Male: 45–60 lb; Female: 35–50 lb

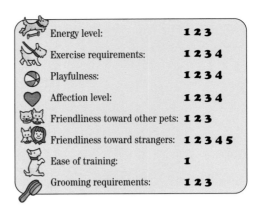

Energy level:	**1 2 3**
Exercise requirements:	**1 2 3 4**
Playfulness:	**1 2 3 4**
Affection level:	**1 2 3 4**
Friendliness toward other pets:	**1 2 3**
Friendliness toward strangers:	**1 2 3 4 5**
Ease of training:	**1**
Grooming requirements:	**1 2 3**

HISTORY During the Alaskan gold rush, dogs became a vital part of life in the Arctic regions, and dog racing became a favorite source of entertainment. The All-Alaska sweepstakes race, covering 408 miles between Nome and Candle, was especially popular, and in 1909 the first team of Chukchi huskies brought over from Siberia was entered. The next year, Siberian Husky teams dominated the race. In 1925 teams of Huskies raced 340 miles with lifesaving serum for diphtheria-stricken Nome and were credited with saving the town. A statue in their honor stands in Central Park. The first Siberian Huskies came to Canada, and then the United States, at around this time. The AKC recognized the breed in 1930. During World War II many Siberians served in the U.S. Army's search and rescue teams.

TEMPERAMENT Siberian Huskies are fun-loving, adventurous, alert, independent, clever, stubborn, mischievous, and obstinate. They love to run and will roam if given the chance. Some howl, dig, and chew.

UPKEEP Siberian Huskies need a long jog or vigorous play session daily. Their coat needs brushing once or twice a week—daily during periods of heaviest shedding.

HEALTH Concerns: PRA, cataract, corneal opacities
Suggested tests: Eye
Life span: 11–13 years

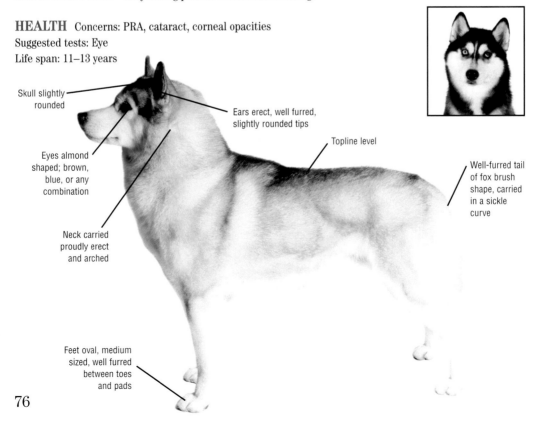

Skull slightly rounded

Ears erect, well furred, slightly rounded tips

Topline level

Eyes almond shaped; brown, blue, or any combination

Well-furred tail of fox brush shape, carried in a sickle curve

Neck carried proudly erect and arched

Feet oval, medium sized, well furred between toes and pads

Standard Schnauzer

Area of Origin: Germany
Original Function: Ratting, guardian
Coat: Harsh, wiry, medium length
Color: Pepper and salt, or pure black
Height: Male: 18.5–19.5″; Female: 17.5–18.5″
Weight: Male: 40–45 lb; Female: 35–40 lb

Energy level:	**1 2 3 4**
Exercise requirements:	**1 2 3**
Playfulness:	**1 2 3**
Affection level:	**1 2**
Friendliness toward other pets:	**1 2 3**
Friendliness toward strangers:	**1**
Ease of training:	**1 2 3**
Grooming requirements:	**1 2 3 4**

HISTORY As long ago as the 14th century the Standard Schnauzer was appreciated as a household pet and hunting companion. The breed is a fortuitous blend of terrier, working, and hunting stock, able to function as a hardy rat catcher as well as capable guard dog. By the beginning of the 20th century, Standard Schnauzers were the most popular dogs for guarding farmers' carts at the marketplace. The first Schnauzers entered the show ring as Wirehaired Pinschers at an 1879 German show. Their smart looks quickly endeared them to the dog fanciers, and they became very popular as show dogs by 1900. The breed was initially classified as a terrier, but it was later reclassified as a working dog. Their alert and intelligent nature gained them a role as dispatch carriers and aides during World War I. The Standard Schnauzer was also used in police work.

TEMPERAMENT Standard Schnauzers are bold, lively, and fun-loving. They are also clever and head-strong, and can be mischievous. They are protective of family, reserved with strangers, and may be aggressive toward strange dogs.

UPKEEP Standard Schnauzers need a long walk or a vigorous game daily. The harsh coat needs combing twice weekly, plus professional scissoring and shaping four times yearly.

HEALTH Concerns: Hip dysplasia, follicular dermatitis
Suggested tests: Hip
Life span: 12–14 years

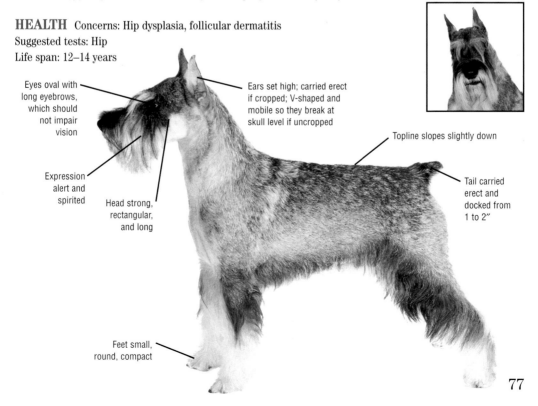

Eyes oval with long eyebrows, which should not impair vision

Ears set high; carried erect if cropped; V-shaped and mobile so they break at skull level if uncropped

Topline slopes slightly down

Expression alert and spirited

Head strong, rectangular, and long

Tail carried erect and docked from 1 to 2″

Feet small, round, compact

77

Tibetan Mastiff

Area of Origin: Tibet
Original Function: Guardian
Coat: Coarse, fairly long
Color: Black, brown, and gray, all with or without tan markings; various shades of gold; white markings on breast and feet acceptable.
Height: Male: 26″, Female: 24″ minimum
Weight: Male: 90–150 lb or more; Female: 80–110 lb

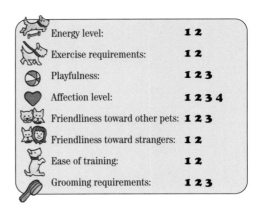

	Energy level:	1 2
	Exercise requirements:	1 2
	Playfulness:	1 2 3
	Affection level:	1 2 3 4
	Friendliness toward other pets:	1 2 3
	Friendliness toward strangers:	1 2
	Ease of training:	1 2
	Grooming requirements:	1 2 3

HISTORY Tibetan Mastiffs may have been developed as camp guardians for nomadic herdsmen on the Himalayan plateaus. They were later used to guard villages and monasteries. Village sentries were usually chained to gates and rooftops by day and allowed to roam at night. With few dogs outside their native country, the breed's future was threatened when China invaded Tibet in the 1950s, displacing the native dogs. Survival depended on fleeing to neighboring countries or retreating to isolated mountain villages. Only in the 1970s did stock from Nepal and India arrive to found breeding programs in America. The imports came from a wide genetic base, accounting for the natural variation in size and style in the breed today. In 2005 the breed entered the AKC Miscellaneous Class. It was admitted into the Working group in 2007.

TEMPERAMENT Tibetan Mastiffs are independent, strong-willed, and territorial. They are aloof toward strangers, but devoted to family. They are generally good with other dogs. They often bark at night.

UPKEEP Tibetan Mastiffs require a moderate to long walk each day. Their coat requires brushing a few times a week (daily during shedding).

HEALTH Concerns: Hip dysplasia
Suggested tests: Hip
Life span: 11–14 years

Deep-set almond-shaped eyes

Strongly defined stop

Topline straight and level

Medium to long tail, set high and curled over

Broad, heavy head; some wrinkling from eyes to mouth corner; moderate flews

Medium-sized V-shaped ears, set high and hanging close to the head

Pronounced tuck-up

Fairly large, compact cat feet; single or double dewclaws may be present on rear feet

Airedale Terrier

Area of Origin: England
Original Function: Versatile hunter: badger and otter hunting, bird flushing and retrieving
Coat: Wiry, medium length
Color: Tan with black or grizzle saddle
Height: Male: 23″; Female: slightly less
Weight: About 55 lb

Energy level:	**1 2 3 4**
Exercise requirements:	**1 2 3**
Playfulness:	**1 2 3 4**
Affection level:	**1 2 3**
Friendliness toward other pets:	**1 2**
Friendliness toward strangers:	**1 2 3**
Ease of training:	**1 2 3**
Grooming requirements:	**1 2 3 4**

HISTORY Known as the "king of terriers," the Airedale is the tallest terrier. In the mid-1800s black-and-tan terriers around the River Aire in South Yorkshire were crossed with Otterhounds in order to improve their hunting ability around water, as well as their scenting ability. The result was a dog adept at otter hunting, originally called the Bingley or Waterside Terrier but recognized as the Airedale Terrier in 1878. As it entered the world of the show dog, crosses to the Irish and Bull Terriers were made to enhance its good looks. The Airedale's size and gameness won it worldwide fame as a hunter, even proving itself as a big-game hunter. Its smart looks and manners won it a place as a police dog and family pet, both roles it still enjoys.

TEMPERAMENT Airedales are bold, playful, and adventurous. They are generally biddable and responsive, but also headstrong. They are protective. They will not back down from a challenge, but get along well with smaller dogs.

UPKEEP Airedales need a long walk or lively play session every day. The wire coat needs combing twice weekly, plus scissoring and shaping every one to two months. Ears may need gluing as puppies in order to ensure proper shape as adults.

HEALTH Concerns: Hip dysplasia, gastric torsion
Suggested tests: Hip
Life span: 10–13 years

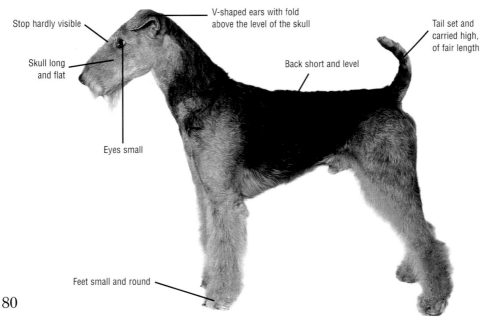

Stop hardly visible

V-shaped ears with fold above the level of the skull

Tail set and carried high, of fair length

Skull long and flat

Back short and level

Eyes small

Feet small and round

American Staffordshire Terrier

	Energy level:	1 2 3
	Exercise requirements:	1 2 3
	Playfulness:	1 2 3
	Affection level:	1 2 3
	Friendliness toward other pets:	1
	Friendliness toward strangers:	1 2 3
	Ease of training:	1 2 3 4
	Grooming requirements:	1

Area of Origin: United States
Original Function: Bull baiting, dog fighting
Coat: Stiff, smooth, short
Color: Any solid or partial color, but more than 80 percent white, black and tan, or liver are less preferred
Height: Male: 18–19″; Female: 17–18″
Weight: 57–67 lb

HISTORY The American Staffordshire Terrier descended from crossing the old Bulldog and old terrier strains to produce the "Bull and Terrier," later to be dubbed the Staffordshire Bull Terrier. The dogs gained fame among dog fighting fans, which gained them passage to America in the late 1800s. Here they became known as the Pit Bull Terrier, American Bull Terrier, and even the Yankee Terrier. Americans favored a bigger dog than the English preferred, and eventually, the American version diverged from its predecessor. The AKC recognized the breed in 1936. Docility and tractability were vital traits in a powerful dog that must be handled even in the midst of a dog fight; therefore, the American Staffordshire evolved to have a trustworthy disposition around people. Since the 1980s the breed has found itself the target of local breed-specific laws aimed at banning it.

TEMPERAMENT American Staffordshire Terriers are devoted, comical, and biddable, but with a stubborn streak. They are a protective breed and can be aggressive and fearless toward other dogs, especially those that challenge them.

UPKEEP Am Staffs, as they are called, need a moderate walk or vigorous play session daily. Their coat needs brushing once a week or so.

HEALTH Concerns: Hip dysplasia, cerebellar ataxia, PRA
Suggested tests: Hip
Life span: 12–14 years

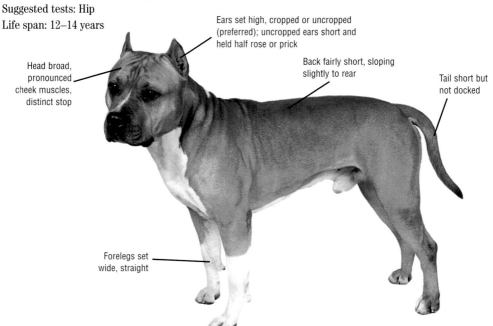

Ears set high, cropped or uncropped (preferred); uncropped ears short and held half rose or prick

Back fairly short, sloping slightly to rear

Tail short but not docked

Head broad, pronounced cheek muscles, distinct stop

Forelegs set wide, straight

81

Australian Terrier

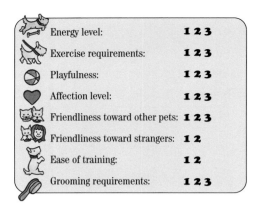

Energy level:	**1 2 3**
Exercise requirements:	**1 2 3**
Playfulness:	**1 2 3**
Affection level:	**1 2 3**
Friendliness toward other pets:	**1 2 3**
Friendliness toward strangers:	**1 2**
Ease of training:	**1 2**
Grooming requirements:	**1 2 3**

Area of Origin: Australia
Original Function: Killing small vermin
Coat: Harsh, straight, medium length
Color: Blue and tan, solid sandy, and solid red
Height: 10–11″
Weight: 12–14 lb

HISTORY The Australian Terrier originated in Tasmania, where its forebears were all-purpose companions, killing vermin and snakes, controlling livestock, and sounding the alarm at intruders. A cornucopia of dogs, mostly terriers, was crossed with this root stock, producing a dog that was both useful and striking in appearance. The first of the breed was shown in the late 1800s as a "broken-coated terrier of blackish blue sheen." The name was soon changed to the Blue and Tan, the Toy, then the Blue Terrier, then in 1900 the Rough-coated Terrier, Blue and Tan. Although mainly known for its blue and tan coloration, a red or sandy color was also found among the early representatives of the breed. Soon afterward the breed made its way to England. It came to America in 1925, and gained AKC recognition in 1960.

TEMPERAMENT Australian Terriers are plucky, tough, fun-loving, and adventurous. They are eager to please, making them one of the more obedient terriers. They get along fairly well with other dogs and household pets. They are reserved with strangers.

UPKEEP Australian Terriers need a moderate walk or a rollicking game daily. Their coat needs weekly combing plus twice yearly stripping of dead hairs.

HEALTH Concerns: Patellar luxation, diabetes
Suggested tests: Knee
Life span: 12–14 years

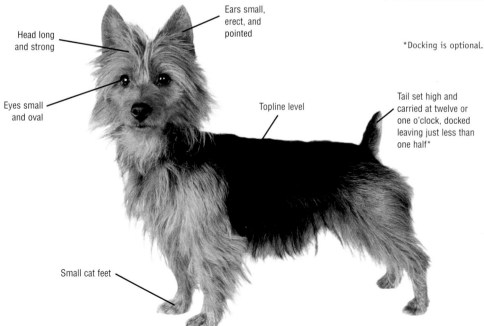

Head long
and strong

Ears small,
erect, and
pointed

Eyes small
and oval

Topline level

*Docking is optional.

Tail set high and
carried at twelve or
one o'clock, docked
leaving just less than
one half*

Small cat feet

Bedlington Terrier

Area of Origin: England

Original Function: Killing rats, badgers, and other vermin

Coat: Mixture of hard and soft hair, tendency to curl, medium length

Color: Blue, sandy, and liver, each with or without tan points. Bedlington puppies are born dark, and lighten to adult color by about one year of age

Height: Male: 16.5″; Female: 15.5″

Weight: 17–23 lb

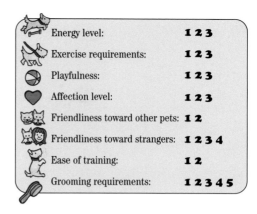

Energy level:	**1 2 3**
Exercise requirements:	**1 2 3**
Playfulness:	**1 2 3**
Affection level:	**1 2 3**
Friendliness toward other pets:	**1 2**
Friendliness toward strangers:	**1 2 3 4**
Ease of training:	**1 2**
Grooming requirements:	**1 2 3 4 5**

HISTORY The Bedlington Terrier hails from the Hanny Hills of Northumberland. In the late 18th century a strain of game terriers was developed that became known as Rothbury Terriers, and the first Bedlingtons came from these dogs and perhaps some other crosses. The result was an agile game terrier that was effective on badgers, foxes, otters, rats, and even rabbits. By the late 1800s the breed had stepped into the show ring as well as into the homes of the elite. At one time the liver color was more popular, although the blue has since passed it in popularity. The Bedlington's lamblike appearance draws many admirers, but the emphasis on show trimming at one time dampened the breed's popularity as a show dog.

TEMPERAMENT Bedlington Terriers are companionable, demonstrative, and loyal. They are fairly quiet house dogs. They can be scrappy fighters when pushed by other dogs.

UPKEEP Bedlingtons need a good long walk or vigorous romp daily. The coat needs combing once or twice weekly, plus scissoring to shape the coat every other month.

HEALTH Concerns: Copper toxicosis, retinal dysplasia, renal cortical hypoplasia

Suggested tests: DNA for copper toxicosis, eye

Life span: 12–14 years

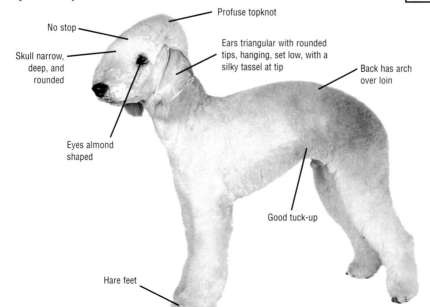

No stop

Profuse topknot

Skull narrow, deep, and rounded

Ears triangular with rounded tips, hanging, set low, with a silky tassel at tip

Back has arch over loin

Eyes almond shaped

Good tuck-up

Hare feet

83

Border Terrier

Area of Origin: Border of Scotland and England
Original Function: Fox bolting, ratting
Coat: Wiry, straight, fairly short
Color: Red, grizzle and tan, blue and tan, or wheaten
Height: 10–11″
Weight: Male: 13–15.5 lb; Female: 11.5–14 lb

Energy level:	**1 2 3**
Exercise requirements:	**1 2 3**
Playfulness:	**1 2 3**
Affection level:	**1 2 3**
Friendliness toward other pets:	**1 2**
Friendliness toward strangers:	**1 2 3**
Ease of training:	**1 2 3 4**
Grooming requirements:	**1 2 3**

HISTORY The Border Terrier originated around the border country between Scotland and England in order to chase and dispatch the fox that were considered a nuisance to farmers. The smallest of the long-legged terriers, the Border had to be fast enough to keep up with a horse yet small enough to go in after the fox once it had gone to ground. The breed was once known as the Coquetdale Terrier (among other names), but the name Border Terrier, taken from the Border Hunt, was adopted in 1870. By this time, the breed had risen from its utilitarian roots to take a valued place alongside the Foxhounds in the gentry's elegant fox hunts. The breed was recognized by the AKC in 1930.

TEMPERAMENT Border Terriers are inquisitive, friendly, and biddable, but independent. They are generally good with other dogs, at least compared to other terriers. They dig, and some bark.

UPKEEP Border Terriers need a good walk or vigorous game session daily. Their harsh coat needs brushing weekly, plus stripping of dead hairs about four times yearly to maintain its clean outline.

HEALTH Concerns: Patellar luxation
Suggested tests: Knee
Life span: 12–15 years

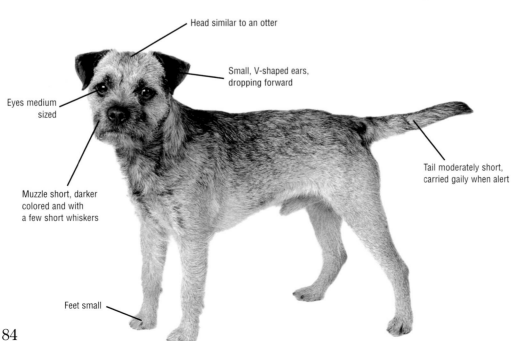

Head similar to an otter

Small, V-shaped ears, dropping forward

Eyes medium sized

Muzzle short, darker colored and with a few short whiskers

Tail moderately short, carried gaily when alert

Feet small

Bull Terrier

Area of Origin: England
Original Function: Companion
Coat: Harsh, smooth, short
Color: White variety: white, with markings on head permissible; colored variety: any color other than white, or any color with white markings; brindle preferred
Height: 21–22″
Weight: Male: 60–70 lb; Female: 50–60 lb

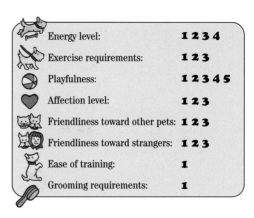

Energy level:	**1 2 3** 4
Exercise requirements:	**1 2 3**
Playfulness:	**1 2 3 4 5**
Affection level:	**1 2 3**
Friendliness toward other pets:	**1 2 3**
Friendliness toward strangers:	**1 2 3**
Ease of training:	**1**
Grooming requirements:	**1**

HISTORY The "Bull and Terrier" was once considered the ultimate pit fighting dog. With the abolition of dog fighting, however, some of their patrons turned to dog shows to compete with their dogs, and they began to breed for appearance. Around 1860, crosses to White English Terriers and Dalmatians produced an all-white strain called Bull Terriers. The new all-white strain became fashionable companions for young gentlemen. The dogs gained the reputation for defending themselves, but not provoking a fight, and were thus dubbed "the white cavalier." Around 1900 crosses with Staffordshire Bull Terriers reintroduced color into the breed. The breed was not well-accepted at first, but it finally gained equal status as a separate AKC variety in 1936. Its comical nature and expression won it many friends, and the breed has proven to be very successful in movies and advertising.

TEMPERAMENT Exuberant, comical, playful, assertive, and very mischievous describes Bull Terriers. They are also sweet-natured, affectionate, and devoted, but stubborn. Some can be aggressive with other dogs.

UPKEEP Bull Terriers need a good exercise session plus mental stimulation every day. Coat care consists of weekly brushing.

HEALTH Concerns: Deafness (in whites), kidney problems, heart problems, patellar luxation
Suggested tests: Hearing (in whites), kidney function, heart
Life span: 11–14 years

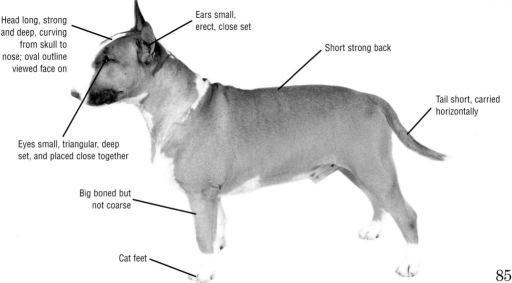

Head long, strong and deep, curving from skull to nose; oval outline viewed face on

Ears small, erect, close set

Short strong back

Tail short, carried horizontally

Eyes small, triangular, deep set, and placed close together

Big boned but not coarse

Cat feet

Cairn Terrier

Area of Origin: Scotland
Original Function: Killing vermin
Coat: Harsh, straight, short to medium length
Color: Any color but white; dark ears, muzzle, tail tip desired
Height: Male: 10″; Female: 9.5″
Weight: Male: 14 lb; Female: 13 lb

Energy level:	**1 2 3 4**	
Exercise requirements:	**1 2 3**	
Playfulness:	**1 2 3**	
Affection level:	**1 2 3**	
Friendliness toward other pets:	**1**	
Friendliness toward strangers:	**1**	
Ease of training:	**1**	
Grooming requirements:	**1 2 3**	

HISTORY Cairns Terriers have existed since the 15th century on the Isle of Skye, where they were used to hunt fox, badger, and otter. The dogs were adept at bolting otters from their cairns (piles of stone that served as landmarks or memorials). The dogs came in a variety of colors, ranging from white to gray to red, and were all considered Scotch Terriers. In 1873 they were divided into Dandie Dinmont and Skye Terriers, with the Cairn in the latter group. At one time, the Cairn was called the Shorthaired Skye, receiving its current name only in 1912. Some of the most influential early Cairns were all white, but white, as well as crossing to West Highland Whites, was banned by the 1920s. The breed gained its greatest fame for the dog playing "Toto" in the *Wizard of Oz*.

TEMPERAMENT Cairns are plucky, spirited, bold, inquisitive, hardy, clever, stubborn, and scrappy. They love to explore and hunt. They can be aggressive with other dogs. They dig, and some bark.

UPKEEP Cairns need either a moderate walk or a fun romp every day. The wire coat needs combing once weekly, plus stripping of dead hair at least twice yearly.

HEALTH Concerns: Liver shunt, glaucoma, jaw problems
Suggested tests: GCL
Life span: 12–14 years

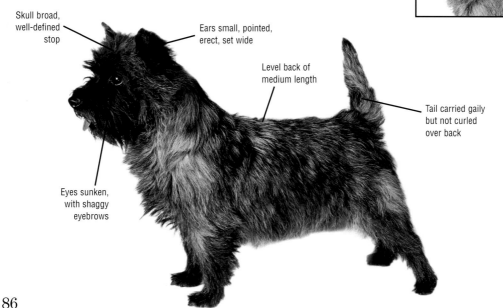

Skull broad, well-defined stop

Ears small, pointed, erect, set wide

Level back of medium length

Tail carried gaily but not curled over back

Eyes sunken, with shaggy eyebrows

Dandie Dinmont Terrier

Area of Origin: Border of Scotland and England
Original function: Otter and badger hunting
Coat: Mixture of hard and soft hair, medium length
Color: Pepper (all shades of gray and silver) or mustard (all shades of brown and fawn). Dandie Dinmont puppies are much darker than adults
Height: 8–11″
Weight: 18–24 lb

Energy level:	**1 2 3**	
Exercise requirements:	**1 2 3**	
Playfulness:	**1 2 3**	
Affection level:	**1 2 3**	
Friendliness toward other pets:	**1 2 3**	
Friendliness toward strangers:	**1**	
Ease of training:	**1 2**	
Grooming requirements:	**1 2 3**	

HISTORY The Dandie Dinmont Terrier first appeared as a distinct type of terrier in the 18th century around the border country of Scotland and England, where farmers and gypsies used them for drawing and killing otters, badgers, and foxes. At one time, they were known as Catcleugh, Hindlee, or Pepper and Mustard Terriers. The best-known of these dogs were owned by James Davidson, who named almost all his dogs either Pepper or Mustard along with some identifying adjective. Davidson and his dogs are believed by some to have been the models for Sir Walter Scott's characters of Dandie Dinmont and his dogs in *Guy Mannering*, published in 1814. The dogs became known as Dandie Dinmont's Terriers. At one time the breed was included in the general family of Scotch Terriers, but was recognized separately from this group in 1873.

TEMPERAMENT Dandie Dinmonts are rough-and-tumble yet dignified, affectionate, but not doting. They tend to be independent, reserved with strangers, and aggressive toward strange dogs. Some dig.

UPKEEP Dandies need a moderate walk or play session daily. The coat needs combing twice weekly, plus scissoring and shaping about four times a year.

HEALTH Concerns: Intervertebral disk disease, glaucoma
Suggested tests: Eye
Life span: 11–13 years

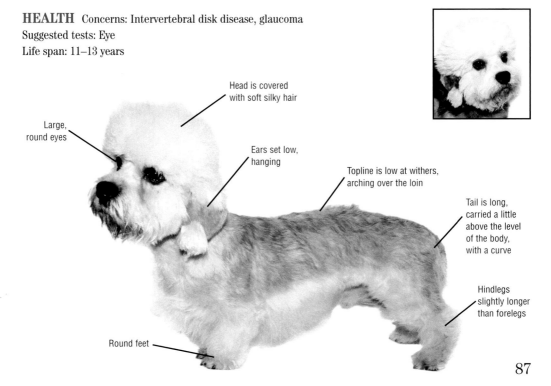

Large, round eyes

Head is covered with soft silky hair

Ears set low, hanging

Topline is low at withers, arching over the loin

Tail is long, carried a little above the level of the body, with a curve

Hindlegs slightly longer than forelegs

Round feet

Terrier Group

Fox Terrier (Smooth)

Area of Origin: England
Original Function: Vermin hunting, fox bolting
Coat: Smooth, hard, short
Color: White should predominate (brindle, red, or liver markings are objectionable)
Height: Male: should not exceed 15.5″; Female: smaller
Weight: Male: 17–19 lb; Female: 15–17 lb

Energy level:		1 2 3 4
Exercise requirements:		1 2 3
Playfulness:		1 2 3 4
Affection level:		1 2 3 4
Friendliness toward other pets:		1 2
Friendliness toward strangers:		1 2 3 4
Ease of training:		1 2 3 4
Grooming requirements:		1

HISTORY The Smooth Fox Terrier was already known by 1800. It accompanied Foxhound packs and dislodged foxes that had taken cover. Predominantly white dogs were preferred because they could be more easily distinguished from the quarry in dim lighting. Some speculation exists that the Smooth and Wire Fox Terriers arose from distinct backgrounds, with the Smooth descending from the smooth-coated Black and Tan, the Bull Terrier, and even the Greyhound and Beagle. The Smooth Fox Terriers were among the first breeds to enter the show ring. The two varieties were interbred extensively at one time, but the practice gradually declined. Because the two breeds had long since ceased to be crossed by the latter part of the 1900s, the AKC divided them into separate breeds in 1985.

TEMPERAMENT Smooth Fox Terriers are energetic, inquisitive, bold, feisty, playful, mischievous, independent, and adventurous. They love to run, chase, and explore. They are usually fairly reserved with strangers, and may challenge other dogs. They tend to bark and dig.

UPKEEP Smooth Fox Terriers need a vigorous game or walk every day. The smooth coat needs weekly brushing to remove shedding hair. The Smooths shed more than the Wires.

HEALTH Concerns: Lens luxation, cataract, Legg-Perthes
Suggested tests: Eye
Life span: 10–13 years

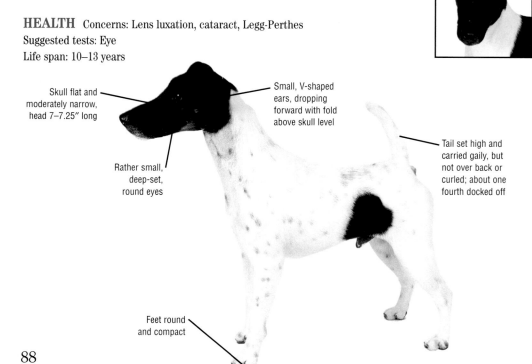

Skull flat and moderately narrow, head 7–7.25″ long

Small, V-shaped ears, dropping forward with fold above skull level

Rather small, deep-set, round eyes

Tail set high and carried gaily, but not over back or curled; about one fourth docked off

Feet round and compact

Fox Terrier (Wire)

Energy level:	**1 2 3 4**	
Exercise requirements:	**1 2 3**	
Playfulness:	**1 2 3 4**	
Affection level:	**1 2 3 4**	
Friendliness toward other pets:	**1 2**	
Friendliness toward strangers:	**1 2 3 4**	
Ease of training:	**1 2 3 4**	
Grooming requirements:	**1 2 3 4**	

Area of Origin: England
Original Function: Vermin hunting, fox bolting
Coat: Wiry, medium length
Color: White should predominate (brindle, red, or liver markings are objectionable)
Height: Male: should not exceed 15.5″; Female: smaller
Weight: Male: 17–19 lb; Female: 15–17 lb

HISTORY The Wire Fox Terrier's forebears were adept at bolting and perhaps dispatching game, especially foxes that had gone to ground. Some speculation exists that the Smooth and Wire Fox Terriers arose from distinct backgrounds, with the Wire descending from the rough-coated Black and Tan Terrier of Wales. The Wire entered the show ring about 15 to 20 years after the Smooth made its debut. The two varieties were interbred extensively at one time, mainly with the objective of improving the Wire variety by decreasing its size, increasing the amount of white on its coat, and imparting a sleeker outline. Wire Fox Terriers became extremely popular in the years following World War II. In 1985, 100 years after the establishment of the American Fox Terrier Club, the AKC divided the Fox Terrier into two separate breeds.

TEMPERAMENT Wire Fox Terriers live to play, explore, run, hunt, and chase. They can be mischievous and independent and may dig and bark. They are usually fairly reserved with strangers. They may be scrappy with other dogs.

UPKEEP Wire Fox Terriers need a moderate walk or good romp daily. The wire coat needs combing two or three times weekly, plus shaping every three months.

HEALTH Concerns: Lens luxation, cataract, Legg-Perthes
Suggested tests: Eye
Life span: 10–13 years

Rather small, deep-set, and round eyes

Small, V-shaped ears, dropping forward with fold above skull level

Tail set high and carried gaily, but not over back or curled; about one fourth docked off

Skull flat and moderately narrow, head 7–7.25″ long

Feet round and compact

89

Glen of Imaal Terrier

Area of Origin: Ireland
Original Function: All-around farm dog, vermin hunting, turnspit dog
Coat: Harsh, medium length
Color: Wheaten, blue, or brindle
Height: 12.5–14″
Weight: Males: about 35 lb; Females: less (actually this is a thin working weight; most are heavier)

Energy level:	**1 2 3**
Exercise requirements:	**1 2 3**
Playfulness:	**1 2 3 4 5**
Affection level:	**1 2 3 4**
Friendliness toward other pets:	**1 2 3**
Friendliness toward strangers:	**1 2 3**
Ease of training:	**1 2 3**
Grooming requirements:	**1 2**

HISTORY The Glen of Imaal Terrier comes from a harsh land, where it earned its keep by tackling rats, badgers, and foxes, fighting in pits by night, and working as turnspit dogs. Here was a dog with courage to face off against a badger underground and the stamina to run for mile after mile in a turnspit of a hot kitchen. Very few turnspit breeds survived into the 20th century, partly because they weren't deemed illustrious or intriguing enough to preserve or develop through dog shows. However, the Glen survived and in 1934 it became one of the first terrier breeds recognized by the Irish Kennel Club. It wasn't until the 1980s that a concerted effort was made to foster the breed in America. The AKC recognized it in 2004.

TEMPERAMENT Glens are an inquisitive and courageous breed, always ready for a game or a hunt. Less excitable than most terriers, they are nonetheless active dogs. They are good-natured and playful. Some can be dog-aggressive.

UPKEEP Glens need moderate exercise but at least a good game every day. They are not good swimmers. The coat needs brushing weekly, and stripping a few times a year.

HEALTH Concerns: PRA, hip dysplasia
Suggested tests: Eye, hip
Life span: 10–14 years

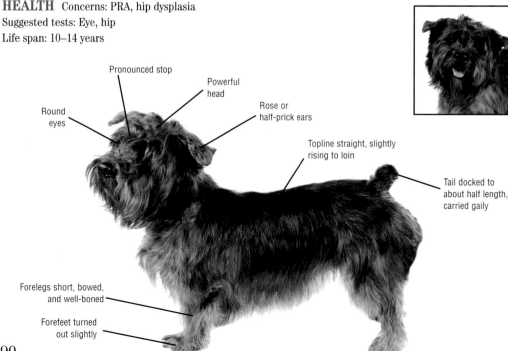

Pronounced stop

Powerful head

Round eyes

Rose or half-prick ears

Topline straight, slightly rising to loin

Tail docked to about half length, carried gaily

Forelegs short, bowed, and well-boned

Forefeet turned out slightly

Irish Terrier

Area of Origin: Ireland
Original Function: Hunting fox, otter, and other vermin
Coat: Wiry, medium length
Color: Red, golden red, red wheaten, or wheaten
Height: About 18″
Weight: Male: ideally 27 lb; Female: ideally 25 lb

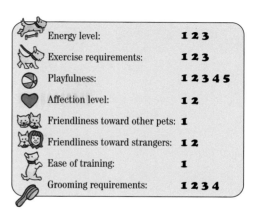

Energy level:	**1 2 3**
Exercise requirements:	**1 2 3**
Playfulness:	**1 2 3 4 5**
Affection level:	**1 2**
Friendliness toward other pets:	**1**
Friendliness toward strangers:	**1 2**
Ease of training:	**1**
Grooming requirements:	**1 2 3 4**

HISTORY The Irish Terrier is the raciest member of the Terrier Group, with a longer body and longer legs than the other terriers. Early Irish Terriers came in a variety of colors, including black and tan, gray, and brindle; only near the end of the 19th century did the solid red color become a fixture of the breed. By the 1880s the breed was the fourth-most popular in England. The breed also became quite popular in America, ranking 13th of all breeds in the late 1920s. It was a dominant force in the show rings of the day. In World War I, the breed proved its mettle by serving as a messenger and sentinel. With such an auspicious beginning, the Irish Terrier seemed certain to remain one of the most popular terriers, but today it is one of the rarer terriers.

TEMPERAMENT Irish Terriers are brash, bold, assertive, playful, inquisitive, independent, and strong-willed. They are usually aggressive toward other dogs and small animals and tend to be reserved with strangers. They like to chase and explore, but can be well mannered indoors.

UPKEEP These dogs need a good walk or a rigorous play session daily. Their wire coat needs combing one or two times weekly, plus scissoring and shaping two to four times yearly.

HEALTH Concerns: Urinary stones
Suggested tests: None
Life span: 12–15 years

Eyes small, with intense expression

Small, V-shaped ears, dropping forward with fold above skull level

Body moderately long

Tail set high but not curled; about one fourth docked off

Head long and fairly narrow

Feet rounded

Kerry Blue Terrier

Area of Origin: Ireland
Original Function: Versatile farm dog
Coat: Soft and wavy, medium length
Color: Any shade of blue-gray in mature (over 18 months) dog; immature dogs may be very dark blue or have tinges of brown
Height: Male: 18–19.5″; Female: 17.5–19″ (optimal)
Weight: Male: 33–40 lb; Female: less

Energy level:	**1 2 3**
Exercise requirements:	**1 2 3**
Playfulness:	**1 2 3 4**
Affection level:	**1 2 3**
Friendliness toward other pets:	**1**
Friendliness toward strangers:	**1 2 3**
Ease of training:	**1 2 3**
Grooming requirements:	**1 2 3 4 5**

HISTORY The Kerry Blue originated in the south and west of Ireland, first gaining notice in the Ring of Kerry. Here the dog had been known for at least a century as a versatile hunter of vermin, small game, and even birds, as well as a land and water retriever and even a sheep and cattle herder. It came on the English and American show scenes around the 1920s. Puppies are born black, the blue coloration not appearing until between nine months and two years of age. It remains a versatile dog, adding police work and trailing to its list of talents. The Kerry Blue can guard, hunt, herd, or just be a fun-loving companion.

TEMPERAMENT Kerry Blues love to run, chase, hunt, explore, play, and dig. They can be wary of strangers and aggressive toward other dogs and small animals. They are clever and independent, often stubborn. Some tend to bark.

UPKEEP Kerry Blues need a long walk on a leash or a vigorous play session daily. Their coat needs combing about twice a week, plus scissoring and shaping every month.

HEALTH Concerns: Cerebellar abiotrophy, cataract, spiculosis, hair follicle tumors, eyelid problems, hip dysplasia
Suggested tests: Eye, hip
Life span: 12–15 years

Head long

Small, V-shaped ears, dropping forward with fold above skull level

Eyes small, keen expression

Back short and straight

Tail set high, carried gaily erect and straight

Feet fairly round and moderately small

Lakeland Terrier

Area of Origin: England
Original function: Vermin hunting
Coat: Wiry, medium length
Color: Solid (blue, black, liver, red, or wheaten); or wheaten or golden tan with a saddle of blue, black, liver, or grizzle
Height: Male: 14.5″; Female: 13.5″
Weight: About 16–17 lb

Energy level:	**1 2 3 4**	
Exercise requirements:	**1 2 3**	
Playfulness:	**1 2 3 4 5**	
Affection level:	**1 2 3**	
Friendliness toward other pets:	**1**	
Friendliness toward strangers:	**1**	
Ease of training:	**1**	
Grooming requirements:	**1 2 3 4**	

HISTORY Lakeland Terriers were kept by farmers who took them along with small packs of hounds in order to kill the foxes and other problem animals. As fox hunting became valued more for its sporting aspect, the Terriers became more fashionable as a part of the fox hunt. Those dogs from the English Lake region gained a reputation as particularly game dogs. Only in 1921 were they recognized as Lakeland Terriers, although Cumberland is considered the exact birthplace of the breed. The breed was accepted for AKC registration in 1934. Since then, the Lakeland Terrier has been a prominent contender in the show ring, combining dapper good looks with unsurpassed showmanship. Its popularity as a pet, however, has remained moderate.

TEMPERAMENT The spunky Lakeland makes the most of every day, always busy investigating, playing and, if it really gets its wish, hunting, running, and chasing. Given daily exercise in a safe area, it settles down in the home and makes an entertaining and endearing house pet. It is reserved with strangers and usually aggressive toward other dogs and small animals. Clever, independent, and stubborn, it can be mischievous. It is nonetheless sensitive and must be trained with patience as well as a sense of humor.

UPKEEP Lakelands need a moderate walk on leash or a rousing game each day. The coat needs combing one or two times weekly, plus scissoring and shaping four times yearly.

HEALTH Concerns: Lens luxation
Suggested tests: Eye
Life span: 12–16 years

Small, V-shaped ears, dropping forward with fold above skull level

Stop barely perceptible

Head appears rectangular from all angles

Eyes moderately small and oval

Topline short and level

Tail set high, carried upright with a slight curve forward; docked to about same height as occiput

Feet round

93

Manchester Terrier

Area of Origin: England
Original function: Ratting, rabbit hunting
Coat: Smooth, short
Color: Black and tan, with a black "thumbprint" patch on the front of each foreleg, and "pencil marks" on the top of each toe
Height: 15–16″
Weight: Standard: over 12 lb to 22 lb (Toy: under 12 lb)

Energy level:	**1 2 3 4**	
Exercise requirements:	**1 2 3**	
Playfulness:	**1 2 3 4**	
Affection level:	**1 2 3 4**	
Friendliness toward other pets:	**1**	
Friendliness toward strangers:	**1**	
Ease of training:	**1 2**	
Grooming requirements:	**1**	

HISTORY The Black and Tan Terrier was a strain of dogs used as early as the 16th century for killing rats. With the advent of industrialization, they became popular as rat killers for sport. They were crossed with another popular working-class dog, the Whippet, to create a faster but still game terrier. They were most popular around Manchester, and were formally dubbed the Manchester Terrier. The name was dropped in favor of Black and Tan Terrier, only to be revived in 1923. The breed has always had a large size range, and until 1959 Standard and Toy Manchesters were shown as two separate breeds, although interbreeding was allowed. In 1959 they were reclassified as one breed with two varieties. Ear cropping is allowed only in the Standard variety.

TEMPERAMENT Manchester Terriers are adventurous and independent, yet sensitive and devoted to family. They are reserved with strangers. More responsive than many terriers, they are generally well-mannered housedogs.

UPKEEP Manchester Terriers need a moderate walk on a leash or a good romp in the yard daily. They like a warm, soft bed. The short coat needs brushing once a week or so.

HEALTH Concerns: Cardiomyopathy, vWD
Suggested tests: Heart, vWD
Life span: 15–16 years

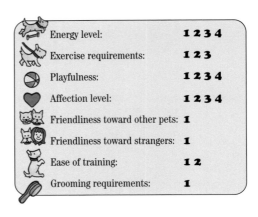

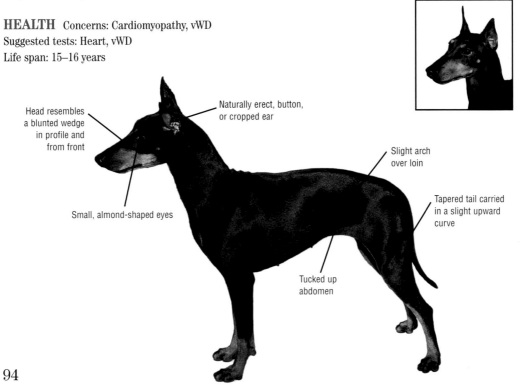

Head resembles a blunted wedge in profile and from front

Naturally erect, button, or cropped ear

Slight arch over loin

Tapered tail carried in a slight upward curve

Small, almond-shaped eyes

Tucked up abdomen

Miniature Bull Terrier

Energy level:	**1 2 3 4**
Exercise requirements:	**1 2 3**
Playfulness:	**1 2 3 4 5**
Affection level:	**1 2**
Friendliness toward other pets:	**1 2 3**
Friendliness toward strangers:	**1 2 3**
Ease of training:	**1**
Grooming requirements:	**1**

Area of Origin: England
Original Function: Companion
Coat: Harsh, smooth, short
Color: White: pure white; Colored: any color to predominate
Height: 10–14″
Weight: 25–33 lb

HISTORY The Miniature Bull Terrier shares the same early history as does its root stock, the Bull Terrier. Bull Terriers have long had smaller specimens among them, with the smallest white Bull Terriers at one time called Coverwood Terriers, after the kennel that produced them. These tiny toys tended to have poor type and interest waned in them, but the Miniatures, rather than Toys, had better type. By 1939 the Miniature Bull Terrier was recognized by the English Kennel Club. Unfortunately, this meant the Miniature could no longer be interbred with standard-sized Bull Terriers, and there were so few Miniatures that considerable inbreeding resulted. The breed gained popular attention slowly, and was finally recognized by the AKC in 1991.

TEMPERAMENT Miniature Bull Terriers are comical, lively, playful, and mischievous. They are devoted, but not fawning, and they tend to be stubborn and independent.

UPKEEP Miniature Bull Terriers need either a moderate walk or a good romp daily. Coat care consists of a weekly brushing.

HEALTH Concerns: Deafness (whites), glaucoma, lens luxation
Suggested tests: Hearing (whites), eye
Life span: 11–14 years

Eyes small, triangular, deep set, and placed close together

Ears small, erect, close set

Short strong back, slight arch over loin

Long, strong, deep head, curving from skull to nose; oval outline viewed face on

Tail short, carried horizontally

Cat feet

95

Miniature Schnauzer

Area of Origin: Germany
Original function: Ratting
Coat: Hard, wiry, medium length
Color: Salt and pepper, black and silver, or black
Height: 12–14″
Weight: 13–15 lb

Energy level:	**1 2 3**	
Exercise requirements:	**1 2 3**	
Playfulness:	**1 2 3 4**	
Affection level:	**1 2 3 4**	
Friendliness toward other pets:	**1 2 3**	
Friendliness toward strangers:	**1 2 3**	
Ease of training:	**1 2 3**	
Grooming requirements:	**1 2 3**	

HISTORY The Miniature Schnauzer was developed in the late 1800s as a small farm dog and ratter in Germany. It was derived from crossing the Standard Schnauzer with the Affenpinscher. The Miniature Schnauzer was exhibited as a breed distinct from the Standard Schnauzer by 1899 in Germany, although it wasn't until 1933 that the AKC divided the Standard and Miniature into separate breeds. The Miniature is the only Schnauzer to remain in the Terrier Group in America. In England it joins the other Schnauzers in the Utility Group. The Miniature Schnauzer came to America long after its Standard and Giant counterparts, but eventually became the third-most popular breed in America at one time.

TEMPERAMENT Miniature Schnauzers are playful, inquisitive, alert, spunky, and companionable. They are less domineering than the larger Schnauzers and less dog-aggressive than most terriers. They can be stubborn, but are generally biddable. Some bark a lot.

UPKEEP Miniature Schnauzers need a moderate walk on a leash or a vigorous pay session in the yard each day. The wire coat needs combing once or twice weekly, plus scissoring and shaping every couple of months.

HEALTH Concerns: Urinary stones, PRA, Schnauzer comedo syndrome, vWD
Suggested tests: Eye, vWD
Life span: 12–14 years

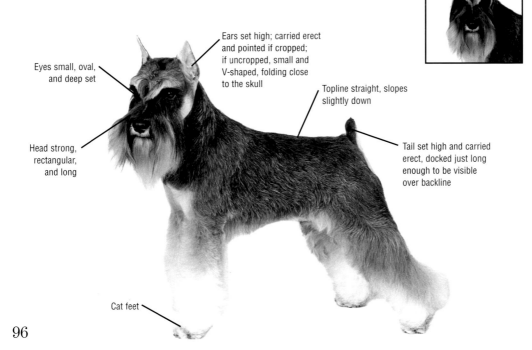

Ears set high; carried erect and pointed if cropped; if uncropped, small and V-shaped, folding close to the skull

Eyes small, oval, and deep set

Head strong, rectangular, and long

Topline straight, slopes slightly down

Tail set high and carried erect, docked just long enough to be visible over backline

Cat feet

Norfolk Terrier

Area of Origin: England
Original Function: Ratting, fox bolting
Coat: Hard, wiry, straight, medium length
Color: All shades of red, wheaten, black and tan, or grizzle
Height: 9–10″
Weight: 11–12 lb

Energy level:	**1 2 3 4**
Exercise requirements:	**1 2 3**
Playfulness:	**1 2 3**
Affection level:	**1**
Friendliness toward other pets:	**1 2 3**
Friendliness toward strangers:	**1 2 3**
Ease of training:	**1 2**
Grooming requirements:	**1 2 3**

HISTORY Short-legged ratting terriers have long been valued in England, but only in the 1880s did the breed that would eventually become both the Norwich and Norfolk Terriers emerge from obscurity. At that time, owning one of these small ratters became a fad among Cambridge University students. During the development of these breeds, both prick and drop ears were seen, and neither could lay claim to being more authentic or original than the other. In the 1930s breeders began to avoid crossing the ear types because the progeny could have uncertain ear carriage. The drop-eared type almost vanished during World War II, but survived largely due to the efforts of one woman. In 1979 the breed was officially changed from one breed with two varieties to two separate breeds.

TEMPERAMENT Norfolks are feisty, bold, inquisitive, game, scrappy, stubborn, and independent. They love to hunt, dig, and investigate. They are amiable, but strong-willed.

UPKEEP Norfolk Terriers need a short to moderate walk or a lively play session daily. Their wire coat needs combing once or twice weekly, plus stripping of dead hairs three to four times yearly.

HEALTH Concerns: Hip dysplasia, allergies
Suggested tests: Hip
Life span: 13–15 years

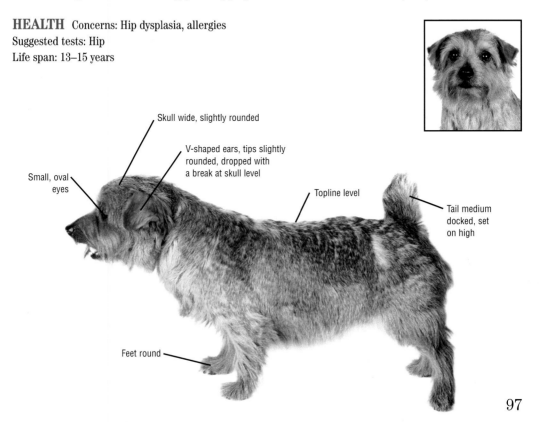

Skull wide, slightly rounded

V-shaped ears, tips slightly rounded, dropped with a break at skull level

Small, oval eyes

Topline level

Tail medium docked, set on high

Feet round

Norwich Terrier

Area of Origin: England
Original Function: Ratting, fox bolting
Coat: Hard, wiry, straight, medium length
Color: All shades of red, wheaten, black and tan, or grizzle
Height: Ideally 10″
Weight: Approximately 12 lb

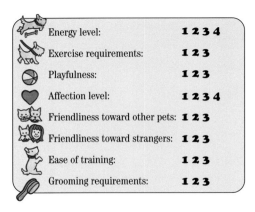

Energy level:	**1 2 3 4**
Exercise requirements:	**1 2 3**
Playfulness:	**1 2 3**
Affection level:	**1 2 3 4**
Friendliness toward other pets:	**1 2 3**
Friendliness toward strangers:	**1 2 3**
Ease of training:	**1 2 3**
Grooming requirements:	**1 2 3**

HISTORY The Norwich Terrier shares an identical early history with the Norfolk Terrier. Around 1900 a dog named Rags came to a stable near Norwich and gained fame as a ratter. He sired countless offspring and is the patriarch of the modern Norwich. One of his sons came to America and proved to be an amiable ambassador for the breed. To this day, many people still refer to the Norwich as the "Jones Terrier," after this dog's owner. The Jones Terrier was incorporated into various foxhound hunt packs. The AKC recognized the breed in 1936. At that time the breed had both prick and drop ears, but in 1979 the drop-ear variety was recognized as a separate breed, the Norfolk Terrier.

TEMPERAMENT Norwich Terriers are always ready for adventure and excitement. They are pert, independent, amusing, but often challenging. They are hunters and may chase small animals.

UPKEEP Norwich Terriers need a short to moderate walk or a good romp each day. Their wiry coat needs combing one to two times weekly, plus stripping of dead hairs three to four times a year.

HEALTH Concerns: Hip dysplasia, allergies, seizures
Suggested tests: Hip
Life span: 13–15 years

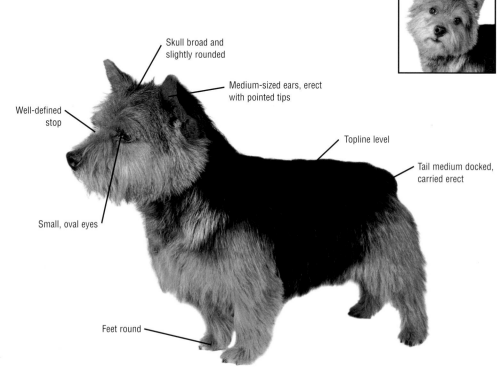

Skull broad and slightly rounded

Medium-sized ears, erect with pointed tips

Well-defined stop

Topline level

Tail medium docked, carried erect

Small, oval eyes

Feet round

Parson Russell Terrier

Area of Origin: England
Original Function: Fox bolting
Coat: Smooth: coarse, flat, short; Broken: harsh, straight, short to medium length
Color: Predominantly white with tan, black, or brown markings, or a combination
Height: 12–14″
Weight: 13–17 lb

Energy level:	**1 2 3 4 5**
Exercise requirements:	**1 2 3 4**
Playfulness:	**1 2 3 4 5**
Affection level:	**1 2 3**
Friendliness toward other pets:	**1**
Friendliness toward strangers:	**1 2 3**
Ease of training:	**1 2 3**
Grooming requirements:	**1 2 3**

HISTORY The Parson Russell Terrier is descended in most part from a dog named Trump, which was obtained by the Parson John Russell of Devonshire, England in the mid-1800s. John Russell was a foxhunting enthusiast, and he sought to develop a line of terriers that could keep up with the horses and bolt and dispatch fox. He declined to show his dogs, and many PRT owners followed that example. Nonetheless, the breed, then called the Jack Russell Terrier, was admitted into the Terrier Group in 1998. In 2003 the AKC-recognized dogs had their name changed from Jack Russell Terrier to Parson Russell Terrier. The PRT has become a popular media dog, and its exposure caused great interest in the breed from pet owners.

TEMPERAMENT PRTs thrive on action and adventure. They explore, wander, chase, and dig when they can. They are playful and energetic. They get along well with children and strangers, but can be scrappy with strange dogs. They may tend to bark and dig.

UPKEEP Parson Russell Terriers need a long walk or strenuous game every day. Coat care for the smooth type consists only of weekly brushing to remove dead hair; for the broken coat it also consists of occasional hand-stripping.

HEALTH Concerns: Lens luxation, patellar luxation
Suggested tests: Eye, knee
Life span: 13–15 years

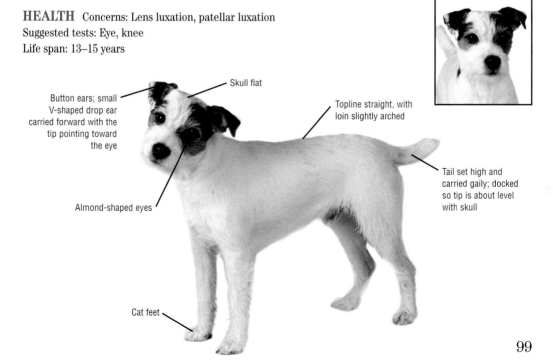

Skull flat

Button ears; small V-shaped drop ear carried forward with the tip pointing toward the eye

Topline straight, with loin slightly arched

Almond-shaped eyes

Tail set high and carried gaily; docked so tip is about level with skull

Cat feet

Scottish Terrier

Area of Origin: Scotland
Original Function: Vermin hunting
Coat: Hard, wiry, straight, medium length
Color: Black, wheaten, or brindle of any color
Height: About 10″
Weight: Male: 19–22 lb; Female: 18–21 lb

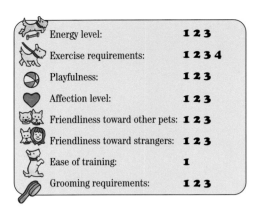

Energy level:	**1 2 3**
Exercise requirements:	**1 2 3 4**
Playfulness:	**1 2 3**
Affection level:	**1 2 3**
Friendliness toward other pets:	**1 2 3**
Friendliness toward strangers:	**1 2 3**
Ease of training:	**1**
Grooming requirements:	**1 2 3**

HISTORY Only in the late 1800s can the Scottish Terrier's history be confidently documented. Of the several short-legged, harsh-coated terriers, the dog now known as the Scottish Terrier was most favored in the Aberdeen area, and so for a time it was called the Aberdeen Terrier. Around 1880 the first breed standard was put forth. The first Scottish Terrier came to America in 1883. It gradually gained popularity until World War II, after which its popularity soared. The best known Scotty in America was Fala, Franklin Roosevelt's dog, who was his constant companion in life and is buried at his side in death. The breed is nicknamed the "Diehard" in reference to its rugged character

TEMPERAMENT Scottish Terriers are tough, determined, and ready for action. They are fearless and feisty and may be aggressive toward other dogs and animals. Although independent and stubborn, they are devoted to family. They tend to dig and bark.

UPKEEP Scotties need a short to moderate walk or a good play session daily. Their wire coat needs combing two to three times weekly, plus shaping every three months.

HEALTH Concerns: vWD, jaw problems, Scotty cramp, patellar luxation, cerebellar abiotrophy
Suggested tests: Knee, vWD
Life span: 11–13 years

Long skull, of medium width

Small, almond-shaped eyes

Small, prick ears, pointed

Uncut tail, about 7″ long, carried with a slight curve but not over the back

Legs, short and heavy boned

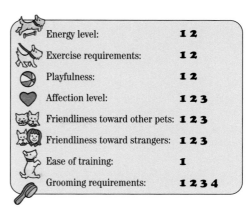

Energy level:	**1 2**	
Exercise requirements:	**1 2**	
Playfulness:	**1 2**	
Affection level:	**1 2 3**	
Friendliness toward other pets:	**1 2 3**	
Friendliness toward strangers:	**1 2 3**	
Ease of training:	**1**	
Grooming requirements:	**1 2 3 4**	

Sealyham Terrier

Area of Origin: Wales
Original Function: Badger, otter, and fox hunting
Coat: Hard, wiry, medium length
Color: All white, or with lemon, tan, or badger markings
Height: Approximately 10.5″
Weight: Male: 23–24 lb; Female: 18–22 lb

HISTORY The documented history of the Sealyham begins in the mid-1800s, when Captain John Edwardes of Sealyham developed the breed. The breeds that went into its makeup are a mystery; some suggest that the Dandie Dinmont Terrier may have played a role. Whatever the ingredients, the result was a plucky terrier that soon gained fame for its ability to face badgers, otters, and foxes. Its smart appearance made it a dog show natural, and it first entered the show ring in 1903. The AKC recognized the Sealyham in 1911. Demand for these terriers quickly grew, especially because they were exceptional hunting dogs as well as extremely competitive show dogs.

TEMPERAMENT Sealyhams are fairly calm, but always ready to investigate, dig, or give chase. They are often aggressive toward other dogs, and are reserved with strangers. They are devoted to family, but tend to be stubborn and independent. They dig and bark.

UPKEEP Sealyham Terriers need a short to moderate exercise session each day. Their coat needs combing two to three times weekly, plus shaping every three months.

HEALTH Concerns: Retinal dysplasia, lens luxation
Suggested tests: Eye
Life span: 11–13 years

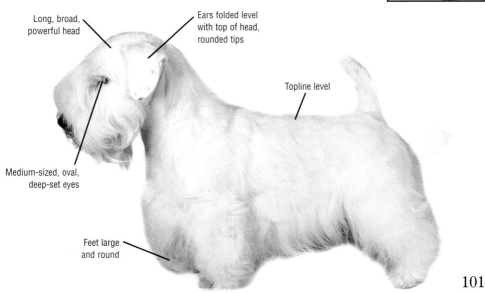

Long, broad, powerful head

Ears folded level with top of head, rounded tips

Topline level

Medium-sized, oval, deep-set eyes

Feet large and round

Skye Terrier

Area of Origin: Scotland
Original Function: Fox and otter hunting
Coat: Coarse, straight, long
Color: Black, blue, gray, silver, fawn, or cream, preferably with black ears, muzzle, and tail tip. Adult color may not be present until 18 months.
Height: Male: 10″; Female: 9.5″ (overall average 10–11″)
Weight: Male: 35–40 lb; Female: 25–30 lb

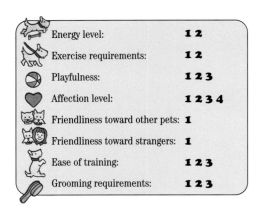

Energy level:	**1 2**
Exercise requirements:	**1 2**
Playfulness:	**1 2 3**
Affection level:	**1 2 3 4**
Friendliness toward other pets:	**1**
Friendliness toward strangers:	**1**
Ease of training:	**1 2 3**
Grooming requirements:	**1 2 3**

HISTORY A plucky strain of terriers developed along the west coastal area of Scotland, where they hunted fox and otter from among the rocky cairns. The purest of these dogs were found on the Isle of Skye, and the dogs were thus dubbed Skye Terriers. It was first described in the 16th century, when it was already noteworthy for its long coat. The breed became prominent in 1840, when Queen Victoria fancied the breed, keeping both drop- and prick-eared dogs. The AKC recognized the breed in 1887, and it quickly rose to the top of the show scene. The most famous Skye of all time was Greyfriar's Bobby, who slept on his master's grave for 14 years until his own death.

TEMPERAMENT Skye Terriers are fearless and tough. They are affectionate with family, but cautious with strangers. They may be aggressive toward strange dogs. They are extremely courageous and make good watchdogs.

UPKEEP Skyes need a short to moderate walk every day. Regular combing (about twice a week) is needed to keep the Skye looking good. The hair around the eyes and mouth may need extra cleaning.

HEALTH Concerns: Premature closure of distal radius
Suggested tests: None
Life span: 12–14 years

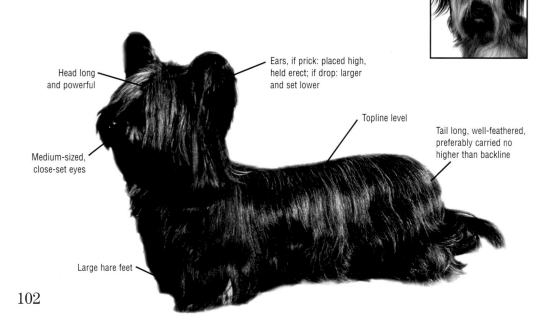

Head long and powerful

Ears, if prick: placed high, held erect; if drop: larger and set lower

Topline level

Tail long, well-feathered, preferably carried no higher than backline

Medium-sized, close-set eyes

Large hare feet

Soft Coated Wheaten Terrier

Area of Origin: Ireland
Original Function: Vermin hunting, herding, guardian
Coat: Soft, silky, fairly long
Color: Any shade of wheaten
Height: Male: 18–19″; Female: 17–18″
Weight: Male: 35–40 lb; Female: 30–35 lb

Energy level:	**1 2 3**
Exercise requirements:	**1 2 3**
Playfulness:	**1 2 3 4**
Affection level:	**1 2 3 4 5**
Friendliness toward other pets:	**1 2 3**
Friendliness toward strangers:	**1 2 3 4**
Ease of training:	**1 2 3**
Grooming requirements:	**1 2 3 4**

HISTORY The Soft Coated Wheaten Terrier originated as an all-around farm dog, perhaps serving in this function for hundreds of years. Besides the ever-essential terrier function of extinguishing vermin, it also helped round up stock and guard the homestead. The Wheaten was a comparative latecomer to the show scene. Only in 1937 was it granted breed status in Ireland. For many years, an Irish championship required that a dog not only prove itself in the ring but also in the field over badger, rat, and rabbit. The English Kennel Club recognized the breed in 1943, and in 1946 the first Wheaten came to America. The breed did not instantly catch the public's attention, but instead it took its time building a firm basis of support. In 1973 the AKC granted recognition.

TEMPERAMENT Wheatens are affectionate, congenial, playful, and much gentler than most terriers. They are generally responsive to their owner's wishes, but can be headstrong at times. They are usually good with other household dogs and pets.

UPKEEP Soft Coated Wheaten Terriers need a moderate to long walk or an invigorating play session every day. Their long coat needs brushing or combing every two days. Bathing and trimming every other month is necessary to maintain the silhouette.

HEALTH Concerns: Protein-losing diseases, renal dysplasia
Suggested tests: Blood and urine protein screens
Life span: 12–14 years

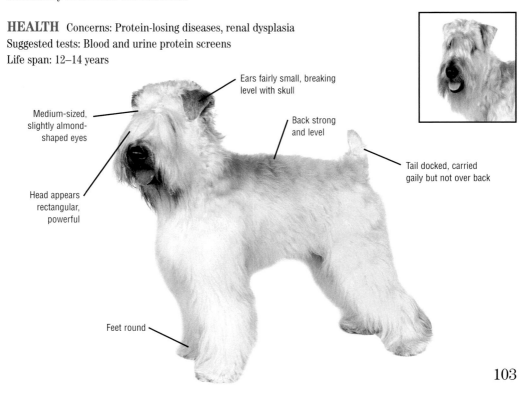

Ears fairly small, breaking level with skull

Medium-sized, slightly almond-shaped eyes

Back strong and level

Head appears rectangular, powerful

Tail docked, carried gaily but not over back

Feet round

Staffordshire Bull Terrier

Energy level:	**1 2 3**	
Exercise requirements:	**1 2 3**	
Playfulness:	**1 2 3 4 5**	
Affection level:	**1 2 3 4**	
Friendliness toward other pets:	**1 2 3**	
Friendliness toward strangers:	**1 2 3**	
Ease of training:	**1 2 3**	
Grooming requirements:	**1**	

Area of Origin: England
Original Function: Ratting, dog fighting
Coat: Smooth, short
Color: Red, fawn, white, black, or blue, solid or with white; any shade of brindle or brindle with white
Height: Male: 18–19″; Female: 17–18″
Weight: Male: 35–40 lb; Female: 30–35 lb

HISTORY In the early 1800s dog fighting became a source of entertainment. Selective breeding resulted in a small nimble dog with incredibly strong jaws that was specifically not aggressive toward people. By the time dog fighting was banned in England, these dogs had so endeared themselves to their fans that they continued to have a loyal following. Concerted efforts to produce a dog more amenable to the ring and attractive as a pet finally resulted in the breed's recognition by the English Kennel Club in 1935, and by the AKC in 1974. In the United Kingdom the Staffordshire Bull Terrier is known as the "Nanny Dog," in reference to its eagerness and ability to assume the role of a child's nursemaid. Although sometimes dogged by breed-specific legislation, the breed is a lover, not a fighter.

TEMPERAMENT Staffordshire Bull Terriers are playful, companionable, amiable, docile, and generally biddable. They are friendly toward strangers. Some can be strong willed. They may not do well around other dogs.

UPKEEP Staffordshire Bull Terriers need a good walk on a leash or a rowdy backyard game every day. Their close coat needs brushing once weekly.

HEALTH Concerns: Hip dysplasia
Suggested tests: Hip
Life span: 12–14 years

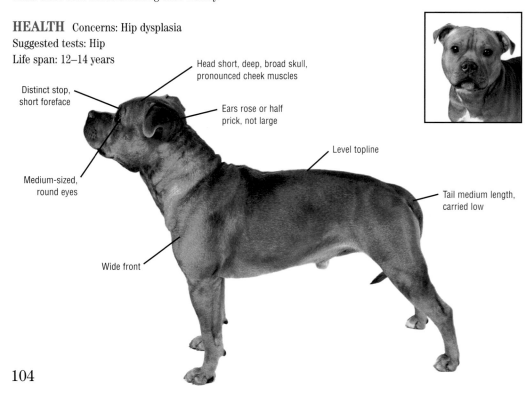

Head short, deep, broad skull, pronounced cheek muscles

Distinct stop, short foreface

Ears rose or half prick, not large

Level topline

Medium-sized, round eyes

Tail medium length, carried low

Wide front

Welsh Terrier

Area of Origin: Wales
Original function: Otter, fox, badger, and rat hunting
Coat: Wiry, medium length
Color: Deep tan with black or grizzle jacket
Height: Male: 15–15.5″; Female: smaller
Weight: 20 lb

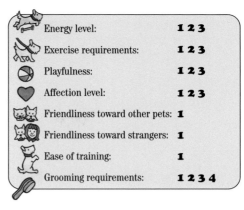

Energy level:	**1 2 3**	
Exercise requirements:	**1 2 3**	
Playfulness:	**1 2 3**	
Affection level:	**1 2 3**	
Friendliness toward other pets:	**1**	
Friendliness toward strangers:	**1**	
Ease of training:	**1**	
Grooming requirements:	**1 2 3 4**	

HISTORY The Welsh Terrier probably descended from the old Black and Tan Rough Terrier that was popular in Britain in the 18th and 19th centuries. By the late 1700s two strains, one known as the "Ynysfor" and the other as the "Old English Broken-Haired Terrier," existed. They eventually merged to become known as Welsh Terriers. In 1886, the English Kennel Club recognized the breed. The early dogs were too rough to be competitive in the show ring, and breeders sought to improve the Welsh's lines not only by selective breeding, but also with crosses to the racier Wire Fox Terrier. The result was a dog that in some ways resembles a miniature Airedale Terrier.

TEMPERAMENT Welsh Terriers are playful and mischievous, yet calm enough to be reliable house pets. They are independent, inquisitive, and sensitive, reserved with strangers, and possibly scrappy with other dogs and pets. They tend to dig and bark.

UPKEEP Welsh Terriers need a moderate walk on a leash every day or an invigorating play session. Their wiry jacket needs combing two to three times weekly, plus shaping every three months.

HEALTH Concerns: Lens luxation, glaucoma
Suggested tests: Eye
Life span: 12–14 years

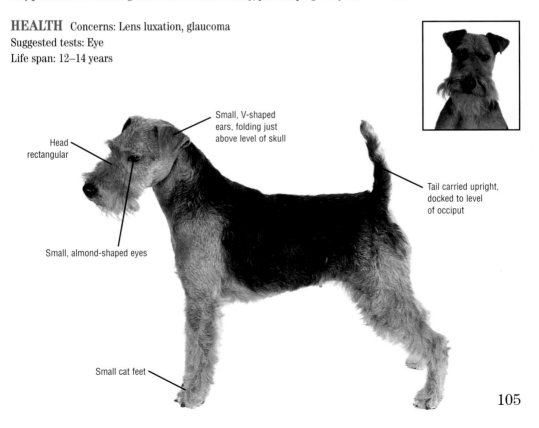

Small, V-shaped ears, folding just above level of skull

Head rectangular

Small, almond-shaped eyes

Tail carried upright, docked to level of occiput

Small cat feet

West Highland White Terrier

Area of Origin: Scotland
Original function: Fox, badger, and vermin hunting
Coat: Straight, hard, medium length
Color: White
Height: Male: 11″; Female: 10″
Weight: 15–21 lb

Energy level:	**1 2 3 4**
Exercise requirements:	**1 2 3**
Playfulness:	**1 2 3**
Affection level:	**1 2 3 4 5**
Friendliness toward other pets:	**1 2 3**
Friendliness toward strangers:	**1 2 3 4**
Ease of training:	**1 2 3 4**
Grooming requirements:	**1 2 3 4**

HISTORY The West Highland White Terrier shares its roots with the other terriers of Scotland, proving itself on fox, badger, and various vermin. At one time it was lumped with several other Scottish Terrier breeds, but selective breeding based on such qualities as coat type or color eventually produced distinctive strains. The short-legged white terriers first gained attention in 1907 as Poltalloch Terriers, named for the home of Colonel E. D. Malcolm, who had been breeding them for the previous 60 years. The breed has gone under several different names, including Roseneath, Poltalloch, White Scottish, Little Skye, and Cairn. In fact, the AKC first registered it as the Roseneath Terrier in 1908, but the name was changed to West Highland White Terrier in 1909.

TEMPERAMENT Westies are happy, curious, independent, and somewhat stubborn. They are affectionate and demanding. They bark and dig.

UPKEEP Westies need either a short walk or a good game every day. Their wire coat needs combing two or three times weekly, plus shaping every three months.

HEALTH Major concerns: Globoid cell leukodystrophy, Legg-Perthes, jaw problems, copper toxicosis, cataract, patellar luxation
Suggested tests: Hip, knee
Life span: 12–14 years

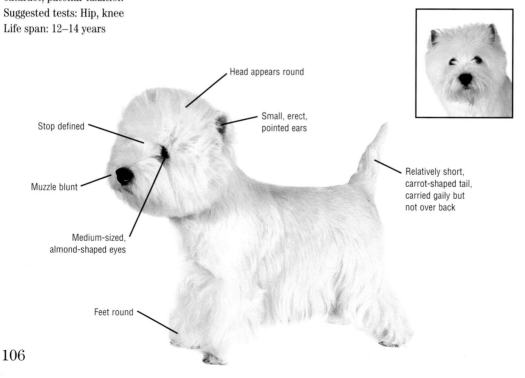

Head appears round

Small, erect, pointed ears

Stop defined

Muzzle blunt

Medium-sized, almond-shaped eyes

Feet round

Relatively short, carrot-shaped tail, carried gaily but not over back

TOY

Affenpinscher

Area of Origin: Germany
Original Function: Small vermin hunting, lap dog
Coat: Harsh, medium length
Color: Black, gray, silver, red, black and tan, or beige; with or without black mask
Height: 9.5–11.5″
Weight: 7–9 lb

Energy level:	**1 2 3 4**
Exercise requirements:	**1 2 3**
Playfulness:	**1 2 3 4**
Affection level:	**1 2 3 4**
Friendliness toward other pets:	**1 2 3**
Friendliness toward strangers:	**1 2 3**
Ease of training:	**1 2 3**
Grooming requirements:	**1 2 3 4**

HISTORY As one of the oldest toy breeds, the Affenpinscher's origins are obscure. Small terriers adept at dispatching rats were abundant in central Europe by the 17th century. In Germany they were used to rid stables and kitchens of rodents. Even smaller versions of these dogs were preferred for ladies' lap dogs, as they were able to kill mice in the home, warm their mistress' laps, and amuse entire households with their antics. This small version eventually became the Affenpinscher. In 1936 the AKC recognized the breed. The Affenpinscher's name describes it well: *affen*, meaning "monkey," and *pinscher*, meaning "terrier." In France the Affenpinscher is known as the *diablotin moustachu*—"moustached little devil"—which also aptly describes it!

TEMPERAMENT Affenpinschers are busy, playful, inquisitive, bold, mischievous, and stubborn. They tend to bark and even climb. They are fairly good with other dogs and pets.

UPKEEP Affenpinschers' exercise needs can be met with vigorous indoor games or romps in the yard, or with short walks. The harsh coat needs combing two or three times weekly, plus shaping every three months.

HEALTH Concerns: Patellar luxation
Suggested tests: Knee
Life span: 12–14 years

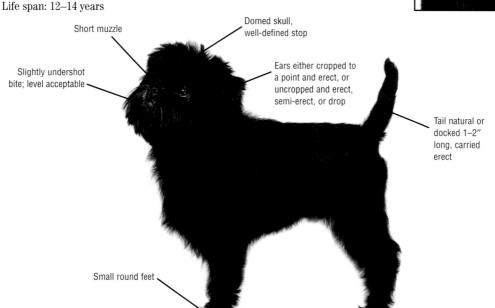

Short muzzle

Domed skull, well-defined stop

Slightly undershot bite; level acceptable

Ears either cropped to a point and erect, or uncropped and erect, semi-erect, or drop

Tail natural or docked 1–2″ long, carried erect

Small round feet

Energy level:	**1 2 3 4**	
Exercise requirements:	**1 2**	
Playfulness:	**1 2 3 4**	
Affection level:	**1 2 3 4**	
Friendliness toward other pets:	**1 2 3**	
Friendliness toward strangers:	**1 2**	
Ease of training:	**1 2 3**	
Grooming requirements:	**1 2 3 4**	

Brussels Griffon

Area of Origin: Belgium
Original Function: Small vermin hunting, companion
Coat: Rough: harsh, medium length; Smooth: soft, short
Color: Red, belge (mixed reddish brown and black),
   black and tan, or black
Height: 9–11″
Weight: 8–10 lb

HISTORY The Brussels Griffon gained favor as a guard or mascot of cabs in Brussels. In the late 1800s this mixture was then crossed with the Pug, at that time extremely popular in neighboring Holland. The pug crosses account for the smooth-coated individuals of the breed, known then (and still in some countries) as the Petit Brabançon. By 1880 the breed was sufficiently established to be recognized at Belgian dog shows. By the early 1900s the little street urchin had risen to the heights of popularity in Belgium and found itself in great demand by nobility. In some countries, only the red longer-coated dogs are classified as the Brussels Griffon; black longer-coated dogs are known as the Belgian Griffon; and smooth-coated dogs are known as the Petit Brabançon.

TEMPERAMENT Brussels Griffons are spunky, brimming with self-confidence and gusto. They are bold, playful, stubborn, and mischievous. They are usually good with other dogs and pets, but tend to bark and climb.

UPKEEP Brussels Griffons need a rousing game or short walk daily. The rough coat needs combing two or three times weekly, plus shaping by stripping every three months. The smooth coat needs only occasional brushing.

HEALTH Concerns: None noted
Suggested tests: None
Life span: 12–15 years

Round skull with deep stop

Very large eyes

Tail docked to about one-third, held high

Undershot

Small round feet

109

Toy Group

Cavalier King Charles Spaniel

Area of Origin: England
Original Function: Flushing small birds, lap dog
Coat: Long, silky
Color: Ruby (solid red), Blenheim (red and white),
  black and tan, tricolor
Height: 12–13″
Weight: 13–18 lb

Energy level:	**1 2 3**	
Exercise requirements:	**1 2 3**	
Playfulness:	**1 2 3 4**	
Affection level:	**1 2 3 4 5**	
Friendliness toward other pets:	**1 2 3 4 5**	
Friendliness toward strangers:	**1 2 3 4 5**	
Ease of training:	**1 2 3 4**	
Grooming requirements:	**1 2 3**	

HISTORY Toy "comforter spaniels" served as lap and foot warmers, companions, and hot water bottles. In the 1700s they were so closely associated with King Charles II that they became known as *King Charles Spaniels.* The King Charles Spaniel continued to grace the homes of the wealthy for generations, but with time a shorter-nosed dog was preferred. By the early 1900s the few dogs that resembled the early members of the breed were considered to be inferior. A wealthy American offered outlandish prize money for the best old-type spaniels, encouraging their preservation. These dogs, named Cavalier King Charles Spaniels in honor of the "cavalier king," eventually outstripped their short-nosed counterparts in popularity, becoming one of the most popular breeds in England. The AKC recognized the breed in 1996.

TEMPERAMENT Cavaliers are sweet, gentle, playful, willing to please, affectionate, and quiet. They are amiable toward other dogs, pets, and strangers.

UPKEEP Cavaliers need a short to moderate walk or a good romp daily. The long coat needs brushing every other day.

HEALTH Concerns: Heart problems, hip dysplasia, syringomelia, patellar luxation
Suggested tests: Heart, hip, knee
Life span: 9–14 years

Ears high set and long

Level topline

Large, round eyes, with cushioning beneath

Full muzzle

Compact seat with long hair

Tail carried happily and in motion when the dog is moving; may be docked with no more than one third removed

Long feathering on feet

110

Chihuahua

Area of Origin: Mexico
Original Function: Ceremonial
Coat: Long-coated: long, soft; Smooth-coated: short, soft
Color: Any
Height: 6–9″
Weight: Not to exceed 6 lb

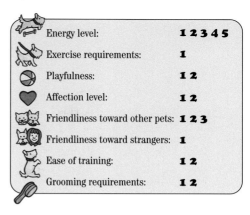

Energy level:	**1 2 3 4 5**
Exercise requirements:	**1**
Playfulness:	**1 2**
Affection level:	**1 2**
Friendliness toward other pets:	**1 2 3**
Friendliness toward strangers:	**1**
Ease of training:	**1 2**
Grooming requirements:	**1 2**

HISTORY The smallest breed of dog, the Chihuahua's ancestors' may have come from China, brought to the New World by Spanish traders. Or its ancestors may have originated entirely in Central and South America, descending from the native Techichi, a small mute dog that was sometimes sacrificed in Toltec religious rituals. Perhaps both theories are correct—the Techichi could have been crossed with tiny Chinese dogs. Whatever the origin, when Cortes conquered the Aztecs in the 16th century, the little dogs were abandoned and left to fend for themselves. About 300 years later, in 1850, three tiny dogs were found in Chihuahua, Mexico. A few were brought to the United States, but they aroused only moderate attention. Only when Xavier Cugat ("the rumba king") appeared in public with a Chihuahua as his constant companion did the breed capture the public's hearts.

TEMPERAMENT Chihuahuas are intensely devoted to one person. They are reserved with strangers but good with other household dogs and pets. Some may be quite bold; others may be timid. Some bark.

UPKEEP Chihuahuas need a short walk or play session every day. The smooth coat needs brushing once a week. The long coat needs brushing two to three times a week.

HEALTH Concerns: Heart problems, hydrocephalus, patellar luxation
Suggested tests: Heart, knee
Life span: 14–18 years

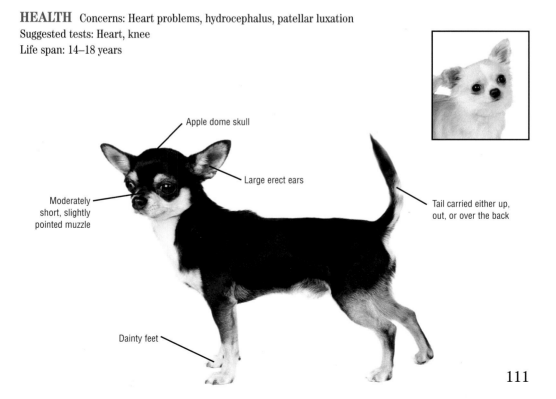

Apple dome skull

Large erect ears

Moderately short, slightly pointed muzzle

Tail carried either up, out, or over the back

Dainty feet

111

Chinese Crested Dog

Area of Origin: China
Original Function: Ratter, lap dog, curio
Coat: Hairless: long, soft hair only on head, feet, and tail;
  Powderpuff: long, straight outer coat, soft undercoat
Color: Any
Height: 11–13″
Weight: 5–12 lb

Energy level:	**1 2 3**	
Exercise requirements:	**1**	
Playfulness:	**1 2 3 4**	
Affection level:	**1 2 3 4**	
Friendliness toward other pets:	**1 2 3 4 5**	
Friendliness toward strangers:	**1 2 3 4 5**	
Ease of training:	**1 2 3**	
Grooming requirements:	**1 2 3**	

HISTORY Hairless dogs seem to arise by mutation all over the world, but they have been principally perpetuated in Central and South America. The Chinese Crested is the exception, apparently existing in China as early as the 13th century. Chinese seafarers are said to have kept the dogs on ship as ratters and curios and to have traded them with local merchants wherever they called. Only in the 1800s were they recorded in Europe, with paintings and later, photographs including dogs of Chinese Crested type. With the help of a handful of committed breeders (including the famed Gypsy Rose Lee), the Chinese Crested gradually gained admirers in both America and Europe. In 1991—after a century of effort—the breed was recognized by the AKC. It comes in both hairless and haired ("powderpuff") versions.

TEMPERAMENT Chinese Cresteds are playful, gentle, biddable, and sensitive. They are devoted to family, and are also good with other dogs, pets, and strangers.

UPKEEP Cresteds need a short walk or good romp daily. The powderpuff coat needs brushing every day or two, plus shaving the muzzle every two weeks. The hairless needs regular skin care, such as the application of moisturizer or sunblock, and bathing to combat blackheads.

HEALTH Concerns: PRA, glaucoma, lens luxation, patellar luxation
Suggested tests: Eye, knee
Life span: 13–15 years

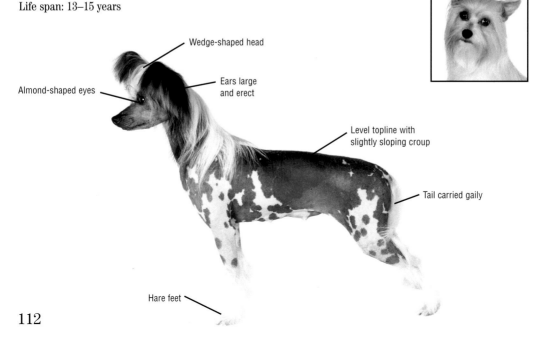

Wedge-shaped head

Almond-shaped eyes

Ears large and erect

Level topline with slightly sloping croup

Tail carried gaily

Hare feet

English Toy Spaniel

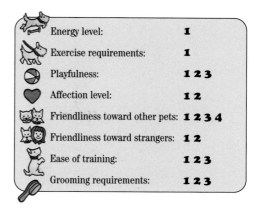

Energy level:	**1**	
Exercise requirements:	**1**	
Playfulness:	**1 2 3**	
Affection level:	**1 2**	
Friendliness toward other pets:	**1 2 3 4**	
Friendliness toward strangers:	**1 2**	
Ease of training:	**1 2 3**	
Grooming requirements:	**1 2 3**	

Area of Origin: England
Original Function: Flushing small birds, lap dog
Coat: Long, silky
Color: Solid red, black and tan, or either of these colors
   on a white background
Height: 10–11″
Weight: 8–14 lb

HISTORY   The English Toy Spaniel and the Cavalier King Charles Spaniel began as one breed, probably resulting from crosses of small spaniels with Oriental toy breeds. These "comforter spaniels" became very popular with the wealthy classes. They were so popular with King Charles II that they were called King Charles Spaniels. These early dogs were all black and tan; other colors were developed later, with the first Duke of Marlborough credited with developing the red-and-white "Blenheims," named after his estate. The King Charles Spaniel was eventually bred down in size and selected for a rounder head and flatter nose. In America, the name was changed to English Toy Spaniel. The breed is shown in two varieties: the red particolored Blenheim and black-and-tan particolored Prince Charles; and the red solid-colored Ruby and black-and-tan solid-colored King Charles.

TEMPERAMENT   English Toy Spaniels are gentle, amiable, calm, and quiet, yet also playful and attentive. They are utterly devoted to family and reserved with strangers. They are somewhat stubborn.

UPKEEP   English Toy Spaniels need only a short walk or romp daily. The long coat needs combing twice weekly.

HEALTH   Concerns: Patellar luxation
Suggested tests: Knee
Life span: 10–12 years

Domed skull with deep stop

Large head with a plush, chubby look

Slightly undershot

Low-set long ears, fringed with heavy feathering

Broad, square jaw

Large eyes

Tail docked 2–4″ in length, carried at or slightly above horizontal, with long silky hair

Havanese

Area of Origin: Cuba
Original Function: Lap dog, performer
Coat: Double coat, with long, wavy outercoat
Color: All colors or combination of colors, including white
Height: 8.5–11.5″
Weight: 7–13 lb

Energy level:	**1 2 3 4**	
Exercise requirements:	**1 2 3**	
Playfulness:	**1 2 3 4 5**	
Affection level:	**1 2 3 4 5**	
Friendliness toward other pets:	**1 2 3 4**	
Friendliness toward strangers:	**1 2 3 4 5**	
Ease of training:	**1 2 3 4**	
Grooming requirements:	**1 2 3**	

HISTORY The Havanese is one of the Barbichon family of small dogs originating in the Mediterranean in ancient times. They were spread by Spanish traders to Cuba, where they became known as Habeneros. Some later found their way back to Europe, where they became popular as pets of the elite and as performing dogs. Their popularity as pets waned, however, and their stronghold remained in the circus, where they performed throughout Europe as trick dogs. Eventually the breed declined in numbers to such an extent that it was almost extinct not only in Europe but also in its native Cuba. A few remained in Cuba, however, and three families with their Havanese left Cuba for the United States during the 1950s and 1960s. Most present-day Havanese descend from these dogs. The Havanese received AKC recognition in 1999.

TEMPERAMENT This is a busy, curious dog; it is happiest when it is the center of attention. It loves to play and clown and is affectionate with its family, children, strangers, other dogs, and pets—basically everyone! The Havanese is willing to please and learn easily, but it tends to be vocal.

UPKEEP Although energetic, the Havanese can have its exercise needs met with a short walk or a good play session. It is not a dog that can live outside. Coat care entails brushing two to four times a week. This is a nonshedding dog, which means that loose hairs are caught in the outer hairs, tending to tangle, unless they are combed out.

HEALTH Concerns: Patellar luxation
Suggested tests: Knee
Life span: 12–14 years

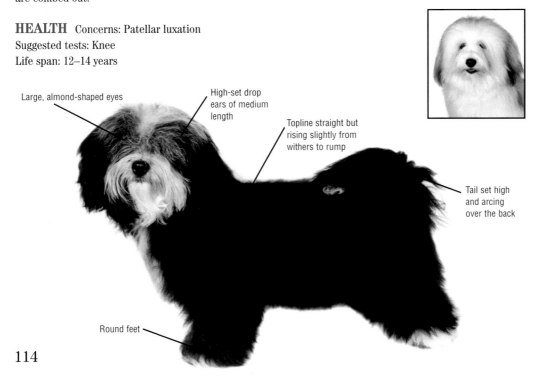

Large, almond-shaped eyes

High-set drop ears of medium length

Topline straight but rising slightly from withers to rump

Tail set high and arcing over the back

Round feet

Italian Greyhound

Area of Origin: Italy
Original Function: Lap dog
Coat: Smooth, short
Color: Any color but brindle or black and tan
Height: 13–15″
Weight: 7–14 lb

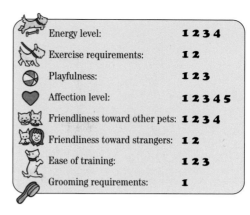

Energy level:	**1 2 3 4**
Exercise requirements:	**1 2**
Playfulness:	**1 2 3**
Affection level:	**1 2 3 4 5**
Friendliness toward other pets:	**1 2 3 4**
Friendliness toward strangers:	**1 2**
Ease of training:	**1 2 3**
Grooming requirements:	**1**

HISTORY Evidence of dogs resembling Italian Greyhounds can be found in art dating nearly 2,000 years ago from Turkey, Greece, and other areas around the Mediterranean. By the Middle Ages, miniaturized Greyhounds could be found throughout southern Europe, but they found special favor with Italian courtiers. The breed came to England in the 17th century, quickly becoming popular with nobility there. In 1820 the Italian Greyhound was one of only two toy breeds mentioned in a book about dogs. The breed's popularity reached its peak during the reign of Queen Victoria. After that time, its numbers declined to such an extent that it almost disappeared in England after World War II. Fortunately, Italian Greyhounds had come to America in the late 1800s. They, along with other imports, helped revive the breed in Europe.

TEMPERAMENT Italian Greyhounds are gentle, sensitive, devoted, and amiable. They are reserved, often timid, with strangers, but demonstrative with family. They love to run and chase.

UPKEEP Italian Greyhounds need a moderate walk or a good chance to run each day. Care of the fine short hair is minimal, consisting only of occasional brushing to remove dead hair.

HEALTH Concerns: Periodontal disease, epilepsy, leg fractures, patellar luxation, PRA
Suggested tests: Knee, eye
Life span: 12–15 years

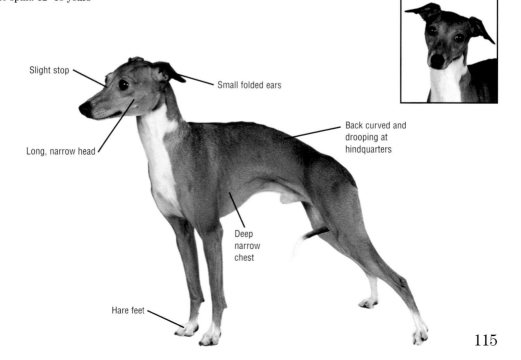

Slight stop

Small folded ears

Long, narrow head

Back curved and drooping at hindquarters

Deep narrow chest

Hare feet

115

Japanese Chin

Area of Origin: Japan
Original Function: Lap dog
Coat: Long, silky
Color: Black and white, red and white, or black and tan and white
Height: 8–11″
Weight: 4–7 lb

Energy level:	**1 2 3**	
Exercise requirements:	**1**	
Playfulness:	**1 2 3 4**	
Affection level:	**1 2 3 4 5**	
Friendliness toward other pets:	**1 2 3 4**	
Friendliness toward strangers:	**1 2 3 4 5**	
Ease of training:	**1 2 3**	
Grooming requirements:	**1 2 3**	

HISTORY The Japanese Chin is actually of ancient Chinese origin, probably sharing a close relationship with the Pekingese. Like the Pekingese, the Chin was kept by Chinese aristocracy, and sometimes presented as a gift to visiting nobility. Once in Japan, it gained great favor with the Japanese Imperial family and was kept as a lap dog and ornament; some particularly small Chins were reportedly kept in hanging "bird" cages. The first record of Chins coming to Europe was in 1853, when Commodore Perry presented a pair from his trip to Japan to Queen Victoria. In the succeeding years, traders brought back many more Chins, selling them in Europe and America. The breed was first recognized by the AKC in the late 1800s as the Japanese Spaniel.

TEMPERAMENT Japanese Chins are devoted, playful, sensitive, and willing to please, tending to shadow their owners. They are a friend to all.

UPKEEP Chins need a short walk, romp, or game every day. The long coat needs combing twice weekly.

HEALTH Concerns: Patellar luxation, dry eye, entropion, cataract
Suggested tests: Knee, eye
Life span: 12–14 years

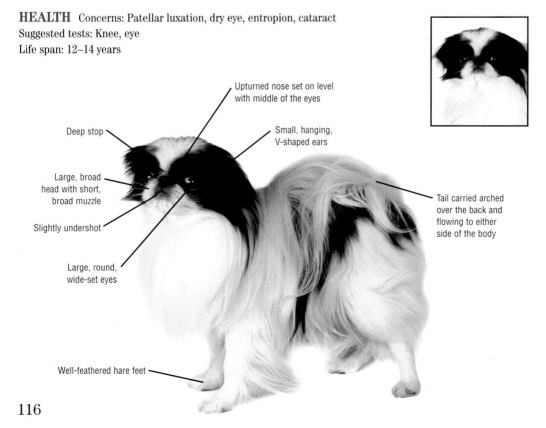

Deep stop

Large, broad head with short, broad muzzle

Slightly undershot

Large, round, wide-set eyes

Well-feathered hare feet

Upturned nose set on level with middle of the eyes

Small, hanging, V-shaped ears

Tail carried arched over the back and flowing to either side of the body

Energy level:	**1 2 3 4**	
Exercise requirements:	**1**	
Playfulness:	**1 2 3 4**	
Affection level:	**1 2 3**	
Friendliness toward other pets:	**1 2 3**	
Friendliness toward strangers:	**1**	
Ease of training:	**1 2 3**	
Grooming requirements:	**1 2 3**	

Maltese

Area of Origin: Malta
Original Function: Lap dog
Coat: Long, silky
Color: White
Height: 9–10″
Weight: Under 7 lb, preferably 4–6 lb

HISTORY The island of Malta was an early trading port, visited by Phoenician sailors by 1500 B.C. Maltese dogs are specifically mentioned in writings as early as 300 B.C. Though the Maltese's hallmark is its long, silky, dazzling white hair, early Maltese came in colors other than white. By the early 14th century, Maltese had been brought to England, where they became the darlings of upper-class ladies. An 1830 painting entitled *The Lion Dog From Malta—Last of His Race* suggests that the breed may have been in danger of extinction. Soon after, two Maltese were brought to England from Manila. Although originally intended as a gift for Queen Victoria, they passed into other hands, and their offspring became the first Maltese exhibited in England. The AKC recognized the Maltese in 1888.

TEMPERAMENT Maltese are bold, feisty, and playful, but also sweet and amiable. They are reserved with strangers. Some bark a lot.

UPKEEP Maltese need only a short walk or romp each day. The coat needs combing every one or two days. The white coat may be difficult to keep clean in some areas. Pets may be clipped for easier care.

HEALTH Concerns: Patellar luxation, hydrocephalus, liver shunt, dental problems, eyelid problems
Suggested tests: Knee
Life span: 12–14 years

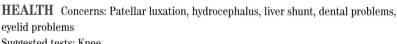

Low-set drop ears covered with long hair

Level topline

Round eyes

Tail carried over the back, its tip lying to the side

Fine muzzle of medium length

Small round feet

Toy Manchester Terrier

Area of Origin: England
Original Function: Hunting small rodents
Coat: Short, sleek
Color: Black and tan, with a black "thumbprint" patch on the front of each foreleg and "pencil marks" on the top of each toe
Height: 10–12″
Weight: under 12 lb (usually 6–8 lb)

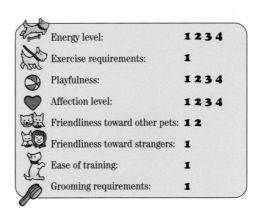

Energy level:	**1 2 3 4**	
Exercise requirements:	**1**	
Playfulness:	**1 2 3 4**	
Affection level:	**1 2 3 4**	
Friendliness toward other pets:	**1 2**	
Friendliness toward strangers:	**1**	
Ease of training:	**1**	
Grooming requirements:	**1**	

HISTORY In Manchester, England, crosses between the Black and Tan Terrier ratters and the Whippet racers created the dog known since about 1860 as the Manchester Terrier. An early standard of 1881 described the existence of a toy variety even then. The smaller dogs were in high demand, and breeders resorted to inbreeding to achieve even smaller specimens, which eventually led to very small frail dogs. Breeders corrected their mistake and bred for a miniature, but not tiny, version. The AKC initially considered the Manchester and Toy Manchester separate but interbreeding breeds. In 1959 they were changed to be two interbreeding varieties of one breed. Besides size, the Toy Manchester differs from its larger counterpart in that cropped ears are not allowed. The Toy Manchester terrier is also known as the English Toy Terrier.

TEMPERAMENT Toy Manchesters are gentle, sensitive, and playful with family, reserved, even timid, with strangers. They can be tough when the need arises, and they retain their hunting instinct.

UPKEEP Toy Manchesters need a short walk and good romp daily. Coat care is minimal, consisting of occasional brushing to remove dead hair.

HEALTH Concerns: vWD, cardiomyopathy
Suggested tests: vWD, heart
Life span: 14–16 years

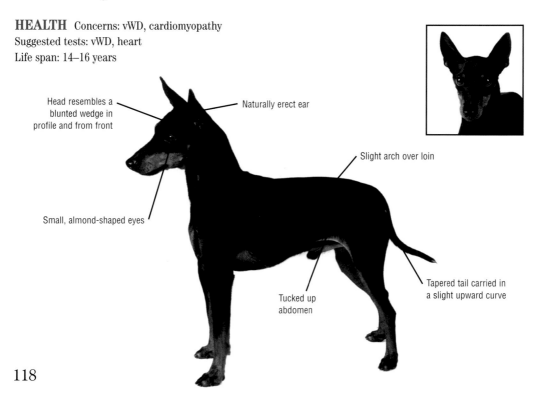

Head resembles a blunted wedge in profile and from front

Naturally erect ear

Slight arch over loin

Small, almond-shaped eyes

Tucked up abdomen

Tapered tail carried in a slight upward curve

Miniature Pinscher

Area of Origin: Germany
Original Function: Small vermin hunting
Coat: Short, sleek
Color: Clear red, stag red, black and tan
Height: 10–12.5″, with 11–11.5″ preferred
Weight: 8–10 lb

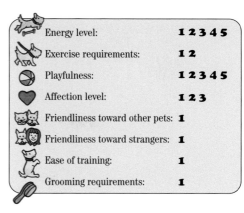

Energy level:	**1 2 3 4 5**
Exercise requirements:	**1 2**
Playfulness:	**1 2 3 4 5**
Affection level:	**1 2 3**
Friendliness toward other pets:	**1**
Friendliness toward strangers:	**1**
Ease of training:	**1**
Grooming requirements:	**1**

HISTORY These little German spitfires were developed into a distinct breed, the *Reh Pinscher* in the early 1800s, so named because of their resemblance to the small red German roe (*reh*) deer. *Pinscher* simply means terrier. The emphasis in the late 1800s was on breeding the tiniest specimens, resulting in crippled ugly dogs. Fortunately, the trend was reversed, and by 1900 the emphasis had returned to elegance and soundness. The Miniature Pinscher quickly became one of the most competitive and popular show dogs in pre-World War I Germany, but after the war, the breed experienced a plunge in numbers. Its future was left to those dogs that had been exported before the war. Its popularity continued to grow in America, and it received AKC recognition in 1929.

TEMPERAMENT Miniature Pinschers are energetic, busy, inquisitive, playful, bold, and brash. They tend to be stubborn and independent. They can be scrappy with other dogs and are reserved with strangers.

UPKEEP Min Pins need a moderate walk and several play sessions daily. The coat is virtually carefree, requiring only occasional brushing.

HEALTH Concerns: Legg-Perthes, patellar luxation, heart defects, mucopolyscharidosis (MPS)
Suggested tests: Hip, knee, DNA for MPS
Life span: 12–14 years

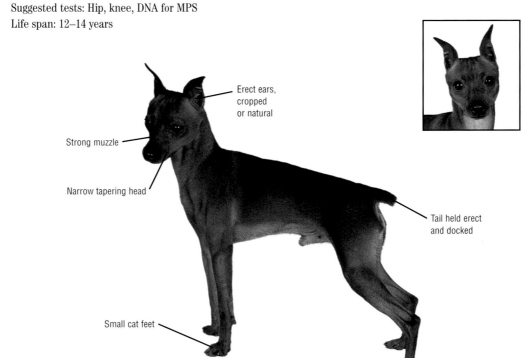

Erect ears, cropped or natural

Strong muzzle

Narrow tapering head

Tail held erect and docked

Small cat feet

Papillon

Area of Origin: France
Original Function: Lap dog
Coat: Long, silky
Color: White with patches of any color
Height: 8–11″
Weight: 4–9 lb

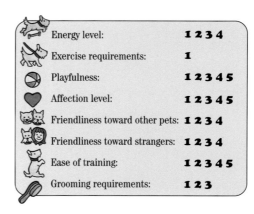

Energy level:	**1 2 3 4**
Exercise requirements:	**1**
Playfulness:	**1 2 3 4 5**
Affection level:	**1 2 3 4 5**
Friendliness toward other pets:	**1 2 3 4**
Friendliness toward strangers:	**1 2 3 4**
Ease of training:	**1 2 3 4 5**
Grooming requirements:	**1 2 3**

HISTORY The Papillon has its roots in the dwarf spaniels that were so popular throughout Europe from at least the 16th century. These little dogs were extremely popular with the nobility; as time went on, Spain and Italy became the centers of dwarf spaniel breeding and trading. The court of Louis XIV of France was particularly fond of Papillons and imported many of them. These early dogs had drooping ears, but eventually drop- and erect-eared Papillons could be found in the same litter. The name Papillon is French for butterfly, because the face with the erect ears gives the impression of one. The drop-eared version is known as the Phalene, which is French for moth. A symmetrically marked face with white blaze adds to the butterfly appearance.

TEMPERAMENT Papillons are obedient and responsive, among the most trainable of Toys. They are gentle, amiable, and playful, friendly toward all.

UPKEEP Papillons need a short walk plus several play or learning sessions a day. The coat needs brushing twice weekly.

HEALTH Concerns: Patellar luxation, seizures, dental problems
Suggested tests: Knee
Life span: 12–15 years

Round eyes

Small rounded head
with fine muzzle

Ears erect
or dropped

Long tail carried
arched over body
and covered with
a long plume

Pekingese

Area of Origin: China
Original Function: Lap dog
Coat: Double coat, with coarse outercoat and soft undercoat
Color: All colors and patterns are allowable
Height: 6–9″
Weight: Not to exceed 14 lb

	Energy level:	1
	Exercise requirements:	1
	Playfulness:	1
	Affection level:	1 2
	Friendliness toward other pets:	1 2 3 4
	Friendliness toward strangers:	1 2
	Ease of training:	1
	Grooming requirements:	1 2 3 4 5

HISTORY The Pekingese owes its existence to the Lamaist form of Buddhism in China, in which the lion was an exalted symbol of Buddha, sometimes appearing in miniaturized form. The Foo dogs then in existence bore some resemblance to a lion and were carefully bred to accentuate this similarity. In fact, these dogs eventually came to be known as "lion dogs." Extensive breeding programs fell under the auspices of palace eunuchs, with no expense spared. In 1860 the British looted the Imperial Summer Palace. Among their loot were five royal lion dogs, which were taken back to England. One was presented to Queen Victoria, and it, along with the other four, caused such interest among dog fanciers that there arose great demand for more of these dogs.

TEMPERAMENT Pekingese are courageous, aloof, and independent. They are devoted to family but not demonstrative. They tend to be stubborn.

UPKEEP Pekingese need a very short walk daily. They do not tolerate heat. The coat will mat unless combed, at the very least, weekly, preferably more often. The over-nose wrinkle should be cleaned daily to avoid infection.

HEALTH Concerns: Brachycephalic syndrome, dry eye, patellar luxation
Suggested tests: Knee
Life span: 13–15 years

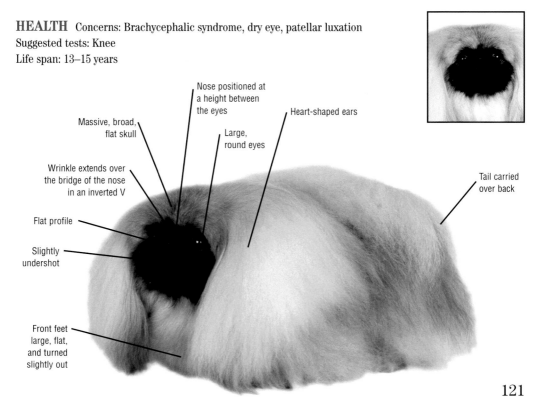

Massive, broad, flat skull

Nose positioned at a height between the eyes

Large, round eyes

Heart-shaped ears

Wrinkle extends over the bridge of the nose in an inverted V

Flat profile

Slightly undershot

Tail carried over back

Front feet large, flat, and turned slightly out

Pomeranian

Area of Origin: Germany
Original Function: Companion
Coat: Double coat, with soft undercoat and long, harsh outercoat
Color: All colors and patterns allowed
Height: 8–11″
Weight: 3–7 lb, preferably 4–5 lb

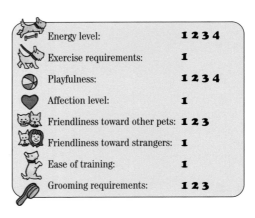

Energy level:	**1 2 3 4**	
Exercise requirements:	**1**	
Playfulness:	**1 2 3 4**	
Affection level:	**1**	
Friendliness toward other pets:	**1 2 3**	
Friendliness toward strangers:	**1**	
Ease of training:	**1**	
Grooming requirements:	**1 2 3**	

HISTORY The smallest member of the spitz family, the Pomeranian boasts tough sledding dog ancestors. Exactly when it began to be bred down in size is not known. Only when the breed was taken to England was it dubbed the Pomeranian, but these early dogs were not the "Poms" known today. They weighed as much as 30 pounds and were often white. Although the Pomeranian was recognized by the English Kennel Club in 1870, it was not until Queen Victoria brought a Pomeranian from Italy that its popularity grew. The queen's new Pom was a small red dog; soon after, fanciers preferred smaller, more colorful specimens. By 1900 Poms had been recognized by the AKC, and dogs were being shown in both England and America in an array of colors.

TEMPERAMENT Bouncy, bold, and busy, Pomeranians are curious, playful, and attentive, ever ready for a game. Some can be aggressive toward other dogs. Some bark a lot.

UPKEEP Pomeranians need a very short walk or several short romps daily. The double coat needs brushing twice weekly, more when shedding.

HEALTH Concerns: Patellar luxation, PRA
Suggested tests: Knee, eye
Life span: 12–16 years

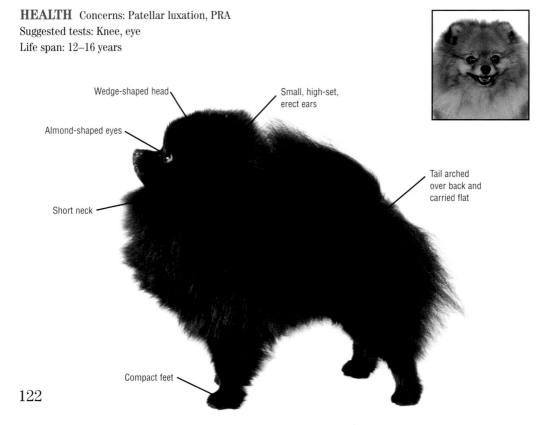

Wedge-shaped head

Small, high-set, erect ears

Almond-shaped eyes

Tail arched over back and carried flat

Short neck

Compact feet

Toy Poodle

Area of Origin: Central Europe
Original Function: Lap dog
Coat: Curly, harsh, long
Color: Any solid color
Height: Not to exceed 10″
Weight: 4–8 lb

Energy level:	**1 2 3** 4
Exercise requirements:	**1 2**
Playfulness:	**1 2 3 4 5**
Affection level:	**1 2 3** 4
Friendliness toward other pets:	**1 2** 3
Friendliness toward strangers:	**1 2 3** 4
Ease of training:	**1 2 3 4 5**
Grooming requirements:	**1 2 3 4 5**

HISTORY The word "poodle" comes from the German word *pfudel*, meaning "puddle" or "to splash," probably reflecting the dog's water abilities. It was a talented water-hunting companion before it became an elegant companion for fashionable ladies. It eventually became the national dog of France. Poodles entered the show ring in the late 1800s and a successful effort was made to perfect the smaller specimens. Some of the early show Poodles were shown in corded coats, in which the hair is allowed to mat in long thin tresses rather than be brushed out. In the early 1900s the corded style was replaced by the bouffant styles still in vogue. Popularity in America waned so that by the late 1920s they had almost died out in North America. They returned to be the most popular breed in America for many years.

TEMPERAMENT Toy Poodles are pert and peppy, among the easiest breeds to train. They are alert, responsive, playful, lively, sensitive, and eager to please. They are devoted to family and often reserved with strangers. They may bark a lot.

UPKEEP Poodles need a short walk or good romp daily. The coat should be combed every day or two. Clipping should be done at least four times a year, with the face and feet clipped monthly.

HEALTH Concerns: PRA, patellar luxation, Legg-Perthes, epilepsy, eyelid problems
Suggested tests: Eye, knee, hip
Life span: 12–14 years

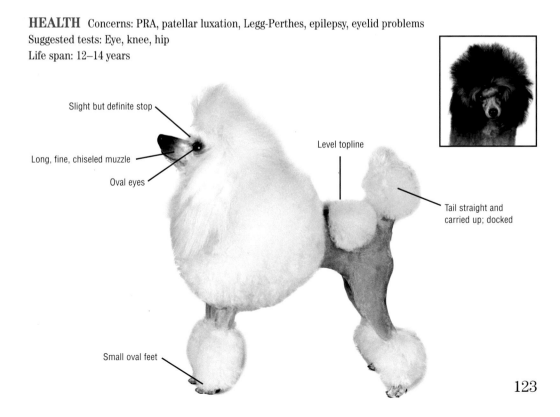

Slight but definite stop

Long, fine, chiseled muzzle

Oval eyes

Level topline

Tail straight and carried up; docked

Small oval feet

Pug

Area of Origin: China
Original Function: Lap dog
Coat: Short, smooth
Color: Silver, apricot-fawn, or black, with black muzzle
or mask, ears, cheek moles, and trace down back
Height: 10–11″
Weight: 14–18 lb

Energy level:		**1 2 3**
Exercise requirements:		**1 2**
Playfulness:		**1 2 3 4**
Affection level:		**1 2 3 4**
Friendliness toward other pets:		**1 2 3**
Friendliness toward strangers:		**1 2**
Ease of training:		**1 2 3**
Grooming requirements:		**1 2**

HISTORY The Pug is the only Toy breed to be descended from mastiff forebears. It originated in China and Tibet. In China the facial wrinkles were an essential breed feature, most notably the "prince mark," or vertical wrinkle on the forehead, which bore a resemblance to the Chinese character for "prince." Pugs probably came to Holland by way of the Dutch East India Trading Company. Pugs were first brought to England during Victorian times and became incredibly popular with the wealthy, displacing the King Charles Spaniel as the favored royal breed. Pugs of Victorian England usually had cropped ears, further accentuating their wrinkled faces. The Pug's official motto, *multum in parvo* ("a lot in a little"), fits it exactly.

TEMPERAMENT Pugs are a blend of dignity and comedy. They are amiable, playful, and confident. They can be stubborn and headstrong, but are generally willing to please.

UPKEEP Pugs need a short to moderate walk or a good play session daily. They do not tolerate heat. They need minimal coat care but daily cleaning of facial wrinkles. They wheeze and snore.

HEALTH Concerns: Brachycephalic syndrome, Pug dog encephalitis, hip dysplasia, patellar luxation, Legg-Perthes, entropion
Suggested tests: Knee, hip, eye
Life span: 12–15 years

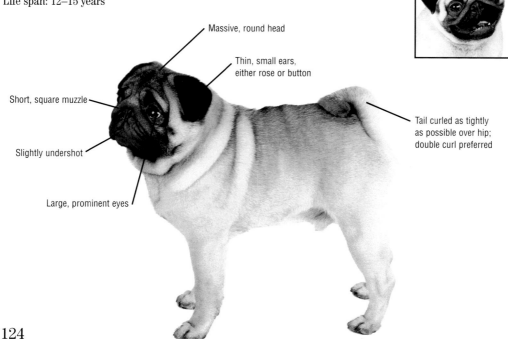

Massive, round head

Thin, small ears, either rose or button

Short, square muzzle

Slightly undershot

Large, prominent eyes

Tail curled as tightly as possible over hip; double curl preferred

Shih Tzu

Area of Origin: China and Tibet
Original Function: Lap dog
Coat: Long, silky
Color: Any
Height: 8–11″ (ideally, 9–10.5″)
Weight: 9–16 lb

Energy level:	**1 2 3**
Exercise requirements:	**1**
Playfulness:	**1 2 3 4**
Affection level:	**1 2 3 4**
Friendliness toward other pets:	**1 2 3 4**
Friendliness toward strangers:	**1 2 3 4**
Ease of training:	**1 2**
Grooming requirements:	**1 2 3 4**

HISTORY Even though the Shih Tzu is most often associated with China, it probably originated in Tibet as early as the 17th century, where it enjoyed status as a holy dog. Shih Tzu means "lion dog," designating the breed as one of the most esteemed animals in China because of its association with Buddhism. The Shih Tzu developed most distinctively in China during the reign of Empress Dowager Cixi (Tz'u-shi, 1861–1908). When the British looted the Imperial Palace, most of the dogs were lost, and the breed suffered a great setback. The Lhasa Apso and Shih Tzu were initially lumped together in England as the Apso, but were acknowledged as two breeds in 1934. In the United States the breed became extremely popular in the 1960s, leading to AKC recognition in 1969.

TEMPERAMENT Shih Tzu are spunky but sweet. They are vivacious, playful, and affectionate. They can be stubborn.

UPKEEP Shih Tzu need a short walk or good play session daily. The luxurious coat needs brushing or combing every other day. Pets may be clipped.

HEALTH Concerns: Hip dysplasia, renal dysplasia, PRA, dry eye, liver shunt, patellar luxation
Suggested tests: Eye
Life span: 11–14 years

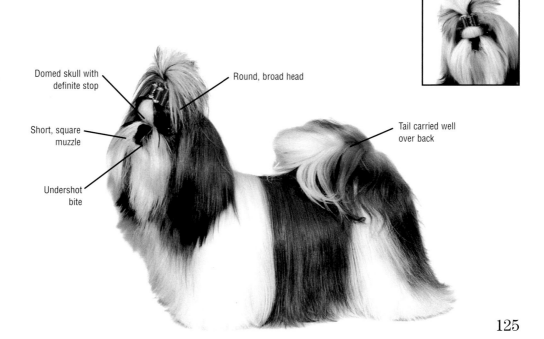

Domed skull with definite stop

Round, broad head

Short, square muzzle

Tail carried well over back

Undershot bite

Silky Terrier

Area of Origin: Australia
Original Function: Companion, small vermin hunting
Coat: Long, silky
Color: Blue and tan
Height: 9–10″
Weight: 8–11 lb

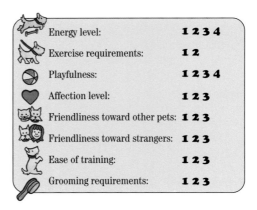

Energy level:	**1 2 3 4**
Exercise requirements:	**1 2**
Playfulness:	**1 2 3 4**
Affection level:	**1 2 3**
Friendliness toward other pets:	**1 2 3**
Friendliness toward strangers:	**1 2 3**
Ease of training:	**1 2 3**
Grooming requirements:	**1 2 3**

HISTORY In the late 1800s Yorkshire Terriers came to Australia, where they were bred with the native Blue and Tan Australian Terriers in an effort to improve the latter's coat color while retaining its more robust conformation. These resulting dogs were intermediate in size and coat length between its parental stock. Because the breed was developed in two separate areas of Australia, separate breed standards were drawn up from each area in 1906 and 1910, with weight being the major disagreement. In 1926 a compromise standard encompassing all areas was accepted. The breed was popularly known as the Sydney Silky Terrier in Australia until its name was changed to Australian Silky Terrier in 1955. In America its name was changed to Silky Terrier in 1955, just prior to its recognition by the AKC.

TEMPERAMENT Silky Terriers are bold, feisty, inquisitive, and playful, ever ready for action, terriers at heart. They can be aggressive toward other dogs or pets. They tend to be stubborn, and can be mischievous. They bark a lot.

UPKEEP Silkies need a moderate walk on leash or a good play session daily. The coat needs combing every other day.

HEALTH Concerns: Patellar luxation, Legg-Perthes
Suggested tests: Knee, hip
Life span: 11–14 years

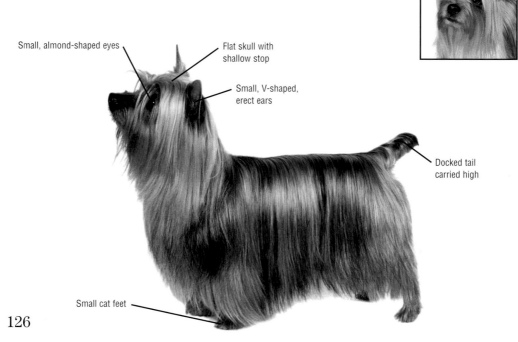

Small, almond-shaped eyes

Flat skull with shallow stop

Small, V-shaped, erect ears

Docked tail carried high

Small cat feet

Toy Fox Terrier

Area of Origin: United States
Original Function: Vermin control
Coat: Short, smooth
Color: Tricolor; white, chocolate and tan; white and tan;
or white and black, all with predominately colored head
and more than 50% white on body
Height: Male: 8.5–11″ (9–11″ preferred)
Weight: 3.5–7 lb

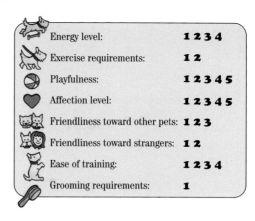

Energy level:	**1 2 3 4**
Exercise requirements:	**1 2**
Playfulness:	**1 2 3 4 5**
Affection level:	**1 2 3 4 5**
Friendliness toward other pets:	**1 2 3**
Friendliness toward strangers:	**1 2**
Ease of training:	**1 2 3 4**
Grooming requirements:	**1**

HISTORY In the early 1900s smaller Smooth Fox Terriers were crossed with several toy breeds, including the Toy Manchester Terrier, Chihuahua, and possibly Italian Greyhound. The result was a smaller version of the Smooth Fox Terrier that was equally adept at catching small rodents and entertaining families, in a handy compact size. The smaller dogs were still registered with the UKC as Smooth Fox Terriers until 1936, when the UKC recognized them as a separate breed. They remain one of the most popular non-AKC companion breeds in the country. In 2003 they entered the AKC show ring for the first time.

TEMPERAMENT Toy Fox Terriers are feisty, fun-loving, and adventurous. They love to play, investigate, and hunt, but also enjoy snuggling on a lap. They are reserved with strangers.

UPKEEP Toy Fox Terriers need a short walk plus at least one play session daily. The short coat needs weekly brushing.

HEALTH Concerns: Patellar luxation, Legg-Perthes
Suggested tests: Knee, hip
Life span: 13–14 years

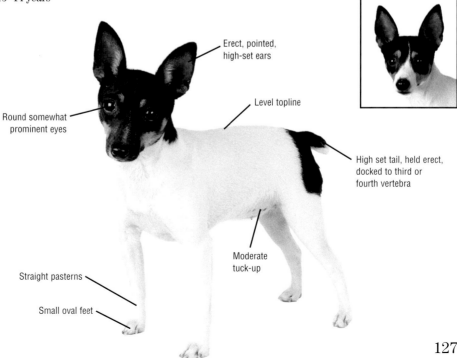

Erect, pointed, high-set ears

Level topline

Round somewhat prominent eyes

High set tail, held erect, docked to third or fourth vertebra

Moderate tuck-up

Straight pasterns

Small oval feet

Toy Group

Yorkshire Terrier

Energy level:	**1 2 3 4**	
Exercise requirements:	**1**	
Playfulness:	**1 2 3 4**	
Affection level:	**1 2 3**	
Friendliness toward other pets:	**1 2**	
Friendliness toward strangers:	**1 2 3**	
Ease of training:	**1 2**	
Grooming requirements:	**1 2 3 4**	

Area of Origin: England
Original Function: Small vermin hunting
Coat: Long, silky
Color: Blue and tan. Yorkshire Terriers are born black, gradually attaining their blue and tan coloration as they mature.
Height: 8–9″
Weight: Not to exceed 7 lb

HISTORY The Yorkshire Terrier originated as a ratter belonging to the working class. Because of its modest roots, the Yorkshire Terrier was initially looked down upon by the wealthier dog fanciers. The breed's beauty soon had it gracing show rings and the laps of wealthy mistresses, however. By 1880 Yorkies had come to America, but the breed varied so much in size that there was great confusion concerning how big a Yorkshire Terrier should be. Many of these early Yorkies weighed between 12 and 14 pounds. By 1900 fanciers on both sides of the Atlantic had decided that the small size was preferable and made a concerted effort to breed a smaller Yorkie with an even longer coat. The modern Yorkshire Terrier is one of the smaller and most luxuriously coated dogs in existence.

TEMPERAMENT Yorkshire Terriers are busy, inquisitive, bold, stubborn, and can be aggressive to strange dogs and small animals. Some tend to bark a lot.

UPKEEP Yorkies need a short walk or a good romp daily. The long coat needs combing every day or two.

HEALTH Concerns: Patellar luxation
Suggested tests: Knee
Life span: 14–16 years

Small head, rather flat on top

Small, V-shaped ears, carried erect

Medium-sized eyes

Level topline

Tail docked to a medium length and carried slightly higher than the level of back

Round feet

American Eskimo Dog

Area of Origin: United States
Original Function: Watchdog, performer, farm worker
Coat: Straight, stand-off double coat, medium length
Color: White, or white with biscuit cream
Height: Standard: 15–19″; Miniature: 12–15″; Toy: 9–12″
Weight: Standard: 20–40 lb; Miniature: 11–20 lb; Toy: 6–10 lb

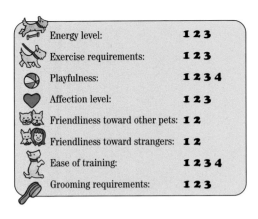

Energy level:	**1 2 3**
Exercise requirements:	**1 2 3**
Playfulness:	**1 2 3 4**
Affection level:	**1 2 3**
Friendliness toward other pets:	**1 2**
Friendliness toward strangers:	**1 2**
Ease of training:	**1 2 3 4**
Grooming requirements:	**1 2 3**

HISTORY The American Eskimo Dog descended from one of the varieties of spitz developed in Germany, with influences from other spitz breeds such as the Keeshond, Pomeranian, and Volpino Italiano. When European workers came to America, they brought these dogs with them. In the 1920s the American Spitz (as it had come to be called) became a favorite circus performer. Spectators often left the circus with an offspring of one of the dazzling performers. Many present-day Eskies can be traced back to circus ancestors. After World War I the breed's name was changed to American Eskimo, to remove any Germanic sound from the name. The breed has historically been registered with the United Kennel Club. Only in 1994 did the AKC recognize the breed.

TEMPERAMENT American Eskimo Dogs are bright, eager to please, lively, and fun-loving—but also independent and tenacious. They are among the most biddable of spitz breeds, and, like all spitz, love cold weather.

UPKEEP Larger Eskies need a good jog or long walk daily. Smaller Eskies need only a short walk or lively romp. The double coat needs brushing and combing twice weekly, more often when shedding.

HEALTH Concerns: Patellar luxation, hip dysplasia, PRA
Suggested tests: Knee, hip, eye
Life span: 12–14 years

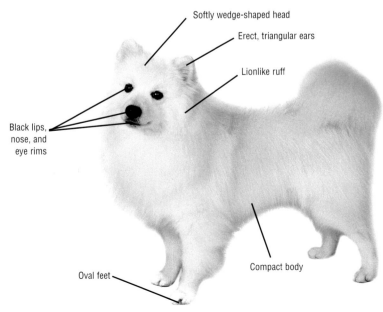

Softly wedge-shaped head

Erect, triangular ears

Lionlike ruff

Black lips, nose, and eye rims

Compact body

Oval feet

Energy level:	**1 2 3 4**
Exercise requirements:	**1 2**
Playfulness:	**1 2 3 4 5**
Affection level:	**1 2 3 4 5**
Friendliness toward other pets:	**1 2 3 4**
Friendliness toward strangers:	**1 2 3 4 5**
Ease of training:	**1 2 3 4**
Grooming requirements:	**1 2 3 4 5**

Bichon Frise

Area of Origin: Mediterranean area
Original Function: Companion, performer
Coat: Undercoat soft; outercoat coarse and curly; medium length
Color: White, may have cream shadings
Height: 9.5–11.5″
Weight: Males: 11–16 lb; Females 10–15 lb

HISTORY The Bichon Frise has its roots in the Mediterranean, from the family of dogs known as Barbichons, which was later shortened to Bichons. The Bichons were divided into four types: the Bichon Maltaise, Bolognese, Havanese, and Teneriffe. The Teneriffe, which was to later become the Bichon Frise, developed on the Canary island of Teneriffe, probably having been taken there by Spanish seafarers in ancient times. In the 14th century Italian sailors brought specimens back from the island to the continent, where they quickly became favored pets of the upper class. In the 19th century they sank from court favorite to common street dogs, and teamed with street peddlers to perform tricks for money. After they were almost decimated by World War I, breeders resurrected them. In 1933 the name officially became Bichon à poil Frise (Bichon of the curly coat).

TEMPERAMENT Perky, bouncy, and playful, Bichons are friends to all. They are sensitive, responsive, and affectionate, as eager to cuddle as play. They can bark a lot, and may be hard to house-train.

UPKEEP Bichons need a vigorous romp or short walk daily. The coat needs combing every other day, plus trimming every two months. It is difficult to keep the beard white.

HEALTH Concerns: Patellar luxation, allergies, cataract, hip dysplasia
Suggested tests: Knee, eye, hip
Life span: 12–15 years

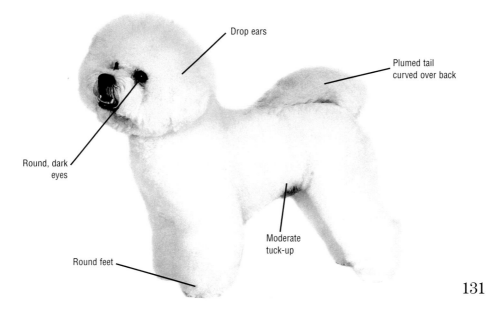

Drop ears

Plumed tail curved over back

Round, dark eyes

Moderate tuck-up

Round feet

Boston Terrier

Area of Origin: United States
Original Function: Ratting, companion
Coat: Smooth, short
Color: Brindle, seal, or black with white markings on muzzle, between eyes, and forechest, and possibly white collar and lower legs
Height: 15–17″
Weight: 10–25 lb (25 lb maximum)

Energy level:	**1 2 3**
Exercise requirements:	**1**
Playfulness:	**1 2 3**
Affection level:	**1 2 3**
Friendliness toward other pets:	**1 2 3 4**
Friendliness toward strangers:	**1 2 3**
Ease of training:	**1 2 3**
Grooming requirements:	**1**

HISTORY Around 1865 the coachmen employed by the wealthy people of Boston began to interbreed some of their employers' fine dogs. One of these crosses, between an English Terrier and a Bulldog, resulted in a dog named Hooper's Judge. His progeny were bred to smaller dogs to decrease size. By 1889 the breed had become sufficiently popular in Boston that fanciers formed the American Bull Terrier Club, but this proposed name for the breed was not well received by Bull Terrier fanciers. The breed's nickname, "roundheads," was similarly inappropriate. Shortly after, the breed was named the Boston Terrier, after its birthplace. AKC recognition came in 1893. The Boston quickly gained favor throughout America, ranking as one of the most popular breeds in the early to middle 1900s.

TEMPERAMENT Bostons are saucy, playful, and devoted, sensitive to their owner's moods. Somewhat stubborn, they nonetheless learn readily. They are reserved with strangers, and may be aggressive toward strange dogs. Some bark a lot.

UPKEEP Bostons love games, and most of their exercise needs can be met with a romp in the yard. Some Bostons wheeze and snore, and most don't tolerate heat well. The coat requires only occasional brushing.

HEALTH Concerns: Patellar luxation, brachycephalic syndrome
Suggested tests: Knee
Life span: 10–14 years

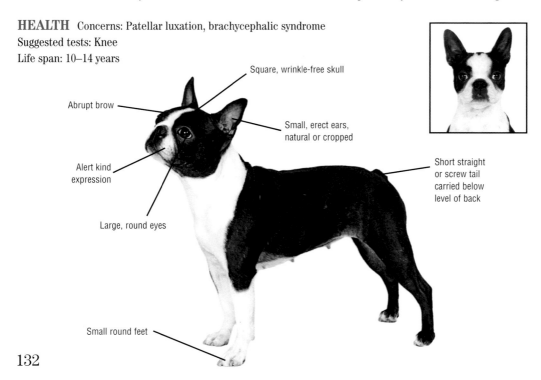

Square, wrinkle-free skull

Abrupt brow

Small, erect ears, natural or cropped

Alert kind expression

Short straight or screw tail carried below level of back

Large, round eyes

Small round feet

Bulldog

Area of Origin: England
Original Function: Bull baiting
Coat: Smooth, short
Color: Brindle, solid white, red, or fawn, or any of these
on a white background
Height: 12–15″
Weight: Male: 50 lb; Female: 40 lb

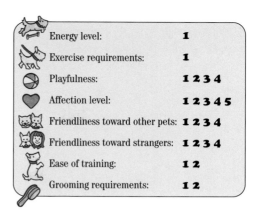

Energy level:	**1**
Exercise requirements:	**1**
Playfulness:	**1 2 3 4**
Affection level:	**1 2 3 4 5**
Friendliness toward other pets:	**1 2 3 4**
Friendliness toward strangers:	**1 2 3 4**
Ease of training:	**1 2**
Grooming requirements:	**1 2**

HISTORY The Bulldog's origin lies in the practice of bull baiting, which originated in England around the 13th century. The dog maddened the bull by grabbing it, usually by the nose, and not releasing. It was thought a bull's meat was tastier if it was baited before being butchered, and some people found it entertaining. In 1835 bull baiting was outlawed. Now a dog without a cause, the breed should have become extinct, except that it had gained so many admirers that they set out to rescue the Bulldog. They selected against ferocity while still accentuating its distinctive physical characteristics. So successful were they that the Bulldog became an extremely amiable character, with a personality not at all like what its "sour mug" would suggest. Its tough, steadfast persona led it to be identified as a national symbol of England.

TEMPERAMENT Bulldogs are jovial, comical, and amiable, among the most docile and mellow of dogs. They are willing to please, though they have a stubborn streak. They are generally good with other pets.

UPKEEP Bulldogs need short walks in cool weather. Overexertion, or exertion in hot, humid weather, is dangerous. Bulldogs cannot swim. Most wheeze, snore, and drool. Tail folds and facial wrinkles should be cleaned daily.

HEALTH Concerns: Brachycephalic syndrome, heart problems, hip dysplasia, dry eye, eyelid problems, internalized tail, shoulder luxation
Suggested tests: Hip, eye, heart
Life span: 8–12 years

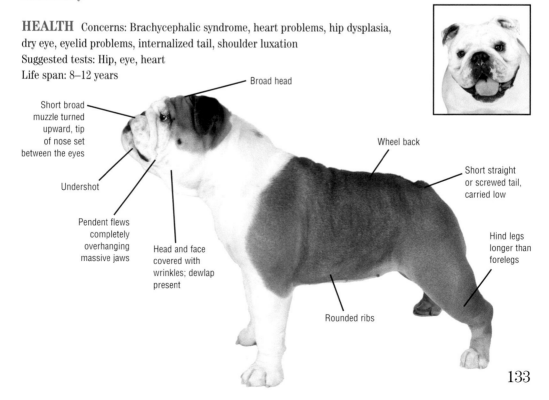

Broad head

Short broad muzzle turned upward, tip of nose set between the eyes

Undershot

Pendent flews completely overhanging massive jaws

Head and face covered with wrinkles; dewlap present

Rounded ribs

Wheel back

Short straight or screwed tail, carried low

Hind legs longer than forelegs

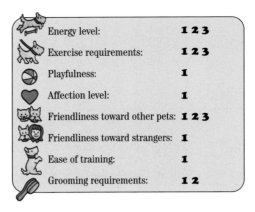

Energy level:	**1 2 3**
Exercise requirements:	**1 2 3**
Playfulness:	**1**
Affection level:	**1**
Friendliness toward other pets:	**1 2 3**
Friendliness toward strangers:	**1**
Ease of training:	**1**
Grooming requirements:	**1 2**

Chinese Shar-Pei

Area of Origin: China
Original Function: Dog fighting, herding, hunting, guardian
Coat: Very harsh, straight, short
Color: Any solid color including sable
Height: 18–20″
Weight: 45–60 lb

HISTORY The Chinese Shar-Pei may have existed in China since 200 B.C., and almost certainly since the 13th century. The Shar-Pei's history is difficult to trace because most records relating to its past were lost when China became communist. At this time Shar-Peis were the working breed of peasant farmers, fulfilling roles of guard dog, wild boar hunter, and dog fighter. After the nation became communist, most of China's dogs were eliminated, with only a few remaining outside of the cities. A few Shar-Peis were bred in British Hong Kong and Taiwan, and the Hong Kong Kennel Club recognized the breed in 1968. Soon after, they became known in America, where so many people wanted one that they went from the brink of extinction to the height of popularity.

TEMPERAMENT Shar-Peis are self-assured, independent, and stubborn. They are devoted to and very protective of family, and reserved, even suspicious, toward strangers. They can be aggressive toward other dogs.

UPKEEP Shar-Peis need a long walk or lively romp daily. The coat needs only weekly brushing, but wrinkles need regular attention to ensure that no irritations develop within the skin folds.

HEALTH Concerns: Eyelid problems, hip dysplasia, patellar luxation, ear problems, allergies
Suggested tests: Hip, knee, eye
Life span: 8–10 years

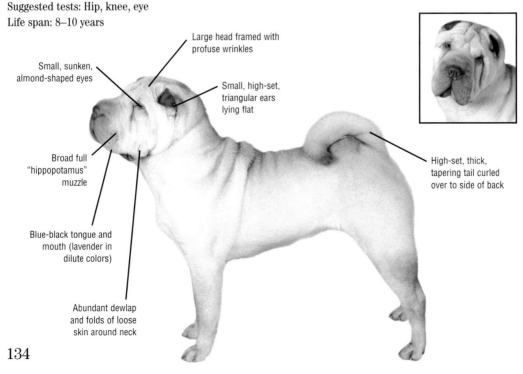

Large head framed with profuse wrinkles

Small, sunken, almond-shaped eyes

Small, high-set, triangular ears lying flat

Broad full "hippopotamus" muzzle

High-set, thick, tapering tail curled over to side of back

Blue-black tongue and mouth (lavender in dilute colors)

Abundant dewlap and folds of loose skin around neck

Chow Chow

Area of Origin: China
Original Function: Guardian, cart puller, food source
Coat: Rough: coarse, medium to long length; Smooth: hard, short to medium length
Color: Solid red, black, blue, cinnamon, and cream
Height: 17–20″
Weight: 45–70 lb

Energy level:		1
Exercise requirements:		1 2
Playfulness:		1
Affection level:		1 2
Friendliness toward other pets:		1 2 3
Friendliness toward strangers:		1
Ease of training:		1
Grooming requirements:		1 2 3 4

HISTORY The Chow Chow has been known in China for thousands of years. Some accounts say it was a hunting dog for the nobility, but after the Imperial hunts were ended only a few descendents were kept in isolated monasteries and wealthy households. Other accounts contend it was a source of fur pelts and food in Manchuria and Mongolia. Only when the dogs were brought to England along with other Chinese importations in the late 1700s was the name Chow Chow adopted. The name is probably derived from a term simply meaning Oriental knick knack and assorted curios, and may have come to be applied to the dogs as they were lumped into a ship's log of cargo. Queen Victoria's interest in these dogs helped draw attention to the breed. The AKC recognized the Chow Chow in 1903.

TEMPERAMENT Chow Chows are reserved, even with family, and somewhat suspicious of strangers. They are serious and protective, and can be aggressive toward other dogs. They are independent and can be stubborn.

UPKEEP Chows need short walks or romps daily, but never in hot weather. The smooth type needs brushing once weekly; the rough type needs brushing at least every other day, daily when shedding. Both types need regular cleaning of facial wrinkles.

HEALTH Concerns: eyelid problems, hip dysplasia, patellar luxation, gastric torsion, elbow dysplasia
Suggested tests: Hip, knee, eye
Life span: 8–12 years

Broad, flat skull

Small, triangular ears carried erect

Padded button of skin above the inner corner of each almond-shaped eye

Tail carried close to back

Blue-black tongue and black mouth

Scowling, dignified expression

Rear legs are almost straight

Round feet

Dalmatian

Area of Origin: Yugoslavia
Original Function: Carriage dog
Coat: Smooth, short
Color: Black or liver spots on white background; spots
   should be round, well defined, and preferably separated.
   Dalmatians are born white and develop spots in 2–3 weeks.
Height: 19–23″
Weight: 40–60 lb

Energy level:	1 2 3 4
Exercise requirements:	1 2 3
Playfulness:	1 2 3
Affection level:	1 2 3 4 5
Friendliness toward other pets:	1 2 3
Friendliness toward strangers:	1 2 3
Ease of training:	1 2 3
Grooming requirements:	1 2

HISTORY The spotted Dalmatian is the most distinctly patterned breed of any dog. It gets its name from Dalmatia, a region in western Yugoslavia, but it probably did not originate there. Although it served a variety of uses, it was as a coach (carriage) dog in Victorian England that the Dalmatian found its niche. The coach dog served both a practical and esthetic role, as it protected the horses from marauding dogs and added a touch of style to the procession. With the advent of the automobile, the Dalmatian lost its place in high society and its popularity declined. It continued as a coach dog for horse-drawn fire engines, and this association led to its adoption as the modern "fire dog."

TEMPERAMENT Dalmatians are playful, eager, and energetic. They can be independent and stubborn. They tend to be reserved toward strangers, and may be aggressive toward strange dogs.

UPKEEP Dalmatians need a long walk or jog, or a vigorous play session, daily. The coat needs occasional brushing to remove dead hair.

HEALTH Concerns: Deafness, urinary stones, allergies
Suggested tests: Hearing
Life span: 12–14 years

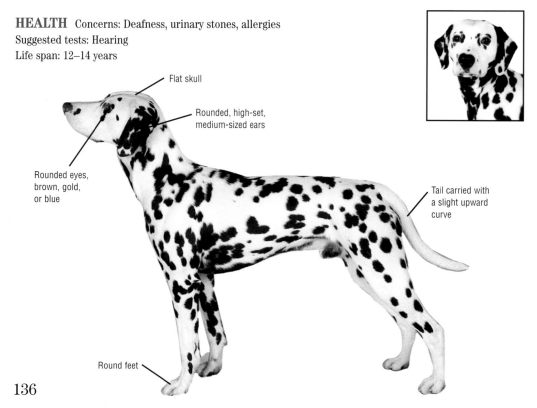

Flat skull

Rounded, high-set,
medium-sized ears

Rounded eyes,
brown, gold,
or blue

Tail carried with
a slight upward
curve

Round feet

Finnish Spitz

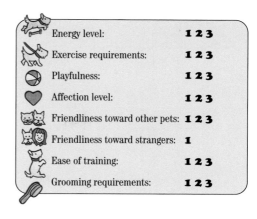

Energy level:	**1 2 3**	
Exercise requirements:	**1 2 3**	
Playfulness:	**1 2 3**	
Affection level:	**1 2 3**	
Friendliness toward other pets:	**1 2 3**	
Friendliness toward strangers:	**1**	
Ease of training:	**1 2 3**	
Grooming requirements:	**1 2 3**	

Area of Origin: Finland
Original Function: Hunting birds and small mammals
Coat: Harsh, straight, medium length
Color: Shades of golden-red (Puppies are born with a black overlay that disappears by around 8 weeks of age.)
Height: Male: 17.5–20″; Female: 15.5–18″
Weight: Male: 31–36 lb; Female: 23–29 lb

HISTORY When early Finno-Ugrian tribes journeyed across Eurasia to Finland, they brought spitz dogs with them. They developed into their own pure strain, but in the early 1800s the influx of other people and dogs threatened to obliterate the pure Finnish Spitz. In the late 1800s, two Finnish sportsmen spotted some dogs that had apparently not been interbred and used them to rescue the breed. It wasn't until the 1960s that Finkies began to be bred in the United States. The breed was recognized by the AKC in 1988. Although prized primarily as a pet in America, it is still used for hunting in Finland. There Finkies hunt the *capercaille* (a turkey-like bird) and black grouse. Their barking talents are so valued that they select a "king barker" each year.

TEMPERAMENT Finnish Spitz are independent and somewhat stubborn. They are alert, inquisitive, and playful, but also sensitive, tending to be devoted to one person. They can be aggressive to strange dogs, and reserved with strange people. They bark a lot.

UPKEEP Finkies need a long walk or a vigorous run daily. The double coat needs brushing one or two times weekly, more often when shedding.

HEALTH Concerns: None noted
Suggested tests: None
Life span: 12–14 years

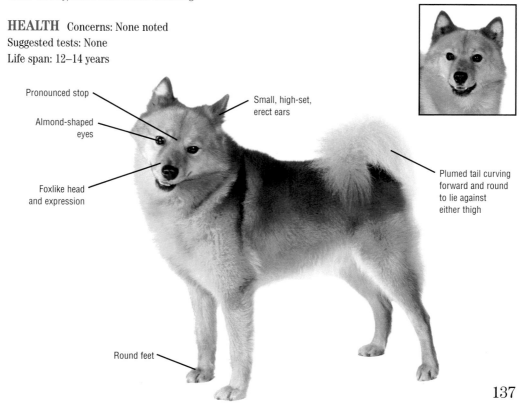

Pronounced stop

Almond-shaped eyes

Foxlike head and expression

Small, high-set, erect ears

Plumed tail curving forward and round to lie against either thigh

Round feet

137

French Bulldog

Area of Origin: France
Original Function: Lap dog
Coat: Smooth, short
Color: Brindle, fawn, white, brindle and white, and any color not specifically mentioned as a disqualification
Height: 11–13″
Weight: Not to exceed 28 lb

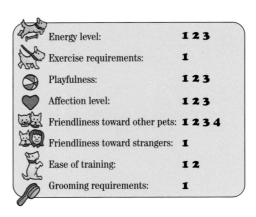

Energy level:	**1 2 3**
Exercise requirements:	**1**
Playfulness:	**1 2 3**
Affection level:	**1 2 3**
Friendliness toward other pets:	**1 2 3 4**
Friendliness toward strangers:	**1**
Ease of training:	**1 2**
Grooming requirements:	**1**

HISTORY Bulldogs, including small Bulldogs, were fairly popular in 19th-century England. When workers went to France in the mid-1800s, they took their small "Toy" Bulldogs with them, where they were a hit with the French women. The dogs were dubbed Bouledogue Français. French breeders sought to consistently produce the erect "bat ears," much to the chagrin of English breeders. By the late 1800s the breed had caught the attention of the upper class, and had moved into some of the finer homes in France. Around this same time, American visitors to France brought several back to America. Amid continued controversy over which ear type was correct, an American club was formed and in 1898 it sponsored gracious shows that attracted high society, and the breed became the darling of wealthy Americans.

TEMPERAMENT French Bulldogs are clowns that enjoy playing as much as cuddling. They are amiable, sweet, companionable, willing to please, but somewhat stubborn.

UPKEEP Frenchies enjoy a romp or short walk, but not in hot weather. They cannot swim. They snore and may wheeze. The coat requires minimal care, but facial wrinkles should be regularly cleaned.

HEALTH Concerns: Brachycephalic syndrome, intervertebral disc disease, hip dysplasia, allergies, patellar luxation
Suggested tests: Hip, knee
Life span: 9–11 years

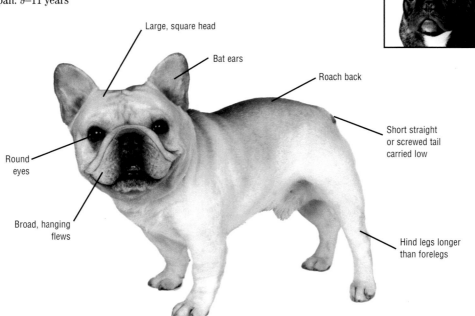

Large, square head

Bat ears

Roach back

Short straight or screwed tail carried low

Round eyes

Broad, hanging flews

Hind legs longer than forelegs

Keeshond

Area of Origin: The Netherlands
Original Function: Barge watchdog
Coat: Harsh, straight, medium length
Color: Mixture of gray, black, and cream. Undercoat is pale, and tips of the outercoat hairs are black. Black muzzle, ears, tail tip, and spectacle lines reaching from the outer eyes corners to the ears. Lighter ruff, shoulders, trousers, legs, feet, and tail plume
Height: Male: 18″ (17–19″ acceptable); Female: 17″ (16–18″ acceptable)
Weight: Male: about 45 lb; Female: about 35 lb

Energy level:	**1 2 3**
Exercise requirements:	**1 2 3**
Playfulness:	**1 2 3**
Affection level:	**1 2 3 4 5**
Friendliness toward other pets:	**1 2 3 4**
Friendliness toward strangers:	**1 2 3 4**
Ease of training:	**1 2 3**
Grooming requirements:	**1 2 3**

HISTORY The Keeshond seems to have been well established in Holland at least since the 18th century as a companion and watchdog. It was often kept as a watchdog on the small vessels navigating the Rhine River. During the French Revolution, the leader of the Patriot faction owned a barge dog named Kees. Kees was chosen to symbolize the Patriot party because the breed was considered a dog of the people. Unfortunately for the Keeshond, as it became known, the Patriots did not prevail, and the breed lost favor and numbers. In 1920 the Baroness van Hardenbroek began an effort to rescue the surviving members. She was so successful at winning friends for the breed that they were in England by 1925 and were recognized by the AKC in 1930. It is now the national dog of Holland.

TEMPERAMENT The Keeshond is energetic and playful, attentive and loving, ready for adventure yet easygoing. It is sensitive and learns readily. It is friendly to all, but nonetheless an alert watchdog.

UPKEEP A good daily walk combined with a vigorous game can satisfy the Keeshond's exercise needs. The double coat needs brushing twice weekly, more when shedding.

HEALTH Concerns: Hip dysplasia, epilepsy, patellar luxation
Suggested tests: Hip, knee
Life span: 12–14 years

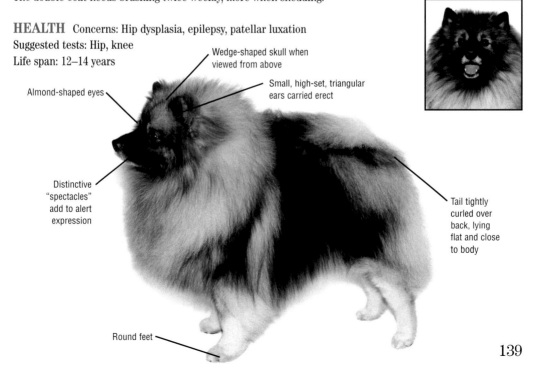

Wedge-shaped skull when viewed from above

Almond-shaped eyes

Small, high-set, triangular ears carried erect

Distinctive "spectacles" add to alert expression

Tail tightly curled over back, lying flat and close to body

Round feet

Non-Sporting Group

Lhasa Apso

Area of Origin: Tibet
Original Function: Companion, watchdog
Coat: Hard, straight, long
Color: Any
Height: 10–11″ (females may be smaller)
Weight: 13–15 lb

Energy level:	**1 2 3**
Exercise requirements:	**1 2**
Playfulness:	**1 2 3**
Affection level:	**1 2 3**
Friendliness toward other pets:	**1 2 3**
Friendliness toward strangers:	**1**
Ease of training:	**1**
Grooming requirements:	**1 2 3 4**

HISTORY The Lhasa Apso is an ancient breed, revered in the villages and monasteries of Tibet. Its history is intertwined with Buddhist beliefs, including the belief that the souls of lamas entered the sacred dogs' bodies upon death. The dogs also performed the role of monastery watchdog, sounding the alert to visitors, thus giving rise to their native name of Abso Seng Kye ("Bark Lion Sentinel Dog"). It is likely that the breed's western name of Lhasa Apso is derived from its native name. The first Lhasa Apsos were seen in the western world around 1930, with some of the first dogs arriving as gifts of the 13th Dalai Lama. The breed was admitted into the AKC Terrier Group in 1935, but reassigned to the Non-Sporting Group in 1959.

TEMPERAMENT Lhasas are independent, stubborn, and bold. They are equally amenable to playing or snoozing. They are somewhat reserved with strangers.

UPKEEP Lhasas need a short walk or a vigorous play session daily. The long coat needs brushing and combing every other day.

HEALTH Concerns: Patellar luxation, eyelid problems, PRA, renal cortical hypoplasia
Suggested tests: Knee, eye
Life span: 12–14 years

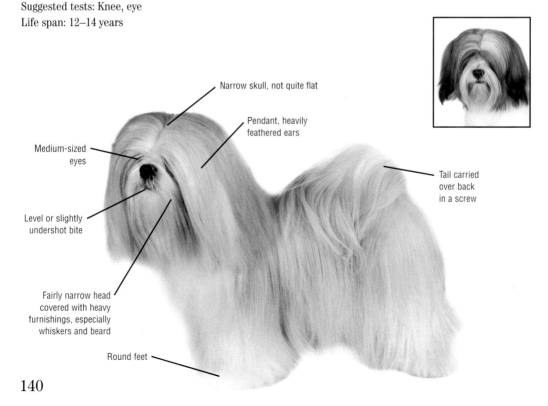

Narrow skull, not quite flat

Pendant, heavily feathered ears

Medium-sized eyes

Tail carried over back in a screw

Level or slightly undershot bite

Fairly narrow head covered with heavy furnishings, especially whiskers and beard

Round feet

Löwchen

Area of Origin: France, Germany
Original Function: Companion
Coat: Slight soft and wavy, long
Color: Any colors or combinations
Height: 12–14″
Weight: 8–18 lb

Energy level:	**1 2 3 4**
Exercise requirements:	**1**
Playfulness:	**1 2 3**
Affection level:	**1 2 3**
Friendliness toward other pets:	**1 2 3 4**
Friendliness toward strangers:	**1 2 3**
Ease of training:	**1 2 3**
Grooming requirements:	**1 2 3 4**

HISTORY Germany, Russia, and France have all laid claim to the Löwchen (or "little lion dog"), which shares common roots with other members of the Bichon family. The exact time and place of its origin is obscure, but dogs resembling the Löwchen, sporting the distinctive lion trim, can be found in 16th-century German art. In the 1960s the breed's numbers had dwindled to perilous numbers; through the efforts of two breeders, several related dogs from Germany were brought to Britain. Because of their small numbers, these dogs were interbred extensively and formed the basis of the breed in Britain as well as America. The Löwchen entered the AKC Miscellaneous Class in 1996 and was admitted as a member of the Non-Sporting Group in 1999.

TEMPERAMENT Löwchens are a mixture of playful spirit and calm soulmate. They are willing to please and responsive to commands, and are devoted to family. Some may bark or dig a lot.

UPKEEP Löwchens need a short to medium-length walk or an active game every day. The coat needs brushing or combing every other day. Clipping to maintain the traditional lion trim must be done every month or two.

HEALTH Concerns: Patellar luxation
Suggested tests: Knee
Life span: 13–15 years

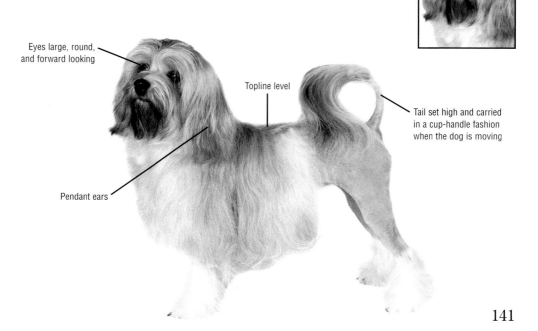

Eyes large, round, and forward looking

Topline level

Tail set high and carried in a cup-handle fashion when the dog is moving

Pendant ears

Energy level:	**1 2** 3
Exercise requirements:	**1 2 3** 4
Playfulness:	**1 2 3** 4
Affection level:	**1 2** 3
Friendliness toward other pets:	**1 2 3** 4
Friendliness toward strangers:	**1 2** 3
Ease of training:	**1 2 3 4 5**
Grooming requirements:	**1 2 3 4 5**

Poodle

Area of Origin: Germany and Central Europe
Original Function: Water retrieving, performer
Coat: Harsh, curly, long
Color: Any solid color
Height: 10–15″
Weight: 12–18 lb

HISTORY The Poodle originated as a water retriever in Germany. Its hair was shorn in a working pattern, clipped close to facilitate swimming, but left longer on the chest for warmth and around joints and tail tip for protection. When the Poodle came to France it was appreciated more as a companion and circus dog than as a retriever. Its characteristic clip was accentuated and a successful effort was made to breed smaller specimens. It eventually became the national dog of France. Many of the early show Poodles were shown in corded coats, in which the hair is allowed to mat in long thin tresses rather than being brushed out. Following World War II the Poodle began its rise to its long-standing placement as one of the most popular dogs in America.

TEMPERAMENT

Miniature: Poodles are amiable, playful, responsive, and obedient. They are sensitive, tending to be devoted to one person, and reserved with strangers. They are good with other pets, but the smaller varieties tend to bark a lot.

Standard: Standard Poodles are playful, adventurous, and responsive. They love to run, swim, and retrieve. They are excellent with other pets and children.

UPKEEP Miniature Poodles need mental and physical exercise every day. Standard Poodles will need long walks, while the smaller varieties can do with short walks or indoor games.

HEALTH Concerns: Eyelid problems, Legg-Perthes, patellar luxation, PRA, epilepsy, sebaceous adenitis (Standards)
Suggested tests: Eye, hip, knee
Life span: 12–15 years

Slight but definite stop

Oval eyes

Level topline

Tail straight and carried up, docked

Long, fine, chiseled muzzle

Small, oval feet

142

Schipperke

Area of Origin: Belgium
Original Function: Barge dog, watchdog, ratter
Coat: Harsh, straight, medium length
Color: Black
Height: Male: 11–13″; Female: 10–12″
Weight: Male: 12–16 lb; Female: 10–14 lb

Energy level:	**1 2 3 4**
Exercise requirements:	**1 2 3**
Playfulness:	**1 2 3**
Affection level:	**1 2 3 4**
Friendliness toward other pets:	**1 2 3**
Friendliness toward strangers:	**1 2**
Ease of training:	**1 2 3**
Grooming requirements:	**1 2**

HISTORY Although small, black, tailless dogs are mentioned in Belgian writings of the 15th and 16th century, definite evidence of Schipperkes is not found until 1690. The Schipperke may have originated as a dog of the boatmen who traveled between Brussels and Antwerp. The Flemish word for boat is *schip*, so Schipperke may mean "little boatman." Another theory of origin is that it was a dog of middle-class households that wanted a small watchdog and ratter. The breed resembles a miniature Belgian Sheepdog, and it is possible that Schipperke derives from the word for shepherd, *scheper*. By the 19th century the breed was so popular in Belgium that it was acknowledged as the national dog. In 1885 Queen Marie Henriette acquired a Schipperke, which drew the elite's attention to the breed. Soon after, the first Schipperkes came to America.

TEMPERAMENT Schipperkes are bold, energetic, independent, and headstrong, happiest when on the lookout for adventure. They are reserved with strangers.

UPKEEP Schipperkes need either a moderate walk on leash or a vigorous romp. The double coat needs weekly brushing, more when shedding.

HEALTH Concerns: Mucopolysacharidosis (MPS), Legg-Perthes, epilepsy
Suggested tests: DNA for MPS, hip
Life span: 13–15 years

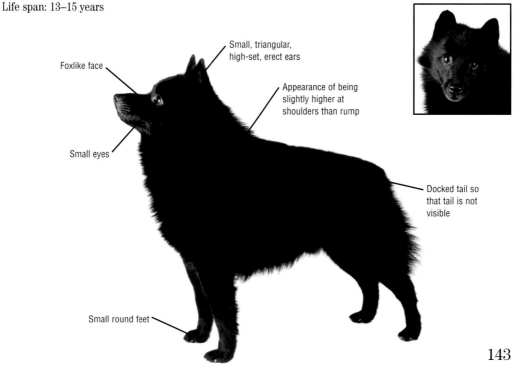

Small, triangular, high-set, erect ears

Foxlike face

Appearance of being slightly higher at shoulders than rump

Small eyes

Docked tail so that tail is not visible

Small round feet

143

Shiba Inu

Area of Origin: Japan
Original Function: Hunting and flushing small game
Coat: Stiff, straight, short to medium length
Color: Red, red sesame (red with black overlay), or black and tan, with cream to white ventral shading
Height: Male: 14.5–16.5″; Female: 13.5–15.5″
Weight: Male: average 23 lb; Female: average 17 lb

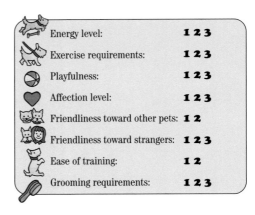

Energy level:	**1 2 3**	
Exercise requirements:	**1 2 3**	
Playfulness:	**1 2 3**	
Affection level:	**1 2 3**	
Friendliness toward other pets:	**1 2**	
Friendliness toward strangers:	**1 2 3**	
Ease of training:	**1 2**	
Grooming requirements:	**1 2 3**	

HISTORY The Shiba Inu may have been used as early as 300 B.C. as a hunting dog. The Shiba is the smallest of the six native Japanese Inu dogs. The name *shiba* may denote "small," or it may mean "brushwood" in reference to the brilliant red brushwood trees that so closely matched the breed's red coat and through which they hunted. The Shiba is sometimes called the "little brushwood dog." Three main types existed, each named for its area of origin: the Shinshu Shiba, the Mino Shiba, and the Sanin Shiba. After World War II the breed was nearly lost, and was further decimated by distemper in 1952. To save the Shiba Inu, the different types were interbred, crossing the heavier-boned dogs from mountainous regions with the lighter-boned dogs from other regions.

TEMPERAMENT Shibas are bold, independent, and headstrong, brimming with self-confidence. Some tend to be domineering, and they may be aggressive with strange dogs. They are territorial, alert, and reserved with strangers. They are quite vocal.

UPKEEP Shiba Inus need a vigorous game, a long walk, or a good run daily. The double coat needs brushing one or two times weekly, more when shedding.

HEALTH Concerns: Patellar luxation, allergies, cataract
Suggested tests: Knee, eye
Life span: 12–15 years

Moderate stop

Small triangular ears, tilting forward

Tail curled over back

Somewhat triangular eyes

Cat feet

Tibetan Spaniel

Area of Origin: Tibet
Original Function: Watchdog, companion
Coat: Silky, medium length
Color: All colors and mixtures; white allowed on feet
Height: About 10″
Weight: 9–15 lb

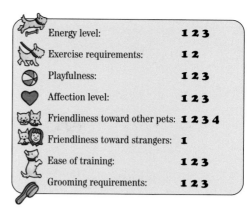

Energy level:	**1 2 3**
Exercise requirements:	**1 2**
Playfulness:	**1 2 3**
Affection level:	**1 2 3**
Friendliness toward other pets:	**1 2 3 4**
Friendliness toward strangers:	**1**
Ease of training:	**1 2 3**
Grooming requirements:	**1 2 3**

HISTORY The Tibetan Spaniel's history is interwoven with Buddhist beliefs that regarded the lion as an important symbol, as it was said to follow Buddha like a dog. The little lionlike dogs that followed their Lama masters were thus regarded as symbols of the sacred lion. The Chinese also cultivated a lion dog, the Pekingese, and dogs from each country were often presented between countries, encouraging some interbreeding. The little dogs perched on the monastery walls and sounded the alarm when strangers approached. They also served as Prayer Dogs, turning the prayer wheels by means of small treadmills. Although the first "Tibby" came to England in the late 1800s, no concerted breeding program was attempted until the 1920s. It wasn't until the 1960s that the breed came to America, and only in 1984 did it receive AKC recognition.

TEMPERAMENT Tibetan Spaniels are independent, bold, and stubborn, but also sensitive, biddable, and happy. They are amiable with other dogs and animals, but reserved with strangers.

UPKEEP The Tibbie's exercise needs can be met by games inside the house or yard, or with a short walk on leash. The coat needs brushing and combing twice weekly.

HEALTH Concerns: Patellar luxation, cataract
Suggested tests: Knee
Life span: 12–15 years

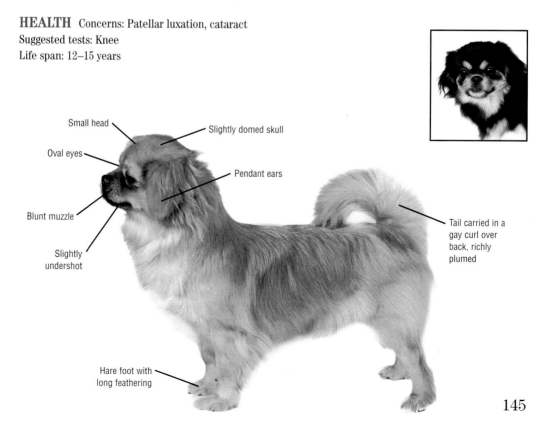

Small head
Slightly domed skull
Oval eyes
Pendant ears
Blunt muzzle
Slightly undershot
Tail carried in a gay curl over back, richly plumed
Hare foot with long feathering

145

Tibetan Terrier

Area of Origin: Tibet
Original Function: Herder, good luck, companion
Coat: Wavy or straight, long
Color: Any
Height: Male: 15–16", Females slightly smaller
Weight: Average 20–24 lb, but may be 18–30 lb

	Energy level:	**1 2 3**
	Exercise requirements:	**1 2 3**
	Playfulness:	**1 2 3**
	Affection level:	**1 2 3 4**
	Friendliness toward other pets:	**1 2 3**
	Friendliness toward strangers:	**1 2**
	Ease of training:	**1 2 3**
	Grooming requirements:	**1 2 3 4**

HISTORY The Tibetan Terrier was bred in Lamaist monasteries nearly 2,000 years ago. The dogs were kept as family companions that might occasionally help out with herding or other farm chores. They were known as "luck bringers." As befitting any bringer of luck, these dogs were never sold, but they were often presented as special gifts of gratitude. In 1920 an Indian physician was given one of the special dogs in return for medical treatment. He obtained additional dogs and began to breed and promote them. The Tibetan Terrier first became recognized in India; by 1937 it had made its way into English dog shows. From there it came to America in the 1950s and was admitted to AKC registration in 1973.

TEMPERAMENT Tibetan Terriers are gentle, amiable, companionable, and willing to please. They tend to be sensitive but somewhat stubborn. They are equally up for an adventure in the field, a game in the yard, or a snooze in the house.

UPKEEP Tibetan Terriers need a moderately long walk or a vigorous game daily. The long coat needs brushing or combing every other day.

HEALTH Concerns: Patellar luxation, epilepsy
Suggested tests: Knee
Life span: 12–15 years

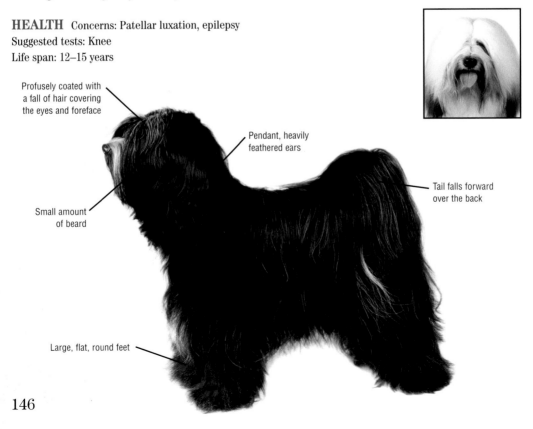

Profusely coated with a fall of hair covering the eyes and foreface

Pendant, heavily feathered ears

Tail falls forward over the back

Small amount of beard

Large, flat, round feet

Australian Cattle Dog

Area of Origin: Australia
Original Function: Cattle herding
Coat: Smooth, hard, fairly short
Color: Blue or blue-mottled with or without other markings;
  red-speckled. Puppies are born white but get their color
  within a few weeks.
Height: Male: 18–20″; Female: 17–19″
Weight: 35–45 lb

Energy level:	**1 2 3 4 5**
Exercise requirements:	**1 2 3 4 5**
Playfulness:	**1 2 3 4**
Affection level:	**1 2 3 4**
Friendliness toward other pets:	**1 2**
Friendliness toward strangers:	**1 2**
Ease of training:	**1 2 3 4 5**
Grooming requirements:	**1 2**

HISTORY In the early 1800s vast land areas in Australia supported unruly cattle that traditional European herding breeds had trouble controlling. Ranchers needed a dog that could travel long distances over rough terrain in hot weather, and that could control cattle without barking (which only served to make wild cattle wilder). Crosses between European herders, Dingos, and assorted other breeds produced a dog with the herding instincts of the Collie and Kelpie, the endurance, ruggedness, and quiet style of the Dingo, and the horse sense and protectiveness of the Dalmatian. As the dogs became increasingly vital to the cattle industry of Queensland, they gained the name Queensland Blue Heelers. They later became known as Australian Heelers, and then Australian Cattle Dogs. A standard for the breed, emphasizing its Dingo characteristics, was drawn up in 1897. The AKC recognized the breed in 1980.

TEMPERAMENT ACDs are smart, hardy, independent, stubborn, tenacious, responsive, energetic, and untiring—all traits essential to a driver of headstrong cattle. They must have a job to do or they can become difficult. They may nip at heels of running children.

UPKEEP The Australian Cattle Dog needs a lot of physical and mental activity. A good jog or long workout every day is essential. The coat needs brushing weekly to remove dead hairs.

HEALTH Concerns: Hip dysplasia, PRA, deafness, elbow dyplasia
Suggested tests: Hearing, eye, hip, elbow
Life span: 10–13 years

Broad skull

Rather small
pricked ears

Tail set low,
hanging in
slight curve

Medium-sized,
oval eyes

Round feet

Australian Shepherd

Area of Origin: United States
Original Function: Sheep herding
Coat: Straight to wavy, medium length
Color: Blue merle, black, red merle, or red, all with
or without white markings and/or tan points
Height: Male: 20–23″; Female: 18–21″
Weight: Male: 50–65 lb; Female: 40–55 lb

Energy level:	**1 2 3 4**
Exercise requirements:	**1 2 3 4 5**
Playfulness:	**1 2 3 4 5**
Affection level:	**1 2 3 4**
Friendliness toward other pets:	**1 2 3**
Friendliness toward strangers:	**1 2**
Ease of training:	**1 2 3 4 5**
Grooming requirements:	**1 2 3**

HISTORY During the 1800s the Basque people of Europe settled in Australia, bringing with them their sheep and sheepdogs. Shortly thereafter, many of these shepherds relocated to the western United States, again, complete with dogs and sheep. American shepherds naturally dubbed their dogs "Australian Shepherds," since that was their immediate past residence. The rugged areas of Australia and western America placed demands on the herding dogs that they had not faced in Europe, but the Basque dogs soon adapted and excelled under these harsh conditions. The breed kept a low profile until the 1950s, when it was featured in a popular trick-dog act that performed in rodeos and was featured in film. A club was formed in 1957, and the first Aussies were registered with the National Stock Dog Registry. The AKC recognized the Australian Shepherd in 1993.

TEMPERAMENT Australian Shepherds are bold, alert, confident, independent, and responsive. Without adequate mental and physical exercise, they can be unruly. They are reserved with strangers. They may try to herd children and small animals. Dogs from working strains are more energetic.

UPKEEP Aussies need a good, strenuous workout every day, preferably combining both physical and mental challenges. The coat needs brushing or combing one to two times weekly.

HEALTH Concerns: Cataract, Collie eye anomaly, hip dysplasia, nasal solar dermatitis, Pelger-Huet syndrome, ivermectin sensitivity
Suggested tests: Eye, hip
Life span: 12–15 years

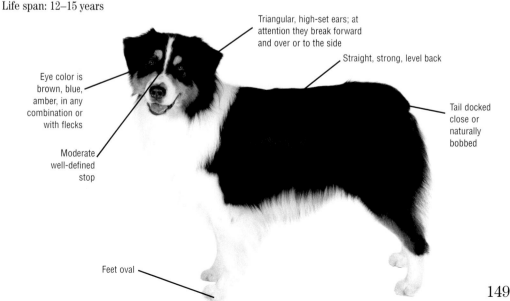

Triangular, high-set ears; at attention they break forward and over or to the side

Straight, strong, level back

Eye color is brown, blue, amber, in any combination or with flecks

Tail docked close or naturally bobbed

Moderate well-defined stop

Feet oval

149

Bearded Collie

Area of Origin: Scotland
Original Function: Sheep herding
Coat: Flat, harsh, long
Color: Any shade of gray or chocolate. White may appear as a blaze, or on tail tip, feet, and chest. Tan points may also occur.
Height: Male: 21–22″; Female: 20–21″
Weight: 45–55 lb

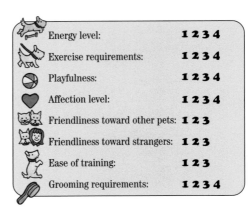

Energy level:	**1 2 3 4**
Exercise requirements:	**1 2 3 4**
Playfulness:	**1 2 3 4**
Affection level:	**1 2 3 4**
Friendliness toward other pets:	**1 2 3**
Friendliness toward strangers:	**1 2 3**
Ease of training:	**1 2 3**
Grooming requirements:	**1 2 3 4**

HISTORY Although dogs strongly resembling Bearded Collies are depicted in art dating from the 18th century, hard evidence of the breed cannot be found until the early 19th century. These dogs were tireless herders of sheep and drovers of cattle over rough terrain in the cold Scottish mists. At first, two strains were known: the Border strain, which was brown and white with a slightly wavy coat, and the Highland strain with a gray and white coat. The two strains have since been interbred and merged into one breed. After World War I the Beardie's value as a stock dog made it difficult for outsiders to acquire one. Despite the difficulty of obtaining foundation stock, eventually a few breeders interested in showing Beardies were able to bring some dogs to England, and then America. The AKC recognized the breed in 1977.

TEMPERAMENT Beardies are exuberant, full of enthusiasm and play. They are biddable, but also independent thinkers with a clownish sense of humor. They especially enjoy herding, and may try to herd children when playing.

UPKEEP Beardies needs a good jog or very long walk daily. The long coat needs brushing or combing every other day.

HEALTH Concerns: Hip dysplasia, epilepsy, colonic disease, pemphigus
Suggested tests: Hip
Life span: 12–14 years

Broad flat skull

Level topline

Low-set tail carried low, with slight upward curve at end

Large, wide-set eyes with soft expression, framed by long eyebrows

Beard

Beauceron

Area of Origin: France
Original Function: Herder, guardian
Coat: Coarse, flat, medium length
Color: Black and tan or black, gray, and tan
(merle with tan points)
Height: Male: 25½–27½″; Female: 24–26½″
Weight: 65–85 lb

Energy level:	**1 2 3 4**
Exercise requirements:	**1 2 3 4**
Playfulness:	**1 2 3**
Affection level:	**1 2 3**
Friendliness toward other pets:	**1 2**
Friendliness toward strangers:	**1**
Ease of training:	**1 2 3 4 5**
Grooming requirements:	**1**

HISTORY The Beauceron originated in the plains area surrounding Paris known as La Beauce, where it was used as a general-purpose farm dog, driving and protecting sheep and sometimes, cattle, and guarding its family. In 1863 two types of plains flock-herding and guarding dogs were differentiated: the long-coated Berger de Brie (Briard) and the short-coated Berger de Beauce (Beauceron). The Société Centrale Canine registered the first Berger de Beauce in 1893, and the first breed club was formed in 1922. The French army employed Beaucerons as messenger dogs on the front lines during both world wars. The breed's extraordinary ability to follow directions, follow trails, and detect mines still makes the Beauceron a respected military and police dog. The AKC admitted the Beauceron into the Miscellaneous class in 2001, and the Herding Group in 2007.

TEMPERAMENT Beaucerons are uncannily intelligent, as well as courageous and calm. They make reliable, thoughtful guardians. They are eager to please family, but may be wary of strangers and do not take to unfamiliar dogs.

UPKEEP Beaucerons need a long walk and good physical and mental workout every day. Coat care is minimal, consisting of brushing once a week.

HEALTH Concerns: Hip dysplasia, gastric torsion
Suggested tests: Hip
Life span: 10–12 years

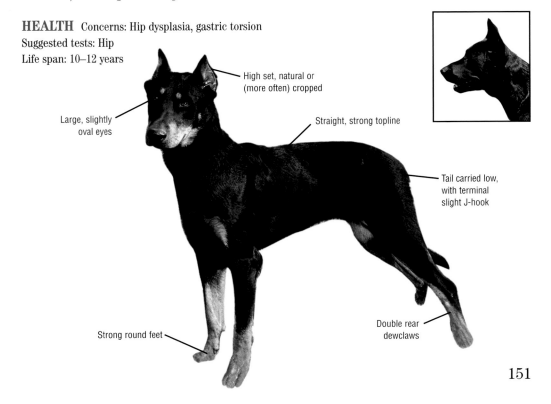

High set, natural or (more often) cropped

Large, slightly oval eyes

Straight, strong topline

Tail carried low, with terminal slight J-hook

Double rear dewclaws

Strong round feet

Belgian Malinois

Area of Origin: Belgium
Original Function: Stock herding
Coat: Straight, fairly short
Color: Rich fawn to mahogany, with black-tipped hairs; black mask and ears
Height: Male: 24–26″; Female: 22–24″
Weight: 60–65 lb

	Energy level:	**1 2 3 4**
	Exercise requirements:	**1 2 3 4 5**
	Playfulness:	**1 2 3 4**
	Affection level:	**1**
	Friendliness toward other pets:	**1 2 3**
	Friendliness toward strangers:	**1**
	Ease of training:	**1 2 3 4 5**
	Grooming requirements:	**1**

HISTORY The Belgian sheepherding breeds, collectively known as Chiens de Berger Belge, shared their early history as general-purpose shepherds and guard dogs of Belgium. The shorthaired variety was developed in the area around Malines, and so became known as the Belgian Malinois. It remains the most popular of the Belgian sheepdog breeds in its native land. Between 1911 and World War II the Malinois enjoyed a good deal of popularity in America. After the war, registrations plummeted, and it was rare to find a Malinois entered in competition. When the breeds were separated in 1959, Malinois registrations began to grow once again. More recently, the Malinois is becoming popular because of its reputation as one of the preeminent police dogs in the world.

TEMPERAMENT Belgian Malinois are intense and high energy. They are alert, smart, and serious, ideal watchdogs. They are aloof with strangers, protective of home and family, and can be aggressive toward other dogs. Some can be domineering.

UPKEEP Malinois need a good jog or a vigorous play session every day, as well as mental challenges. They especially enjoy herding. The coat needs weekly brushing, more when shedding.

HEALTH Concerns: Hip dysplasia, elbow dysplasia
Suggested tests: Hip, elbow
Life span: 10–12 years

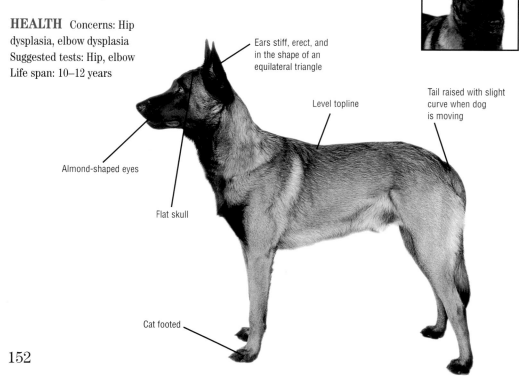

Ears stiff, erect, and in the shape of an equilateral triangle

Level topline

Tail raised with slight curve when dog is moving

Almond-shaped eyes

Flat skull

Cat footed

Belgian Sheepdog

Area of Origin: Belgium
Original Function: Stock herding
Coat: Straight, fairly long
Color: Black
Height: Male: 24–26″; Female: 22–24″
Weight: Male: 55–75 lb; Female: 40–60 lb

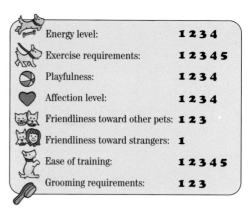

Energy level:	**1 2 3 4**
Exercise requirements:	**1 2 3 4 5**
Playfulness:	**1 2 3 4**
Affection level:	**1 2 3 4**
Friendliness toward other pets:	**1 2 3**
Friendliness toward strangers:	**1**
Ease of training:	**1 2 3 4 5**
Grooming requirements:	**1 2 3**

HISTORY The Belgian Sheepdog was originally known as the Groenendael variation of the Belgian Shepherd, or Chiens de Berger Belge. Like all of the Belgian shepherds, it was a working farm dog expected to both herd and guard. It differed from the others in having a rather long, black coat. In 1910 these dogs were officially dubbed Groenendael after the kennel that had selectively bred the black dogs since 1893. By this time the breed had gained some repute as a police dog, and was already employed in this capacity in America. In World War I they continued to shine as sentry dogs, messengers, and even draft dogs. They once again rose to the challenge of service during World War II. In 1959 the three Belgian shepherd breeds were divided into separate breeds.

TEMPERAMENT Belgian Sheepdogs are playful, alert, watchful, and protective. They are aloof with strangers, and can be aggressive toward other dogs. Some can be domineering. They are intelligent and biddable, but independent. They are protective of home and family.

UPKEEP Belgian Sheepdogs need a lot of strenuous exercise daily. They also profit from mental challenges. The double coat needs brushing and combing twice weekly, more when shedding.

HEALTH Concerns: Seizures, allergies
Suggested tests: Hip
Life span: 10–12 years

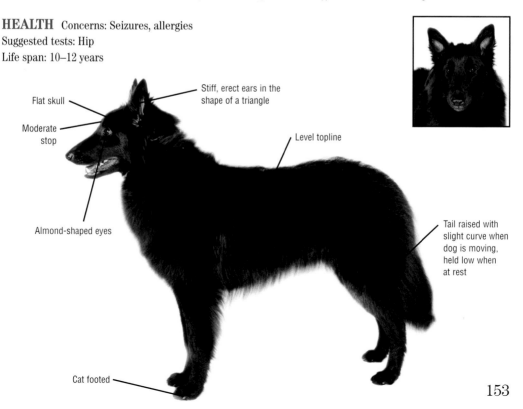

Flat skull

Moderate stop

Almond-shaped eyes

Stiff, erect ears in the shape of a triangle

Level topline

Tail raised with slight curve when dog is moving, held low when at rest

Cat footed

153

Belgian Tervuren

Energy level:		1 2 3 4
Exercise requirements:		1 2 3 4 5
Playfulness:		1 2 3 4
Affection level:		1 2 3 4
Friendliness toward other pets:		1 2 3
Friendliness toward strangers:		1
Ease of training:		1 2 3 4 5
Grooming requirements:		1 2 3

Area of Origin: Belgium
Original Function: Stock herding
Coat: Straight, fairly long
Color: Rich fawn to russet mahogany with black overlay
  (becoming darker with maturity); black mask and ears
Height: Male: 24–26″; Female: 22–24″
Weight: Male: 55–65 lb; Female: 40–50 lb

HISTORY The Belgian Tervuren is one of four Belgian shepherd breeds, all sharing the same origins but distinguished by different coat types and colors. They are the wire-haired Laekenois, the shorthaired Malinois, the long black-haired Groenendael, and the long anything-but-black-haired Tervuren. The Tervuren was named after the village of Tervuren, where one of the breed's earliest proponents lived. The first Terv was registered in America in 1918, but the breed's numbers remained so low that they died out by the Depression. The Tervuren had to be almost recreated after World War II from longhaired offspring of Malinois parents. In 1959 the Belgian Shepherd was divided into three breeds, and the Tervuren was on its way. It is a versatile dog and is used less in guard work, but more in herding, than are their Belgian shepherd counterparts.

TEMPERAMENT Tervurens are alert, watchful, and energetic. They enjoy playing and herding, but may nip at the heels of playing children in an attempt to herd them. They are biddable but independent. They are aloof with strangers, and can be aggressive toward other dogs.

UPKEEP Tervs needs strenuous activity, either a long walk or jog or invigorating play or work session every day. The double coat needs brushing and combing twice weekly, more often when shedding.

HEALTH Concerns: Seizures, hip dysplasia, elbow dysplasia, PRA
Suggested tests: Hip, elbow, eye
Life span: 10–12 years

Flat skull

Stiff, erect, triangular ears

Level topline

Moderate stop

Almond-shaped eyes

Tail raised with slight curve when dog is moving, held low when at rest

Cat footed

Energy level:	**1 2 3 4 5**	
Exercise requirements:	**1 2 3 4 5**	
Playfulness:	**1 2 3 4**	
Affection level:	**1 2 3**	
Friendliness toward other pets:	**1**	
Friendliness toward strangers:	**1 2**	
Ease of training:	**1 2 3 4 5**	
Grooming requirements:	**1 2 3**	

Border Collie

Area of Origin: Great Britain
Original Function: Sheep herder
Coat: Rough: flat to slightly wavy, medium length;
Smooth: short
Color: Solid, bicolor, tricolor, merle, and sable, of various
colors; solid white not allowed
Height: Male: 20–23″; Female: 18–21″
Weight: 30–45 lb

HISTORY In the 1800s a variety of sheepherding dogs with differing herding styles existed in Great Britain. Some were "fetching" dogs, which circle stock and bring them back toward the shepherd. Most of them tended to nip and bark as they fetched. A dog named Hemp distinguished himself in herding trials by herding not by barking and nipping, but by calmly staring at the sheep ("giving eye"), intimidating them into moving. Hemp is considered to be the father of the Border Collie. In 1906 the first standard was drawn up, but unlike the physical standards of most breeds, this was a description of working ability, with no regard to physical appearance. The Border Collie came to America and instantly dazzled serious shepherds with its quick herding and obedience capabilities. In 1995 the AKC recognized the breed.

TEMPERAMENT Border Collies are a bundle of mental and physical energy awaiting a chance to be unleashed. Biddable and smart, they are nonetheless a disastrous housedog if not given a challenging job every day. They are reserved, even protective, toward strangers.

UPKEEP Border Collies do best when they work every day. They need a lot of vigorous physical activity as well as mental activity. The coat needs brushing or combing twice weekly.

HEALTH Concerns: Hip dysplasia, PRA, lens luxation, Collie eye anomaly, seizures, heart defects
Suggested tests: Eye, hip, heart
Life span: 10–14 years

Ears carried erect or semierect

Topline level with
slight arch over loins

Tail set and
carried low

Blue eyes
allowed in
merles only

Feet oval

155

Bouvier des Flandres

Area of Origin: Belgium
Original Function: Cattle herding
Coat: Harsh, tousled, medium to long
Color: From fawn to black, including salt and pepper, gray, and brindle
Height: Male: 24.5–27.5"; Female: 23.5–26.5"
Weight: 69–90 lb

Energy level:	**1 2 3**
Exercise requirements:	**1 2 3 4**
Playfulness:	**1 2**
Affection level:	**1 2 3**
Friendliness toward other pets:	**1 2 3**
Friendliness toward strangers:	**1 2 3**
Ease of training:	**1 2 3**
Grooming requirements:	**1 2 3 4**

HISTORY The Bouvier des Flandres served farmers and cattle merchants in southwest Flanders and on the French northern plain. *Bouvier* means oxherd in French, although the dogs were more often called *Vuilbaard* (dirty beard) or *Koe Hond* (cow dog). Besides its main duty as a cattle drover, the Bouvier was an all-round farm dog, functioning also as a livestock and farm guard and draft dog. The first breed standard, drawn up in 1912, reflected the diversity of types expected of a breed with so many functions. In the midst of rising popularity, most of the Bouviers were lost in World War I. One of the few survivors was of such superior quality that the breed was successfully revived through his progeny. This dog, Ch. Nic de Sottegem, can be found in virtually every modern Bouvier pedigree.

TEMPERAMENT Bouviers are loyal, devoted, fearless, and protective. They are independent and confident, yet biddable and willing to please. They can be domineering. They are reserved, even protective, toward strangers, and can be aggressive with strange dogs.

UPKEEP Bouviers need a good jog or a vigorous play session daily. The harsh coat needs combing twice weekly, plus scissoring and shaping (clipping for pets, stripping for show dogs) every three months.

HEALTH Concerns: Hip dysplasia, elbow dysplasia, heart defects, glaucoma
Suggested tests: Hip, elbow, heart
Life span: 10–12 years

Flat skull

High-set, rough-coated ears; if cropped, triangular

Oval eyes

Thick beard, mustache, and eyebrows

Tail docked to two or three vertebrae, carried upright when in motion

Rounded feet

Briard

Area of Origin: France
Original Function: Herding and guarding sheep
Coat: Coarse, slightly wavy, long
Color: All uniform colors except white (includes black, tawny, and gray shades)
Height: Male: 23–27″; Female: 22–25.5″
Weight: Male: 75–100 lb; Female: 50–65 lb

Energy level:	**1 2 3**
Exercise requirements:	**1 2 3 4**
Playfulness:	**1 2 3**
Affection level:	**1 2 3**
Friendliness toward other pets:	**1 2 3**
Friendliness toward strangers:	**1**
Ease of training:	**1**
Grooming requirements:	**1 2 3 4**

HISTORY Dogs resembling Briards are depicted in art from as long ago as the 8th century, with more definitive evidence by the 14th century. These early dogs were known as Chiens Berger de Brie (Shepherd Dogs of Brie); the name Briard was not used until 1809. Originally herd protectors, Briards were expected to tackle wolves if the need arose. After the French Revolution, which resulted in the land being divided into smaller sectors, it was important that the flocks be kept close to home. The Briard turned its talents to herding, rather than guarding, sheep. Briards came to America very early, with evidence that both Lafayette and Thomas Jefferson imported them. After World War I American soldiers brought some Briards to America, and this was the beginning of the modern American Briard.

TEMPERAMENT Briards are independent and self-assured, but willing to please. Devoted and faithful, they are loving and protective companions. They are reserved with strangers, and can be aggressive with other dogs.

UPKEEP Briards need a long walk or jog daily. The long coat needs brushing or combing every other day or mats can form.

HEALTH Concerns: Hip dysplasia, gastric torsion
Suggested tests: Hip
Life span: 10–12 years

Large, calm eyes

High-set ears; natural ear is straight, lying away from the head and covered with hair, cropped ear is long with rounded tip.

Wide muzzle with mustache and beard

Tail carried low and ending in curve (called a crochet)

Rear toes turn out slightly

Two dewclaws on each hindleg

157

Canaan Dog

Area of Origin: Israel
Original Function: Sentry, messenger, and assistance
Coat: Straight, harsh, flat, short
Color: May be either predominantly white with mask with or without additional color patches, or solid color with or without white trim. The mask should be symmetrical and must completely cover both eyes and ears.
Height: Male: 20–24″; Female: 19–23″
Weight: Male: 45–55 lb; Female: 35–45 lb

Energy level:	**1 2 3**
Exercise requirements:	**1 2 3 4**
Playfulness:	**1 2 3**
Affection level:	**1 2 3**
Friendliness toward other pets:	**1 2 3 4**
Friendliness toward strangers:	**1 2**
Ease of training:	**1 2 3 4**
Grooming requirements:	**1**

HISTORY Canaan Dogs are thought to have originated in the land of Canaan, where they were called Kelev Kanani (Dog of Canaan). When the Israelites left the area 2,000 years ago, they also left the dogs, which became feral. Bedouins captured male puppies to raise as guards and livestock dogs. When the Israeli Defense Force tried to develop service dogs for World War II, the traditional European service breeds could not adapt to the harsh climate. As an experiment, they captured native feral dogs and found they could be trained as sentry dogs, messengers, mine detectors, and even locators of wounded soldiers. The first Canaan Dogs came to America in 1965 and the AKC recognized the breed in 1997.

TEMPERAMENT Canaan Dogs are devoted, willing to please, and tractable. They excel as herders and at almost any task involving dependability and obedience. They are aloof toward strangers and protective of family. They may be aggressive toward strange dogs. They are natural guardians and tend to bark.

UPKEEP Few breeds can claim as pure a working heritage as the Canaan Dog. This dog will not be happy just sitting around. They need lots of exercise and mental and physical challenges. These needs can be met with herding exercise, a long jog, a strenuous game session, along with a challenging training session. They can live outdoors in warm to cool climates, but also make excellent housedogs. The coat needs brushing about once a week to remove dead hairs.

HEALTH Concerns: None reported
Suggested tests: None
Life span: 12–13 years

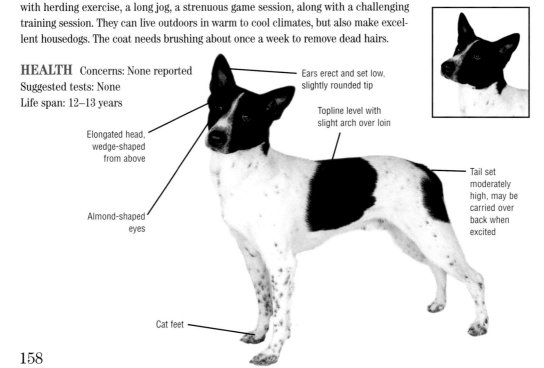

Ears erect and set low, slightly rounded tip

Topline level with slight arch over loin

Elongated head, wedge-shaped from above

Almond-shaped eyes

Tail set moderately high, may be carried over back when excited

Cat feet

Collie

Area of Origin: Scotland
Original Function: Sheep herder
Coat: Rough: straight, harsh, long; Smooth: hard, short
Color: Sable and white; tricolor, blue merle; white
  (predominantly white, preferably with markings)
Height: Male: 24–26″; Female: 22–24″
Weight: Male: 60–75 lb; Female: 50–65 lb

Energy level:	**1 2 3**
Exercise requirements:	**1 2 3**
Playfulness:	**1 2 3**
Affection level:	**1 2 3**
Friendliness toward other pets:	**1 2 3 4**
Friendliness toward strangers:	**1 2 3**
Ease of training:	**1 2 3**
Grooming requirements:	**1 2 3 4**

HISTORY Both rough- and smooth-coated "Scotch" Collies existed by 1800, but they apparently were derived from different crosses. Queen Victoria became enthusiastic about the breed in the late 1800s; under her sponsorship its popularity grew with the upper class. Meanwhile, as sheep herding became more important in America, settlers brought Collies with them to the New World. In 1878 Queen Victoria once again put the breed in the limelight by entering two Collies in the Westminster Dog Show. This provided the impetus for America's social elite to join the Collie clan. Later, the Collie found a champion in Albert Payson Terhune, whose stories about Collies heightened their popularity. Lassie further popularized the breed, helping to make the Rough Collie one of the all-time favorite breeds in America. The Smooth Collie has never shared the popularity of the Rough.

TEMPERAMENT Collies are sensitive, devoted, gentle, and willing to please, a mild-mannered friend to all. They can be stubborn, and may nip at heels in play. They bark a lot.

UPKEEP Collies need a good walk or jog or a fun play session every day. The Smooth coat needs weekly brushing; the Rough needs brushing every other day, more when shedding.

HEALTH Concerns: Collie eye anomaly, PRA, gastric torsion, dermatomyositis, ivermectin sensitivity
Suggested tests: Eye
Life span: 8–12 years

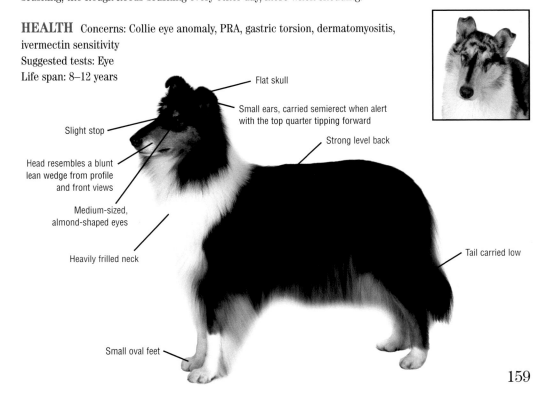

Flat skull

Small ears, carried semierect when alert with the top quarter tipping forward

Slight stop

Strong level back

Head resembles a blunt lean wedge from profile and front views

Medium-sized, almond-shaped eyes

Heavily frilled neck

Tail carried low

Small oval feet

German Shepherd Dog

Area of Origin: Germany
Original Function: Sheep herder, guardian, police dog
Coat: Straight, harsh, fairly short
Color: Most colors, other than white, are permissible
Height: Male: 24–26″; Female: 22–24″
Weight: 75–95 lb

Energy level:	**1 2 3**
Exercise requirements:	**1 2 3 4**
Playfulness:	**1 2**
Affection level:	**1 2 3**
Friendliness toward other pets:	**1 2 3**
Friendliness toward strangers:	**1 2**
Ease of training:	**1 2 3 4 5**
Grooming requirements:	**1 2**

HISTORY The German Shepherd Dog is the result of a conscious effort to produce the ideal shepherd, capable of herding and guarding flocks. In 1899 the Verein fur Deutsche Scharferhunde SV was formed to oversee the breeding of the German Shepherd Dog. Their efforts created a dog that is a capable flock shepherd, but a gifted police dog. When World War I broke out, it was the obvious choice for a war sentry. The greatest boon to the Shepherd's popularity came in the form of two movie stars, Strongheart and Rin Tin Tin. The German Shepherd Dog held the number one spot in American popularity for many years. It remains as one of the most versatile dogs ever created, also proving its worth as a guide dog, search and rescue dog, and contraband detection dog.

TEMPERAMENT German Shepherd Dogs are devoted, dependable, and biddable. They are aloof and suspicious toward strangers, protective of home and family. They can be domineering, as well as aggressive toward other dogs.

UPKEEP Shepherds need a long walk or jog daily, along with challenging mental stimulation. The coat needs brushing one or two times weekly.

HEALTH Concerns: Hip dysplasia, elbow dysplasia, panosteitis, vWD, degenerative myelopathy, skin problems, dermatitis, hemangiosarcoma, pannus, cataract, gastric torsion, perianal fistulas
Suggested tests: Hip, elbow, vWD, eye
Life span: 10–12 years

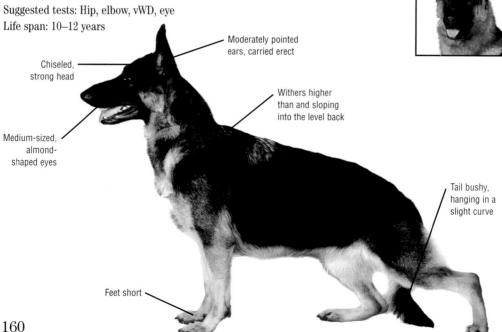

Moderately pointed ears, carried erect

Chiseled, strong head

Withers higher than and sloping into the level back

Medium-sized, almond-shaped eyes

Tail bushy, hanging in a slight curve

Feet short

Old English Sheepdog

Area of Origin: England
Original Function: Sheep herding
Coat: Shaggy, neither straight nor curly, long
Color: Any shade of gray, grizzle, blue, blue merle with or without white markings
Height: Male: 22″ and up; Female: 21″ and up
Weight: Male: 70–90 lb; Female: 60–80 lb

Energy level:	**1 2 3**	
Exercise requirements:	**1 2 3**	
Playfulness:	**1 2 3**	
Affection level:	**1 2 3 4 5**	
Friendliness toward other pets:	**1 2 3 4 5**	
Friendliness toward strangers:	**1 2 3 4**	
Ease of training:	**1**	
Grooming requirements:	**1 2 3 4**	

HISTORY The Old English Sheepdog was the answer to the need for a strong dog capable of defending the flocks and herds from the wolves that existed at one time in England. By the middle of the 19th century these dogs were used mainly to drive cattle and sheep to market. As working dogs, they were exempt from dog taxes, but their tails had to be docked as proof of their occupation. This custom continues in modern times, and has led to their nickname, Bobtail. The Old English was recognized by the AKC in 1905. Although the modern Bobtail is very similar to the early specimens, it has a more profuse coat and more compact body. Popularity as a pet was slower to grow, until the 1970s when the breed became a favorite media animal.

TEMPERAMENT Old English Sheepdogs are easygoing and peaceful. They have a comic streak, and can be stubborn. They are devoted to and protective of family members, sometimes tending children as flock members.

UPKEEP Old English Sheepdogs require a moderate walk or a vigorous romp daily. The coat needs brushing or combing every one to two days or it will form mats. The coat may tend to track in debris.

HEALTH Concerns: Hip dysplasia, gastric torsion, ear infections, retinal detachment, cataract, PRA, cerebellar ataxia
Suggested tests: Hip, eye
Life span: 10–12 years

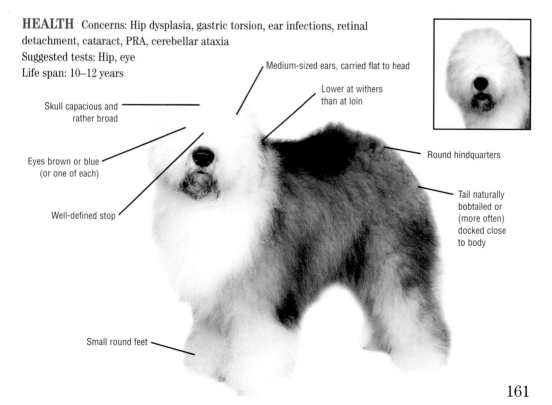

Skull capacious and rather broad

Medium-sized ears, carried flat to head

Lower at withers than at loin

Eyes brown or blue (or one of each)

Round hindquarters

Well-defined stop

Tail naturally bobtailed or (more often) docked close to body

Small round feet

Polish Lowland Sheepdog

Area of Origin: Poland
Original Function: Sheep herding
Coat: Fairly straight, long
Color: All colors are acceptable
Height: Male: 18–20″; Female: 17–19″
Weight: 30–35 lb

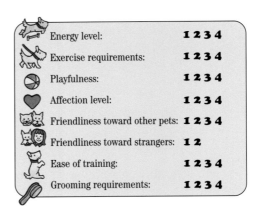

Energy level:	**1 2 3 4**
Exercise requirements:	**1 2 3 4**
Playfulness:	**1 2 3 4**
Affection level:	**1 2 3 4**
Friendliness toward other pets:	**1 2 3 4**
Friendliness toward strangers:	**1 2**
Ease of training:	**1 2 3 4**
Grooming requirements:	**1 2 3 4**

HISTORY The Polish Lowland Sheepdog is known in much of the world as the Polski Owczarek Nizinny (pronounced *pole-ski off-chair-ick na-gin-nee*), and even in America it goes by its nickname, the PON. While large flock-guarding dogs staved off large predators, the smaller PONs worked with shepherds to move and control sheep, and also kept watch against intruders. Unlike larger dogs, they didn't scare the sheep. In the late 1800s and early 1900s several PONs left the plains to live and work on large estates. When Germany invaded Poland in 1939, most dogs had to be abandoned. Only about 150 PONs remained after World War II, but several fanciers sought to reconstitute the breed. In 2001 the PON was admitted to the AKC under the English translation of its name, Polish Lowland Sheepdog.

TEMPERAMENT PONs are lively and loyal, affectionate to family but wary of strangers. They have an independent and even willful side. They bark a lot.

UPKEEP PONs need a good workout every day. The coat needs considerable care, preferably brushing every couple of days.

HEALTH Concerns: None reported
Suggested tests: None
Life span: 10–14 years

Heart-shaped drop ears

Level topline

Oval eyes

Short low-set tail, no longer than two vertebra; may be docked

Oval feet

Heavy bone

Puli

Area of Origin: Hungary
Original Function: Sheep herding
Coat: Wavy or curly, clumping to form long cords
Color: Solid black, rusty black, gray, and white
Height: Male: ideally 17″; Female: ideally 16″
Weight: 25–35 lb

Energy level:	**1 2 3 4**
Exercise requirements:	**1 2 3**
Playfulness:	**1 2 3**
Affection level:	**1 2**
Friendliness toward other pets:	**1 2 3**
Friendliness toward strangers:	**1**
Ease of training:	**1 2**
Grooming requirements:	**1 2 3 4 5**

HISTORY Around the 9th century the Magyar tribes came from the eastern Urals to occupy the central Danube area, bringing with them various sheepdogs, including small black dogs that could turn a sheep by jumping on its back. After the decimation of Hungary by invaders in the 16th century, the country was repopulated by people, sheep, and dogs from Western Europe. These dogs interbred with the native Pulik to produce the Pumi, and then the Puli and Pumi were interbred so much that the original Puli breed was nearly lost. In the early 1900s an effort began to resurrect the Puli. In 1935 the United States Department of Agriculture imported several Pulik to improve herding dogs in America. This effort was thwarted by the war, but the breed's working ability became known in America. The AKC recognized the breed in 1936.

TEMPERAMENT Pulik are busy and curious, and also headstrong and tough. Alert and watchful, they are protective of family and can be aggressive toward other dogs. They bark a lot.

UPKEEP Pulik need a good walk or a lively game every day. The nonshedding coat can be brushed or corded; if brushed, it needs brushing every one to two days. If corded, the cords must be regularly separated and bathing and drying are time-consuming.

HEALTH Concerns: Hip dysplasia
Suggested tests: Hip
Life span: 10–15 years

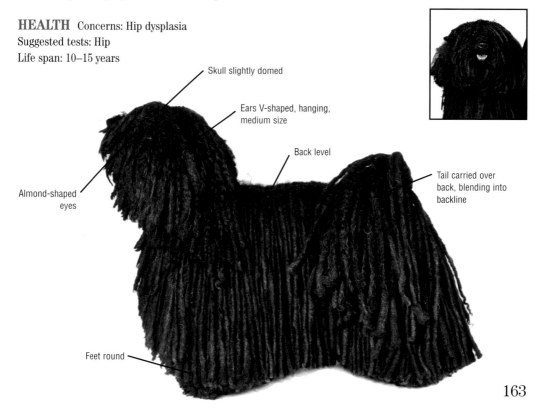

Skull slightly domed

Ears V-shaped, hanging, medium size

Back level

Tail carried over back, blending into backline

Almond-shaped eyes

Feet round

Shetland Sheepdog

Area of Origin: Origin: Scotland (Shetland Islands)
Original Function: Sheep herder
Coat: Harsh, straight, long
Color: Black, blue merle, and sable, marked with varying
   amounts of white and/or tan
Height: 13–16″
Weight: About 20 lb

Energy level:	1 2 3	
Exercise requirements:	1 2 3	
Playfulness:	1 2 3	
Affection level:	1 2 3	
Friendliness toward other pets:	1 2 3 4	
Friendliness toward strangers:	1	
Ease of training:	1 2 3 4 5	
Grooming requirements:	1 2 3 4	

HISTORY The Shetland Sheepdog almost certainly is derived from ancestral Collie-type dogs, which then were further developed on the Shetland Islands. The paucity of vegetation favored smaller livestock, and the animals needed to herd them were proportionately smaller. In a land with few fences, an adept herder was essential to keep livestock away from cultivated land. Due to their isolation from the rest of the world, the breed was able to breed true in a comparatively short time. The British naval fleet used to frequent the Islands for maneuvers, and often bought puppies to take home to England. Early dogs were referred to as Toonie dogs (*toon* being the local Shetland word for farm), but they were initially shown (around 1906) as Shetland Collies. Collie fanciers objected to the name, so it was changed to Shetland Sheepdog.

TEMPERAMENT Shetland Sheepdogs are obedient, quick to learn, willing to please, and sensitive. They are gentle, playful, amiable, and companionable with family; but reserved, and often timid toward, strangers. They bark a lot.

UPKEEP Shelties need a good walk, short jog, or active game and training session daily. The thick coat needs brushing or combing every other day.

HEALTH Concerns: Dermatomyositis, Collie eye anomaly, PRA, cataract, hip dysplasia, Legg-Perthes, patellar luxation, ivermectin sensitivity
Suggested tests: Eye, hip
Life span: 12–14 years

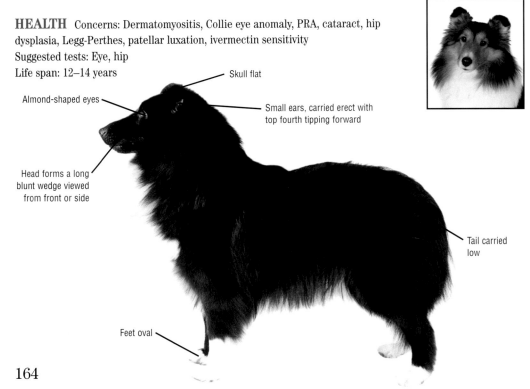

Skull flat

Almond-shaped eyes

Small ears, carried erect with
top fourth tipping forward

Head forms a long
blunt wedge viewed
from front or side

Tail carried
low

Feet oval

Welsh Corgi (Cardigan)

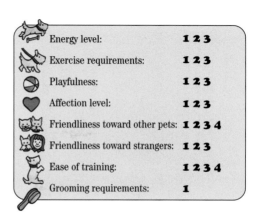

Energy level:	**1 2 3**	
Exercise requirements:	**1 2 3**	
Playfulness:	**1 2 3**	
Affection level:	**1 2 3**	
Friendliness toward other pets:	**1 2 3 4**	
Friendliness toward strangers:	**1 2 3**	
Ease of training:	**1 2 3 4**	
Grooming requirements:	**1**	

Area of Origin: Wales
Original Function: Cattle drover
Coat: Straight, slightly harsh, fairly short
Color: All shades of red, sable, and brindle; also blue merle or black, both with or without tan or brindle points; white flashings common
Height: 10.5–12.5″
Weight: Male: 30–38 lb; Female: 25–34 lb

HISTORY The Cardigan Welsh Corgi was brought from central Europe to Cardiganshire, South Wales, centuries ago. In a time when the land available to tenant farmers was determined by how much acreage their cattle occupied, it was to the farmer's advantage to have scattered, far-ranging stock. Thus, a dog that would drive, rather than herd, the cattle was an invaluable aid, and the Corgi stepped right into this role, nipping at the cattle's heels and ducking their kicks. The original Corgis were supposed to measure a Welsh yard from nose to tail tip, and the breed was sometimes called the "yard-long dog" or "Ci-llathed." The first Cardigans were shown around 1925. Until 1934 the Cardigan and Pembroke Corgis were considered one breed, and interbreeding between the two was common. AKC recognized the breed in 1935.

TEMPERAMENT Fun-loving and high-spirited, yet easygoing, Cardigans are devoted and amusing companions. They are inclined to bark, and can be scrappy with other dogs.

UPKEEP Cardigans need a moderate walk or vigorous play session every day. The coat needs brushing once a week to remove dead hair.

HEALTH Concerns: Hip dysplasia, degenerative myelopathy
Suggested tests: Hip
Life span: 12–14 years

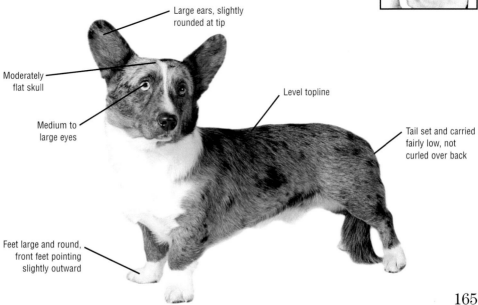

Large ears, slightly rounded at tip

Moderately flat skull

Medium to large eyes

Level topline

Tail set and carried fairly low, not curled over back

Feet large and round, front feet pointing slightly outward

Welsh Corgi (Pembroke)

Energy level:	**1 2 3**
Exercise requirements:	**1 2 3**
Playfulness:	**1 2 3**
Affection level:	**1 2 3 4**
Friendliness toward other pets:	**1 2 3 4**
Friendliness toward strangers:	**1 2 3 4**
Ease of training:	**1 2 3 4**
Grooming requirements:	**1**

Area of Origin: Wales
Original Function: Cattle drover
Coat: Straight, slightly harsh, fairly short
Color: Red, sable, fawn, black and tan, all with or without white flashings
Height: 10–12″
Weight: Ideally, male: 27 lb, Female: 25 lb

HISTORY The Corgi was an essential helper to the farmers of South Wales. Although it certainly shares its past with the Cardigan Welsh Corgi, the Pembroke was developed separately, in Pembrokeshire, Wales. Only in 1926 did a club form and the breed enter the show ring. The obvious differences between the Pembroke and Cardigan were troublesome to judges—the Pembroke is smaller, with sharper features, a more foxlike expression, and characteristically no tail. In 1934 the Cardigan and Pembroke Corgis were divided into two separate breeds, after which the Pembroke soared in popularity. Its appeal was heightened when it became the favorite of King George VI, and subsequently, Queen Elizabeth II. By the 1960s the Pembroke had become one of the most poplar pet breeds all over the world, but especially in Britain.

TEMPERAMENT Pembroke Welsh Corgis are quick-witted, fun-loving, and companionable. They are devoted and willing to please. They can nip at heels in play, and many bark a lot.

UPKEEP Pembrokes need a moderate walk on leash or a good play and training session daily. Coat care consists only of brushing once a week.

HEALTH Concerns: Intervertebral disc disease, hip dysplasia, epilepsy, degenerative myelopathy
Suggested tests: Hip
Life span: 11–13 years

Flat skull

Eyes oval and medium sized

Ears erect, tapering to rounded point

Head foxy in shape and appearance

Tail docked as short as possible

Forearms turned slightly inward

Feet oval, turned neither in nor out

Dogue de Bordeaux

Area of Origin: France
Original Function: Guardian, hunter, fighter
Coat: Short, fine
Color: All shades of fawn, with or without a dark mask
Height: Male: 23–27″; Female: 23–26″
Weight: Male: at least 110 lb; Female: at least 99 lb

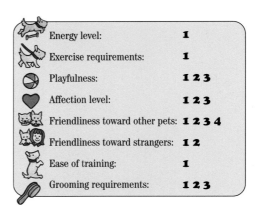

Energy level:	**1**
Exercise requirements:	**1**
Playfulness:	**1 2 3**
Affection level:	**1 2 3**
Friendliness toward other pets:	**1 2 3 4**
Friendliness toward strangers:	**1 2**
Ease of training:	**1**
Grooming requirements:	**1 2 3**

HISTORY The Dogue de Bordeaux originated in France as a guardian, hunter, and fighter. Its ancestry is uncertain, but it may descend from the Tibetan Mastiff, the Roman Mollusus, or the Spanish Alano. The Dogue participated in bull and bear baiting, boar hunting, and cattle guarding. It was prized by both nobility and working class. Those owned by the nobility met untimely deaths during the French Revolution. However, the working-class Dogues survived. The first specific mention of the breed was not until 1863. Dogues came to America in the latter part of the 20th century, but remained obscure until the breed received some recognition as the star of the 1980s movie *Turner and Hooch*. The breed entered the AKC Miscellaneous class in 2006.

TEMPERAMENT Dogues are devoted, affectionate, playful, and even-tempered. They can be stubborn. Without early training, they may not be good with other dogs. Some can be reserved, but not aggressive, with strangers. They are natural and courageous guardians.

UPKEEP Dogues require weekly or so brushing, plus bathing every two to three weeks to prevent odors. Wrinkles should be cleaned regularly and eyes should be wiped several times daily. They require minimal exercise and do not tolerate heat well.

HEALTH Concerns: Gastric torsion, heart disease, lymphoma, kidney disease, hip dysplasia, elbow hygroma, arthritis, epilepsy, entropion, osteosarcoma
Suggested tests: Heart, hips, eyes, thyroid
Lifespan: 5–7 years

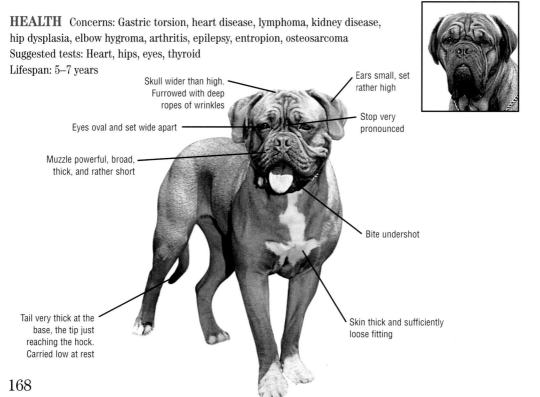

Skull wider than high. Furrowed with deep ropes of wrinkles

Ears small, set rather high

Eyes oval and set wide apart

Stop very pronounced

Muzzle powerful, broad, thick, and rather short

Bite undershot

Tail very thick at the base, the tip just reaching the hock. Carried low at rest

Skin thick and sufficiently loose fitting

Irish Red and White Setter

Area of Origin: Ireland
Original Function: Bird setting and retrieving
Coat: Medium length, straight
Color: White with solid red patches. Flecking permitted around the face and on lower legs.
Height: Male: 24–26″; Female: 22–24″
Weight: Male: 65–75 lb; Female: 55–65 lb

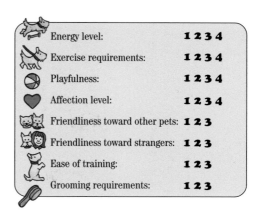

Energy level:	**1 2 3 4**	
Exercise requirements:	**1 2 3 4**	
Playfulness:	**1 2 3 4**	
Affection level:	**1 2 3 4**	
Friendliness toward other pets:	**1 2 3**	
Friendliness toward strangers:	**1 2 3**	
Ease of training:	**1 2 3**	
Grooming requirements:	**1 2 3**	

HISTORY Setters almost certainly derived from Spaniels, but only in the 16th century did the term "setting dogs" come into use. Although the beginnings of the Irish Red and White Setter are unknown, paintings and writings from the 17th and 18th centuries seem to describe the breed. By the 18th century, setters were popular with Ireland's sporting gentry. Red and White Setters were well established, with different strains in different areas of Ireland. Some were patched, some had a shower of red ticking, and some were nearly all white or all red. Originally, the Red and White Setters were more popular than the solid red ones, but by 1900 the red and whites were hard to find. After World War I efforts began to revive the breed; they entered the AKC's Miscellaneous class in 2007.

TEMPERAMENT Red and White Setters are high-spirited, friendly, and active, sometimes to the point of being boisterous. They get along well with other dogs and animals.

UPKEEP These hunting dogs need a good jog or tiring run every day. The coat requires brushing once weekly.

HEALTH Concerns: Cataracts
Suggested tests: Eye, DNA for canine leucocyte adhesion deficiency
Lifespan: 10–12 years

Skull broad and domed

Stop distinct but not exaggerated

Eyes round

Ears set level with eyes, lying close to the head

Topline level

Muzzle square

Chest deep

Tail of moderate length, carried level with or below the back

169

Norwegian Buhund

Area of Origin: Norway

Original Function: Protection, cattle and sheep herding, hunting large animals

Coat: Medium length; outercoat thick and hard, undercoat soft

Color: Black or wheaten (light cream to bright orange), the latter with or without black tips or mask. As little white as possible.

Height: Male: 17–18″; Female: 16–17″

Weight: Male: 31–40 lb; Female: 26–35 lb

Energy level:	**1 2 3 4**	
Exercise requirements:	**1 2 3**	
Playfulness:	**1 2 3 4**	
Affection level:	**1 2 3 4**	
Friendliness toward other pets:	**1 2 3 4**	
Friendliness toward strangers:	**1 2 3**	
Ease of training:	**1 2 3**	
Grooming requirements:	**1 2 3**	

HISTORY The Norwegian Buhund's ancestors rode with the Vikings over land and sea, even accompanying them to the grave where they were expected to continue serving their masters in the afterlife. The Buhund's services included protecting farms, herding cattle and sheep, and hunting large animals such as bear. The Buhund belongs to the large spitz family of dogs. *Bu* means homestead, or may refer to the mountain huts shepherds lived in. Buhunds are still used to gather sheep from the rocky mountainsides in Norway. They often bark to make the sheep move so they can spot them behind boulders, then bring them down on their own. The first Buhund shows were held in the 1920s in Norway. A national Buhund club was formed in the United States in 1983, and the breed was admitted to the AKC Miscellaneous Class in 2007.

TEMPERAMENT Buhunds are active, affectionate, and playful. As members of the Spitz family, they can be independent, but they are among the most trainable of Spitz breeds. They are good watchdogs but may bark a lot.

UPKEEP Buhunds need a long walk or a good play session every day, preferably both. The coat requires brushing once weekly, more when shedding twice yearly.

HEALTH Concerns: Cataracts
Suggested tests: Eye, hip
Lifespan: 11–13 years

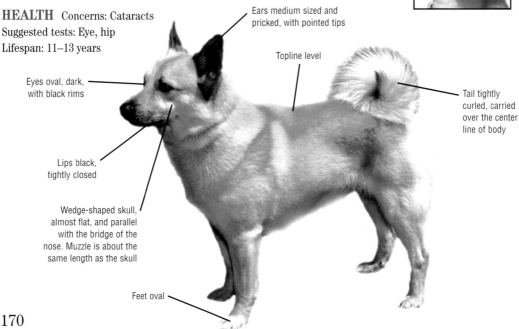

Ears medium sized and pricked, with pointed tips

Topline level

Tail tightly curled, carried over the center line of body

Eyes oval, dark, with black rims

Lips black, tightly closed

Wedge-shaped skull, almost flat, and parallel with the bridge of the nose. Muzzle is about the same length as the skull

Feet oval

Pyrenean Shepherd

Area of Origin: France
Original Function: Herding
Coat: Rough: long or demi-long, harsh with slight wave;
 Smooth: medium short, fine and soft
Color: Fawn to gray; brindle, merle, black, black with white
 markings not exceeding 30% of the body surface
Height: Rough: Male: 15–18″; Female 15–18″;
 Smooth: Male: 15–21″; Female 15–20″
Weight: 18–32 lb; with just enough flesh to cover the bones

Energy level:	**1 2 3 4 5**	
Exercise requirements:	**1 2 3 4**	
Playfulness:	**1 2 3 4**	
Affection level:	**1 2 3 4**	
Friendliness toward other pets:	**1 2 3 4**	
Friendliness toward strangers:	**1 2 3**	
Ease of training:	**1 2 3 4 5**	
Grooming requirements:	**1 2 3**	

HISTORY The exact origin of the Pyrenean Shepherd, or Berger des Pyrénées, is not known but is probably ancient. Such dogs are mentioned in Medieval writings and described more thoroughly in the ensuing centuries. They were used solely for herding, not protection, traditionally working in conjunction with Great Pyrenees dogs, which provided protection against predators. Pyrenean Shepherds served during World War II as couriers, search and rescue dogs, and alert dogs. They were considered among the best breeds of those used in the war effort. The breed was first granted official recognition in 1926, in France. Although a few Pyrenean Shepherds accompanied sheep to North America in the 1800s, not until a century later were efforts made to foster the breed in the United States. They joined the AKC Miscellaneous Class in 2007. The breed has two varieties, the rough face (and coat) and the smooth face (and coat).

TEMPERAMENT Pyrenean Shepherds are extremely energetic and alert. They are obedient and devoted, always ready to join in activities. They are aloof with strangers, but good with other dogs and pets.

UPKEEP Pyrenean Shepherds need a long walk or a vigorous play session every day, preferably both. The rough face's coat needs brushing once a week; the smooth face's coat even less.

HEALTH Concerns: None
Suggested tests: Hip, eye
Lifespan: 14–15 years

Eyes almond shaped

Head triangular, rather small

Ears cropped or uncropped.
Ears are cropped straight across
and stand erect. Uncropped
ears are semi-prick

Feet oval

Level back with slightly arched loin

Tail docked,
natural bob, or
naturally long.
The natural tail
has a crook at
the end

Dewclaws single in front,
either single, double,
or absent in rear

171

Redbone Coonhound

Area of Origin: United States
Original Function: Raccoon hunting
Coat: Smooth, short
Color: Solid red preferred; dark muzzle and small amount of white on brisket and feet permissible
Height: Male: 22–27"; Female: 21–26"
Weight: 45–65 lb

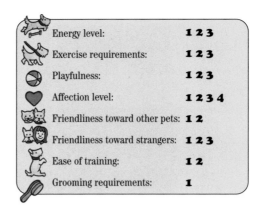

Energy level:	**1 2 3**
Exercise requirements:	**1 2 3**
Playfulness:	**1 2 3**
Affection level:	**1 2 3 4**
Friendliness toward other pets:	**1 2**
Friendliness toward strangers:	**1 2 3**
Ease of training:	**1 2**
Grooming requirements:	**1**

HISTORY The Redbone derives from foxhound ancestors. The breed's development was heavily influenced by Georgia hunters in the 1840s. As more coon hunters became interested in the breed, they set about to create a faster, hotter-nosed dog that was even quicker to locate and tree raccoons. They crossed the existing dogs with later imports of hot, swift Red Irish Foxhounds. These early dogs were sometimes called Saddlebacks because they tended to be red with black saddles. The black saddle was bred out and the breed became known as Redbone Coonhounds, either in recognition of its color or after Peter Redbone, a Tennessee promoter of the breed. In 1902 the Redbone became the second coonhound breed recognized by the United Kennel Club. In 2001 the AKC admitted it into its Miscellaneous Class.

TEMPERAMENT Redbones are generally easygoing gentle dogs. They are eager to please but can become bored with formal training. Redbones get along well with people, children, and dogs. They tend to follow a scent, and have a loud voice when excited.

UPKEEP Redbones need a long walk or a vigorous workout daily. Coat care consists of weekly brushing.

HEALTH Concerns: None noted
Suggested tests: None
Life span: 12–14 years

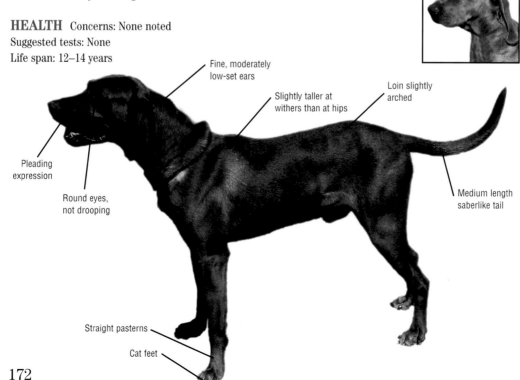

Fine, moderately low-set ears

Slightly taller at withers than at hips

Loin slightly arched

Pleading expression

Round eyes, not drooping

Medium length saberlike tail

Straight pasterns

Cat feet

Swedish Vallhund

Area of Origin: Sweden

Original Function: Cattle herding, vermin control, watchdog

Coat: Harsh, medium length

Color: Sable in colors of gray through red. Lighter harness markings are essential. A well-defined mask with lighter hair around eyes, on the muzzle and under the throat is highly desirable. White markings, if any, should not be in excess of one third of the dog.

Height: Male: 12.5–13.5″; Female: 11.5–12.5″

Weight: 22–35 lb

Energy level:	**1 2 3** 4
Exercise requirements:	**1 2 3** 4
Playfulness:	**1 2 3** 4
Affection level:	**1 2 3 4 5**
Friendliness toward other pets:	**1 2** 3
Friendliness toward strangers:	**1 2 3** 4
Ease of training:	**1 2 3** 4
Grooming requirements:	**1** 2

HISTORY The Swedish Vallhund has been used for centuries, possibly since Viking times, as an all-around farm dog, herding cattle, controlling vermin, and acting as watchdog. Little is known of its early history. By 1942 the breed was almost extinct. Two Swedish enthusiasts, Count Bjorn Von Rosen and Karl Gustav Zettersten, located one male and three females and used them to revive the breed. The breed was recognized by the Swedish Kennel Club in 1943. At this time, the SV was known as the Svensk Vallhund (Swedish Vallhund), where *Vallhund* meant "herding dog." In 1964, with the Swedish standard revised, the breed became known as *Västgötaspets* after the Swedish province Vastergotland, where the revived breeding program originated. They were admitted into the AKC Miscellaneous Class in 2006.

TEMPERAMENT Vallhunds are alert, active, courageous, and eager to please. They are devoted to family and friendly to strangers.

UPKEEP Vallhunds need a moderate walk and a good play session every day. The coat requires brushing once weekly.

HEALTH Concerns: None noted

Suggested tests: Eye, hips

Lifespan: 15–17 years

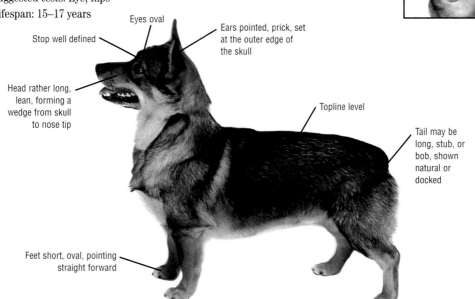

Eyes oval

Stop well defined

Ears pointed, prick, set at the outer edge of the skull

Head rather long, lean, forming a wedge from skull to nose tip

Topline level

Tail may be long, stub, or bob, shown natural or docked

Feet short, oval, pointing straight forward

Definitions of Medical Conditions

ABBREVIATIONS USED IN THIS BOOK

ASD: Atrial septal defects

BAER: Brainstem Auditory Evoked Potential

CEA: Collie eye anomaly

CHD: Canine hip dysplasia

CPRA: Central progressive retinal atrophy

CTP: Thrombocytopenia

HOD: Hypertrophic osteodystrophy

KCS: Keratoconjunctivitis sicca

MPS: Mucopolysacharidosis

MVI: Mitral valve insufficiency

OCD: Osteochondritis dissecans

PDA: Patent ductus arteriosus

PFK: Phosphofructokinase deficiency

PK: Pyruvate kinase deficiency

PPM: Persistent pupillary membrane

PRA: Progressive retinal atrophy

VKH: Vogt-Koyanagi-Harada-like syndrome

vWD: von Willebrand's disease

Achondroplasia: (Skeletal) Type of dwarfism with shortened limbs.

Acute moist dermatitis (pyotraumatic dermatitis): (Skin) Also called "hot spots." An area of extremely itchy and inflamed skin that is exacerbated by the animal licking at it.

Addison's (hypoadrenocorticism): (Endocrine) Insufficient secretions by the adrenal cortex. Special Diagnostics: blood test.

Albinism: (Multiple sites) Deficiency of pigmentation, resulting in white fur color, pink skin, and pink or blue eyes.

Amyloidosis: Abnormal deposits of a type of protein (amyloid) in various tissues or organs, resulting in progressive organ dysfunction. In renal amyloidosis (which is the most common type in some breeds) the kidney is the site of amyloid accumulation. Special Diagnostics: biopsy.

Ataxia: (Neural) Incoordination.

Atrial septal defects (ASD): (Heart) Hole in the wall separating the right and left atria of the heart. Special Diagnostics: ultrasound of heart.

Axonal dystrophy: (Neural) Problem affecting neural impulses.

Basenji enteropathy: (Digestive) Also called immunoproliferative small intestinal disease. Severe progressive intestinal malabsorption resulting in protein loss, intractable diarrhea, and loss of body weight.

Blood platelet abnormality: An abnormality in the clotting components of the blood.

Brachycephalic syndrome: (Respiratory) Group of upper airway abnormalities, including stenotic nares and elongated soft palate, often seen in flat-faced dogs.

Canine hip dysplasia (CHD): (Skeletal) Abnormal development of the hip assembly wherein the head of the femur does not fit snugly into the pelvic socket. Special Diagnostics: hip radiograph.

Cardiomyopathy: (Heart) Enlargement of the heart resulting from dysfunction of the heart muscle. Special Diagnostics: heart ultrasound.

Cataract: (Eye) Opacities of the lens of the eye; juvenile cataracts are present in young dogs and have a hereditary basis. Special Diagnostics: ophthalmoscopic exam.

Cauda equina syndrome: (Neural) Group of neurological signs resulting from compression of the spinal nerves of the lumbosacral vertebral region. Special Diagnostics: radiographs.

Central progressive retinal atrophy (CPRA): (Eye) Degeneration of retinal cells beginning with those serving central areas of vision. Special Diagnostics: retinoscopic exam, electroretinogram.

Cerebellar abiotrophy: (Brain) Degeneration of brain neurons in the cerebellum, resulting in progressively worsening incoordination. Caused by a recessive gene.

Cerebellar ataxia: (Neural) An undefined problem in the part of the brain that controls coordination.

Ceroid lipofuscinosis: (Neural) Metabolic disorder in which a waste product (ceroid lipofuscin) accumulates in the cells, eventually destroying brain cells and leading to abnormal neurologic function.

Cherry eye: (Eye) Tear gland protrudes beyond the "third eyelid," resulting in bright red bulge in the inner corner of the eye.

Chondrodysplasia: (Skeletal) Type of dwarfism. Special Diagnostics: radiograph of foreleg.

Ciliary dyskinesia: Deformation and rigidity of cells that normally have cilia, small hair-like appendages that aid in movement of the cells themselves (such as sperm) or mucous (such as in the lungs and nose).

Colitis: (Digestive) Inflammation of the large bowel, often resulting in diarrhea.

Collie eye anomaly (CEA): (Eye) Congenital abnormalities of varying degrees found in the posterior part of the eye. Special Diagnostics: ophthalmoscopic exam.

Colonic disease: (Digestive) Disease of the large bowel.

Compulsive behavior: (Neural) Behavior that is repeated to excess, often in inappropriate situations, to the extent that it interferes with normal behavior.

Copper toxicosis: (Liver) Accumulation of copper in the liver, resulting in chronic hepatitis. Special Diagnostics: DNA test.

Corneal erosion: (Eye) Loss of the outer layers of the cornea; if progressive, can lead to ulceration of the cornea.

Corneal opacities (corneal dystrophy): (Eye) Deposits of white or silver spots on the central area of the cornea.

Craniomandibular osteopathy: (Skeletal) Abnormal development of the jaw involving excessive bone formation. Due to a recessive gene.

Cushing's (hyperadrenocorticism): (Endocrine) Excessive secretion of cortisol from the adrenal gland.

Deafness: (Ear) Inability to hear in either one or both ears. Special Diagnostics: BAER test (Brainstem Auditory Evoked Potential).

Degenerative myelopathy: (Neural) Progressive loss of coordination and strength beginning in the hind quarters.

Demodicosis: (Skin) Generalized demodectic mange, a condition caused by the *Demodex* mite to which certain breeds are more susceptible. Special Diagnostics: skin scraping.

Dermatitis: (Skin) An inflammation of the skin.

Dermatomyositis: (Skin and muscle) Systemic connective disease causing inflammation of both skin and muscles.

Dermoid sinus: (Skin) Tubular indentation leading from the skin along the midline of the back, sometimes extending into the spinal canal. Special Diagnostics: visual exam.

Diabetes mellitus: (Endocrine system) Deficiency in insulin production or utilization causing glucose to be utilized abnormally.

Digital hyperkeratosis: (Skin) Thickening of the foot pads leading to cracked, infected, and painful pads.

Distichiasis: (Eye) Abnormal origin of eyelashes along the lid margin, often resulting in irritation to the eye.

Ectropion: (Eye) Eversion of the eyelids, so that they roll out from the eye, leaving a gap between the lid and eye.

Elbow dysplasia (ununited anconeal process): (Skeletal) Elbow joint laxity resulting from improper development, and eventually leading to arthritic changes. Special Diagnostics: elbow radiograph.

Elongated soft palate: (Respiratory) Abnormal extension of the soft palate, such that it interferes with breathing.

Entropion: (Eye) Inversion of the eyelids, so that they roll inward, often irritating the eye.

Epilepsy: (Neural) Brain disorder resulting in periodic seizures.

Esophageal achalasia: (Digestive) Failure of the walls of the esophagus to relax enough to allow food to pass into the stomach, resulting in regurgitation of ingested food. Special Diagnostics: radiograph or endoscopic exam.

Eye lid problems: (Eyes) Any condition in which the eyelids are misshapen and interfere with the health of the eye.

Familial nephropathy: (Kidney) Hereditary impaired kidney function.

Fanconi's syndrome: (Kidney) Reabsorptive defects resulting in kidney failure. Special Diagnostics: urine test, renal clearance test.

Follicular dermatitis: (Skin) An inflammation of the hair follicles.

Fragmented coronoid process: (Skeletal) Developmental flaw in which a fragment of the ulnar bone of the foreleg never fuses, leaving a chip floating in the region of the elbow, resulting in lameness. Special Diagnostics: radiograph of elbow.

Gastric torsion (gastric dilation-volvulus): (Digestive) Often called "bloat"; twisting of the stomach that traps the stomach contents and gases, and can lead to death if untreated. It is most common in large, deep-chested breeds.

Glaucoma: (Eye) Increased intraocular pressure, most often due to an abnormality in the drainage of aqueous fluid from the eye. Special Diagnostics: tonometry (eye pressure measurement).

Globoid cell leukodystrophy: (Neural) Gradual destruction of white matter in the brain, eventually fatal.

Glycogen storage disease: (Metabolic) Deficiency of enzymes required for normal glycogen metabolism, resulting in variable symptoms including weakness. Special Diagnostics: blood test.

Hemangiosarcoma (Blood vessels, skin, organs): Malignant tumor of the lining of blood vessels, often affecting the heart or spleen, and usually fatal.

Hemivertebra: (Skeletal) Partially formed wedge-shaped vertebrae. Special Diagnostics: radiographs.

Hemophilia A (factor VIII deficiency): (Blood) Deficiency in clotting factor VIII leading to excessive bleeding. Special Diagnostics: blood test.

Hemophilia B (factor IX deficiency): (Blood) Deficiency in clotting factor IX leading to excessive bleeding. Special Diagnostics: blood test.

Histiocytosis: (Multiple sites) Rapidly progressive malignant cancer infiltrating many parts of body, often including the lungs, liver, spleen, and central nervous system. Special Diagnostics: radiograph and biopsy.

Hot spots: (Skin) A skin infection usually caused by a cycle of itching, licking, and biting.

Hydrocephalus: (Brain) Increased accumulation of cerebrospinal fluid in the ventricles of the brain. Highest incidence in toy and brachycephalic breeds. Special Diagnostics: radiograph of skull; also MRI or CT scan.

Hypertrophic osteodystrophy (HOD): (Skeletal) Inflammation of the bone growth plates during periods of rapid growth in large breeds, resulting in lameness. Special Diagnostics: radiographs.

Hypoglycemia: (Metabolic) Abnormally low level of glucose in the blood. Special Diagnostics: blood test.

Hypomyelination: (Neural) Abnormally low amounts of myelin (the insulator surrounding nerve fibers) in peripheral nerves, resulting in weakness of limbs. Special Diagnostics: nerve conduction tests.

Hypothyroidism: (Endocrine) Decreased production of thyroid hormone, often caused by an autoimmune response. One of the most widespread disorders in dogs. Special Diagnostics: blood test.

Inguinal hernia: (Body wall) Protrusion of abdominal contents through the inguinal canal.

Intervertebral disk disease: (Skeletal) Abnormality of the cartilaginous disks that normally provide cushioning between the vertebra. Special Diagnostics: radiograph of spine.

Intracutaneous cornifying epithelioma: Benign skin tumor.

Iris coloboma: (Eye) Pits in the iris (colored portion) of the eye.

Ivermectin sensitivity: (Neural) A mutation that causes a defect in the blood-brain barrier and renders affected dogs overly sensitive to certain drugs, including ivermectin. Ivermectin is used in many heartworm and mite therapies, but is usually safe at normal doses. A DNA test can detect the mutation.

Keratoconjunctivitis sicca (KCS): (Eye) Decreased tear production of the eye causing a dry eye and damage to the cornea. Special Diagnostics: tear test.

Lacrimal duct atresia: (Eye) Abnormally small or malformed duct that normally drains tears from the eye. Special Diagnostics: tear drainage test.

Laryngeal paralysis: (Respiratory) Paralysis of the larynx, causing noisy or difficult breathing.

Legg-Perthes disease (Legg-Calvé-Perthes): (Skeletal) Destruction of the head of the femur bone due to decrease in blood supply. Special Diagnostics: radiograph of hip.

Lens luxation: (Eye) Displacement of the lens of the eye. Special Diagnostics: retinoscopic exam.

Lick granuloma: (Skin, behavior) Thickened area of skin, usually of a leg, caused by excessive and often compulsive licking.

Lip fold pyoderma: (Skin) Infection of the skin around the folds of the lips due to moisture and bacteria.

Lumbar-sacral syndrome: (Neural) Group of neurological signs resulting from compression of the spinal nerves of the lumbosacral vertebral region. Special Diagnostics: radiographs.

Lupus: (Skin or multiple) Autoimmune condition affecting the skin or entire system.

Lymphedema: (Lymph system) Swelling due to improper drainage of the lymph system.

Lymphosarcoma: A malignant cancer affecting the lymph system.

Mast cell tumors: A type of malignant skin cancer, usually appearing as lumps.

Megaesophagus: (Digestive) Paralysis and enlargement of the esophagus, resulting in regurgitation of food. Special Diagnostics: radiograph of throat.

Meningitis: Inflammation of the membranes surrounding the brain and spinal cord.

Mitral valve insufficiency (MVI): (Heart) Degeneration of the mitral valve of the heart, allowing blood to flow backward into the left atrium and resulting in enlargement of the heart. Special Diagnostics: auscultation (listening to heart), radiographs or ultrasound of heart.

Mucopolysacharidosis IIIB (MPS IIIB): Recessively inherited fatal disease resulting from the lack of an enzyme, giving rise to brain disease. Special Diagnostics: DNA test.

Muscular dystrophy: (Muscles) Progressive degeneration of skeletal muscles. Special Diagnostics: blood test and electromyography.

Narcolepsy: (Neural) Condition in which the dog has episodes of sudden deep sleep.

Narrow palpebral fissure: (Eye) Abnormally small opening between the eyelids.

Nasal solar dermatitis: (Skin) Inflammation of the nose surface from exposure to sunlight.

Necrotic myelopathy: (Neural) Loss of insulating myelin from the spinal cord, resulting in paralysis.

Open fontanel: (Skeletal) Incomplete closure of the bones of the skull, resulting in a soft spot on top of the head.

Osteochondritis dissecans (OCD): (Skeletal) Degeneration of bone underlying the cartilage of joint areas, most often seen in young, fast growing dogs of larger breeds. Special Diagnostics: radiographs of suspected joints; often inconclusive.

Osteosarcoma: (Skeletal) Malignant bone cancer. More common in large and giant breeds. Special Diagnostics: radiograph and biopsy of suspected area.

Otitis externa: (Ear) Infection of the outer ear, including the ear canal. Most common in dogs with long, hanging ears receiving little ventilation.

Pancreatic insufficiency: (Digestive) Inadequate digestive enzyme production by the pancreas, resulting in poor nutrient absorption. Special Diagnostics: blood test.

Pancreatitis: (Pancreas) Inflammation of the pancreas.

Pannus (chronic superficial keratitis): (Eye) Potentially blinding inflammation of the cornea, including abnormal growth of vascularized pigment over the cornea.

Panosteitis: (Skeletal) Excessive formation of bone growth of different maturity around some joints of young dogs resulting in intermittent lameness. Special Diagnostics: radiograph of suspected joints.

Patellar luxation: (Skeletal) Abnormally shallow groove in the knee, so that the knee cap (patella) slips in and out of position, causing lameness. Though seen in many breeds, it is most common in small dogs. Special Diagnostics: radiograph of stifle (knee)—though not always necessary.

Patent ductus arteriosus (PDA): (Heart) Failure of the embryonic blood vessel connecting the pulmonary artery to the aorta to go away in the postnatal dog, resulting in improper circulation of blood. Special Diagnostics: auscultation (listening to the heart), radiographs or ultrasound of heart.

Pelger-Huet: (Blood) Abnormal development of neutrophils. Special Diagnostics: blood test.

Pemphigus: (Skin) Autoimmune disease of the skin.

Perianal fistula: (Skin) Draining tract in the area around the anus.

Persistent pupillary membrane (PPM): (Eye) Developmental abnormality in which a few strands of iris tissue may be stretched over the pupillary opening.

Persistent right aortic arch: (Heart) Failure of the embryonic right aorta to go away in the postnatal dog, resulting in constriction of the esophagus. Special Diagnostics: radiograph of esophagus.

Phosphofructokinase deficiency: (Blood) Deficiency in a red blood cell enzyme (phosphofructinase), causing a type of anemia. Special Diagnostics: blood test; DNA test (English Springer Spaniel).

Polyneuropathy: (Neural) Weakness or paralysis of limbs due to problems in peripheral nerves.

Portacaval shunt (portasystemic shunt): (Liver) Failure of embryonic blood vessel within the liver to go away in the postnatal dog, allowing blood to bypass the liver processing, resulting in neurological and other symptoms. Special Diagnostics: radiograph or ultrasound of liver, ammonia tolerance test.

Premature closure of distal radius: (Skeletal) One side of the radius bone of the foreleg stops growing before the other, resulting in malformation of the leg. Special Diagnostics: radiograph.

Progressive posterior paresis: (Neural) Paralysis of one or both hind limbs.

Progressive retinal atrophy (PRA): (Eye) A family of diseases all involving gradual deterioration of the retina. Symptoms begin with night blindness and progress to total blindness. Special Diagnostics: retinoscopic exam or electroretinogram; DNA test in some breeds.

Prolapse of nictitans gland: (Eye) Hypertrophy of the gland of the third eyelid.

Protein wasting disease: (Digestive) Loss of protein through the kidneys (protein-losing nephropathy: PLN) or intestines (protein-losing enteropathy: PLE) resulting in diarrhea and weight loss. Special Diagnostics: blood and urine tests, including urine protein creatinine ratio.

Pug dog encephalitis: (Neural) Fatal inflammation of the brain seen in some young Pugs.

Pulmonic stenosis: (Heart) Congenital narrowing of the opening in the heart between the right ventricle and pulmonary artery, eventually causing right-sided heart failure. Special Diagnostics: auscultation (listening to heart), ultrasound or angiography.

Pyruvate kinase deficiency (PK): (Blood) Deficiency of a particular red blood cell enzyme (pyruvate kinase), causing premature destruction of red blood cells and resulting in anemia. Special Diagnostics: blood test; DNA test (Basenji).

Rage syndrome: (Neurological) Sudden episode of aggression without apparent warning.

Renal cortical hypoplasia: (Kidney) Failure of both kidneys to function normally. Special Diagnostics: urine test.

Renal disease: (Kidney) Unspecified kidney disease.

Renal dysplasia: (Kidney) Abnormal development and function of the kidneys.

Retinal detachment: (Eye) Detachment of the retina from the back of the eye, leading to partial visual loss. Special Diagnostics: retinoscopic exam.

Retinal dysplasia: (Eye) Abnormal development of the retina. Special Diagnostics: retinoscopic exam, electroretinogram.

Retinal folds: (Eye) Folds in the retinal layer, often caused by differences in growth of different layers of the eye. Many disappear with maturity.

Schnauzer comedo syndrome (follicular dermatitis): (Skin) Skin disease characterized by blackhead formation.

Scotty cramp: (Neuromuscular) Periodic generalized cramping of the muscles, usually precipitated by excitement; associated with problem with metabolism of a neurotransmitter (serotonin).

Sebaceous adenitis: (Skin) Inflammation of the sebaceous glands, resulting in scaly debris, hair loss, and infection. Special Diagnostics: skin biopsy.

Seborrhea: (Skin) Abnormal secretions form the sebaceous glands, causing dandruff or greasy scaling.

Shaker syndrome: (Neural) Episodic diffuse muscular tremors and incoordination, seen mostly in some white dogs.

Shar-pei fever: (Systemic) Recurrent bouts of unexplained fever, often with joint inflammation.

Shoulder luxation: (Skeletal) Dislocation of the shoulder. Special Diagnostics: radiograph of shoulder.

Skinfold dermatitis: (Skin) Skin infection caused by moisture and bacteria trapped within deep folds of skin.

Skin fragility (Ehlers-Danlos syndrome, cutaneous asthenia): (Skin) Tissue disease causing extremely fragile skin. Special Diagnostics: skin biopsy.

Spiculosis: (Skin) Abnormally bristle- or spike-like hairs interspersed among normal hairs.

Stenotic nares: (Respiratory) Abnormally small nostrils, sometimes interfering with breathing.

Subvalvular aortic stenosis: (Heart) Abnormally narrow connection between the left ventricle and the aorta, eventually leading to heart failure. Special Diagnostics: auscultation (listening to heart), ultrasound of heart.

Syringomyelia: (Neural) Cyst formation in the spinal cord, which destroys the center of the cord and causes pain, stiffness, and weakness.

Tailfold dermatitis: (Skin) Infection of the skin around the tail due to excessive skin folds or an "inset" tail.

Tetralogy of Fallot: (Heart) Pulmonic stenosis combined with a defect in the ventricular septum results in de-oxygenated blood being pumped throughout the body. Special Diagnostics: blood test, blood gas measurements, and ultrasound of heart.

Thrombocytopenia (CTP): (Blood) Lowered platelet number in the blood, leading to excessive bleeding. Special Diagnostics: blood test.

Thrombopathy: (Blood) Abnormality of blood platelets.

Tracheal collapse: (Respiratory) Loss of rigidity of the trachea, leading to weakness of the trachea and susceptibility to collapse. Most common in small breeds. Special Diagnostics: radiograph or endoscopic exam of trachea.

Trichiasis: (Eye) Eyelashes arising from normal origin are misdirected into the eye, causing irritation.

Tricuspid valve dysplasia: (Heart) Malformation of one of the valves in the heart.

Urethral prolapse: (Urinary) Protrusion of part of the mucosal lining of the urethra through the external urethral orifice.

Uric acid calculi: (Urinary) Bladder stones resulting from an abnormality in the excretion of uric acid. Special Diagnostics: radiograph.

Urolithiasis: (Urinary) Formation of urinary stones. Special Diagnostics: radiograph.

Vaginal hyperplasia: (Reproductive) Vaginal tissue becomes overly enlarged, especially with estrogen stimulation, sometimes protruding through the vulva. More common in giant breeds.

Vogt-Koyanagi-Harada-like syndrome (VKH) (uveodermatologic syndrome): (Many structures) Autoimmune disease leading to progressive destruction of melanin containing tissues, including those in the eye and skin.

von Willebrand's disease (vWD): (Blood) Defective blood platelet function resulting in excessive bleeding, caused by a deficiency in clotting factor VIII antigen (von Willebrand factor). Special Diagnostics: blood test.

Wobbler's syndrome (cervical vertebral instability): (Skeletal) Abnormality of the neck vertebrae causing rear leg incoordination or paralysis.

Zinc responsive dermatosis: (Skin) Thickened, scaly skin condition that responds to zinc supplementation.

Definitions of Color Terms

Belton: Intermingled colored and white hairs.

Black and tan: Black body with tan on feet and lower legs, cheeks, and eyebrows.

Blue: Gray.

Brindle: Irregular vertical bands of dark hair overlaid on lighter hair.

Grizzle: Intermingled gray or black with white hair; or may refer to a pattern with a dark body but lighter legs, chest, and face with a widows peak mask.

Harlequin: Spotted coloration, used specifically for the Great Dane.

Hound colored: Black, tan, and white, with a black saddle.

Liver: Brown.

Merle: Dark patches overlaid on a lighter background of the same pigment type; also called dapple.

Particolor: Spotted.

Piebald: Black patches on a white background.

Roan: Intermingled white and dark hairs.

Sable: Black-tipped hairs in which the undercoat is of lighter color.

Saddle: Dark patch over the back.

Spectacles: Dark markings around the eyes.

Tan pointed: Tan points on feet and lower legs, cheeks, and eyebrows.

Ticking: Small flecks of coloring on a white background.

Tricolor: Tan pointed dog, usually black and tan, with white feet, tail tip, chest, and possibly muzzle and collar.

Wheaten: Pale yellow color.

Genetic Health Resources

AKC Canine Health Foundation
www.akcchf.org
888-682-9696
Current research

American Veterinary Medical Association
www.avma.org
Information on finding specialists

Canine Eye Registration Foundation (CERF)
www.vmdb.org
Eye clearances

Canine Health Information Center (CHIC)
www.caninehealthinfo.org
Parent club-suggested tests and list of tested dogs

Institute for Genetic Disease Control in Animals
www.vetmed.ucdavis.edu/gdc/gdc.html
603-456-2350
Tumor registry; other information

Morris Animal Foundation
www.morrisanimalfoundation.org
800-243-2345
Current research

Orthopedic Foundation for Animals (OFA)
www.offa.org
573-442-0418
Hip, elbow, thyroid, cardiac, and several other disease registries

Pennsylvania Hip Improvement Program (PennHip)
www.pennhip.org
Alternative hip evaluation method

DNA TESTS Besides DNA tests to determine parentage, DNA tests to check for the presence of certain disease-causing genes are also available. Each test must be developed and tested for each breed, but the list of available tests continues to grow. Note that the presence of a DNA test for a particular disease in a breed does not necessarily indicate that disease is widespread in that breed. Listed below are the current tests available. The letters in parentheses behind PRA indicates the particular type of PRA test available; some breeds may have more than one type of PRA.

American Eskimo Dog: PRA (prcd), PK
Australian Cattle Dog: PRA (prcd)
Basset Hound: Several combined immune deficiency
Basenji: PK
Beagle: PK
Bedlington Terrier: Copper toxicosis
Bernese Mountain Dog: vWD
Briard: Congenital stationary night blindness
Bullmastiff: PRA (dominant)
Cardigan Welsh Corgi: PRA (rcd3)
Cairn Terrier: Globoid cell leukodystrophy
Chesapeake Bay Retriever: PRA (prcd)
Chihuahua: PK
Cocker Spaniel: PFK, coat color
Curly-Coated Retriever: Coat color
Dachshund: Narcolepsy, PK
Dalmatian: Coat color
Doberman Pinscher: Narcolepsy, vWD, coat color
English Cocker Spaniel: PRA (prcd)
English Springer Spaniel: PDF, fucosidosis, coat color
Flat-Coated Retriever: Coat color
German Pinscher: vWD
German Shepherd Dog: MPS VII
German Shorthaired Pointer: Cone degeneration
Golden Retriever: Muscular dystrophy
Gordon Setter: Coat color
Irish Setter: PRA (rcd1), canine leukocyte adhesion deficiency
Irish Red and White Setter: PRA (rcd1), canine leukocyte adhesion deficiency
Kerry Blue Terrier: vWD
Labrador Retriever: PRA (prcd), narcolepsy, cystinuria, coat color
Lhasa Apso: Renal dysplasia
Manchester Terriers: vWD

Mastiff: PRA (dominant)
Miniature Pinscher: MPS VI
Miniature Schnauzer: PRA (type A), myotonia congenita
Newfoundland: Cystinuria, coat color
Nova Scotia Duck Tolling Retriever: PRA (prcd)
Papillon: vWD
Pembroke Welsh Corgi: Severe combined immune deficiency
Poodle (all): vWD, coat color
Poodle (miniature): PRA (prcd)
Poodle (toy): PRA (prcd)
Portuguese Water Dog: PRA (prcd)
Samoyed: PRA (prcd), PRA (XL)
Schipperke: MPS IIIB, coat color
Scottish Terrier: vWD, coat color
Shetland Sheepdog: vWD
Shih Tzu: Renal dysplasia
Siberain Husky: PRA (XL)
Soft Coated Wheaten Terrier: Renal dysplasia
West Highland White Terrier: Globoid cell leukodystrophy, PK

DNA TESTS LABORATORIES

Note: Most laboratories do not offer every test.

HealthGene
www.healthgene.com
1-877-371-1551

OptiGen
www.optigen.com
607-257-0301

PenGen
www.vet.upenn.edu/research/centers/
 penngen/services/
888-PENNGEN

Veterinary Diagnostics Center
www.vetdnacenter.com
800-625-0874

VetGen
www.vetgen.com
800-483-8436

Wegner Lab
Department of Neurology
Jefferson Medical College
1020 Locust Street, 394
Philadelphia, PA 19107

Dog Anatomy

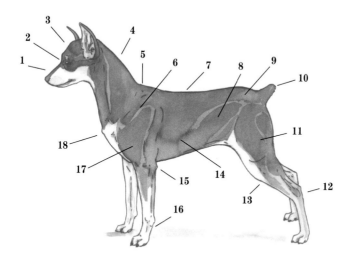

The External Anatomy of the Dog

1. Foreface or muzzle
2. Stop
3. Skull
4. Neckline
5. Withers
6. Shoulder
7. Back
8. Loin
9. Croup
10. Tail
11. Thigh
12. Hock
13. Knee
14. Rib cage
15. Elbow
16. Pastern
17. Upper arm
18. Forechest

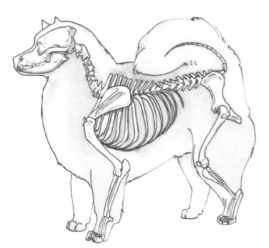

The Skeleton of the Dog

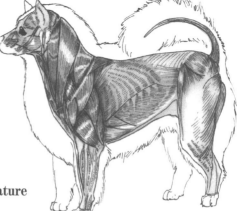

The Musculature of the Dog

Index

Affenpinscher 108
Afghan Hound 30
Airedale Terrier 80
Akita 54
Alaskan Malamute 55
American Eskimo Dog 130
American Staffordshire Terrier 81
Anatolian Shepherd Dog 56
Australian Cattle Dog 148
Australian Shepherd 149
Australian Terrier 82

Basenji 31
Basset Hound 32
Beagle 33
Bearded Collie 150
Beauceron 151
Bedlington Terrier 83
Belgian Malinois 152
Belgian Sheepdog 153
Belgian Tervuren 154
Bernese Mountain Dog 57
Bichon Frise 131
Black and Tan Coonhound 34
Black Russian Terrier 58
Bloodhound 35
Border Collie 155
Border Terrier 84
Borzoi 36
Boston Terrier 132
Bouviers des Flandres 156
Boxer 59
Briard 157
Brittany 2
Brussels Griffon 109
Bulldog 133
Bullmastiff 60
Bull Terrier 85

Cairn Terrier 86
Canaan Dog 158

Cavalier King Charles Spaniel 110
Chihuahua 111
Chinese Crested Dog 112
Chinese Shar-Pei 134
Chow Chow 135
Collie 159

Dachshund 37
Dalmatian 136
Dandie Dinmont Terrier 87
Doberman Pinscher 61
Dogue de Bordeaux 168

English Toy Spaniel 113

Finnish Spitz 137
Fox Terrier (Smooth) 88
Fox Terrier (Wire) 89
Foxhound (American) 38
Foxhound (English) 39
French Bulldog 138

German Pinscher 62
German Shepherd Dog 160
Giant Schnauzer 63
Glen of Imaal Terrier 90
Great Dane 64
Great Pyrenees 65
Greater Swiss Mountain Dog 66
Greyhound 40

Harrier 41
Havanese 114

Ibizan Hound 42
Irish Red and White Setter 169
Irish Terrier 91
Irish Wolfhound 43
Italian Greyhound 115

Japanese Chin 116

Keeshond 139
Kerry Blue Terrier 92
Komondor 67
Kuvasz 68

Lakeland Terrier 93
Lhasa Apso 140
Löwchen 141

Maltese 117
Manchester Terrier (Standard) 94
Manchester Terrier (Toy) 118
Mastiff 69
Miniature Bull Terrier 95
Miniature Pinscher 119
Miniature Schnauzer 96

Neapolitan Mastiff 70
Newfoundland 71
Norfolk Terrier 97
Norwegian Buhund 170
Norwegian Elkhound 44
Norwich Terrier 98

Old English Sheepdog 161
Otterhound 45

Papillon 120
Parson Russell Terrier 99
Pekingese 121
Petit Basset Griffon Vendéen 46
Pharaoh Hound 47
Plott 48
Pointer (German Shorthaired) 4
Pointer (German Wirehaired) 5
Pointer 3
Polish Lowland Sheepdog 162
Pomeranian 122

Poodle (Toy) 123
Poodle 142
Portuguese Water Dog 72
Pug 124
Puli 163
Pyrenean Shepherd 171

Redbone Coonhound 172
Retriever (Chesapeake Bay) 6
Retriever (Curly-Coated) 7
Retriever (Flat-Coated) 8
Retriever (Golden) 9
Retriever (Labrador) 10
Retriever (Nova Scotia Duck Tolling) 11
Rhodesian Ridgeback 49
Rottweiler 73

Saint Bernard 74
Saluki 50
Samoyed 75
Schipperke 143
Scottish Deerhound 51
Scottish Terrier 100
Sealyham Terrier 101
Setter (English) 12
Setter (Gordon) 13
Setter (Irish) 14
Shetland Sheepdog 164
Shiba Inu 144
Shih Tzu 125
Siberian Husky 76
Silky Terrier 126
Skye Terrier 102
Soft Coated Wheaten Terrier 103
Spaniel (American Water) 15
Spaniel (Clumber) 16
Spaniel (Cocker) 17
Spaniel (English Cocker) 18
Spaniel (English Springer) 19
Spaniel (Field) 20
Spaniel (Irish Water) 21
Spaniel (Sussex) 22

Spaniel (Welsh Springer) 23
Spinone Italiano 24
Staffordshire Bull Terrier 104
Standard Schnauzer 77
Swedish Vallhund 173

Tibetan Mastiff 78
Tibetan Spaniel 145
Tibetan Terrier 146
Toy Fox Terrier 127
Toy Manchester Terrier 118
Toy Poodle 123

Vizsla 25

Weimaraner 26
Welsh Corgi (Cardigan) 165
Welsh Corgi (Pembroke) 166
Welsh Terrier 105
West Highland White Terrier 106
Whippet 52
Wirehaired Pointing Griffon 27

Yorkshire Terrier 128